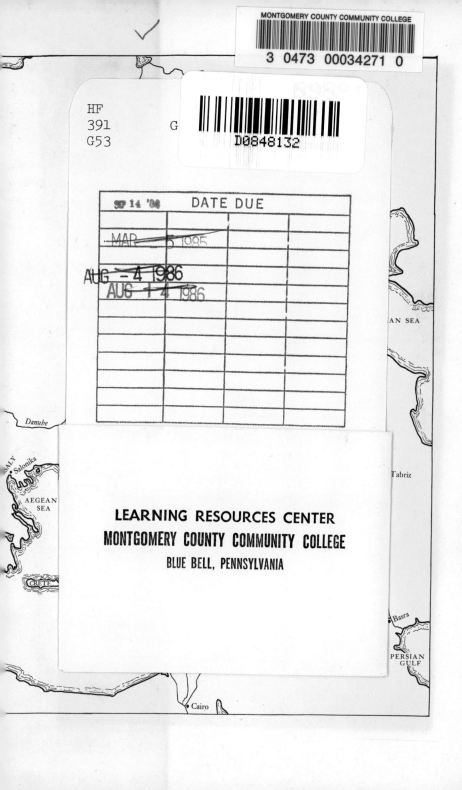

MERCHANTS AND MONEYMEN

The Commercial Revolution, 1000-1500

The Polos—Niccolo, Maffeo, and young Marco—presenting documents and gifts from Pope Gregory to Kublai Khan. The gifts included the vial, in the Khan's left hand, containing sacred oil from the Church of the Holy Sepulchre at Jerusalem. (Bodleian Library)

Merchants and Moneymen

The Commercial Revolution, 1000-1500

JOSEPH and FRANCES GIES

THOMAS Y. CROWELL COMPANY
New York   Established 1834

By the Authors

Life in a Medieval City
Leonard of Pisa and the New Mathematics of the Middle Ages
Merchants and Moneymen: The Commercial Revolution, 1000–1500

Designed by Abigail Moseley

Manufactured in the United States of America

L. C. Card 78-184976
ISBN 0-690-53177-X

1 2 3 4 5 6 7 8 9 10

To
Jenny and Paul

ACKNOWLEDGMENTS

The authors wish to express their thanks to Professor David Herlihy of the University of Wisconsin and Professor Harry A. Miskimin of Yale University for many helpful suggestions and corrections; to the Sterling Library of Yale, and the Northwestern University Library; to Kenneth and Brenda Davis, wardens of Wensum Lodge, Norwich; to the staff of the Datini archive in Prato; and to many others in Venice, Genoa, Florence, Prato, Amalfi, and elsewhere who assisted in various ways, especially in picture research.

CONTENTS

ILLUSTRATIONS

MAPS

by Jane Orth Ware

MERCHANTS AND MONEYMEN

The Commercial Revolution, 1000-1500

I

STIRRINGS

In 568 the Lombards, a pastoral people who had been living for some time along the upper Danube, were driven out of their lands by the Avars, who had poured into the Balkans impelled by the pressure of still other vast migrations in Central Asia. Numbering perhaps two hundred thousand, the army of Lombard men, women, and children wound up and over the Julian Alps into the Italian plain. Taking advantage of the Roman roads, they spread through Venetia and along the Po Valley.

The invaders found a country weakened by three centuries of economic depression, shrinking population, and the incursions of earlier migrations. In the face of the crowds of hungry immigrants who, themselves displaced, had little regard for other people's property, the native Italians turned refugee, packed their belongings and hastened out of reach. Fugitives from the town of Milan, including the archbishop, fled south, finding temporary asylum in Genoa, a port at the junction of two Roman roads; later, Genoa, too, fell to the Lombard king Rothari, who demolished its walls.

Other natives from the Po Valley, including a number of wealthy landowners, retreated in the opposite direction, gaining safety on the islands of Venetia, under Byzantine protection. This marshy archipelago existed in a state of innocence described by Cassiodorus, minister of the Ostrogoth king Theodoric, in 531: "Here where the tides alternately cover and uncover the fields you live like waterfowl. What is at one moment mainland suddenly becomes an island, as if one were in the Cyclades. Among the waters rise your scattered houses, built on man-made foundations; twisted and knotted osier holds the earth in a solid mass, so that it can resist the waves. . . . The only wealth of the inhabitants is fish; rich and poor live on equal terms, eat the same food, live in the same kind of house. . . . Your energies are concentrated on the saltworks. Instead of pushing ploughs and wielding sickles, you turn your salt cylinders. . . ." The islands had seen refugees before in the centuries of migrations; but this time the arrivals were so numerous and included so many men of talent that they took over leadership of communities on the islands of Grado, Torcello, Burano, Heraclea, and Rialto, and began to work a transformation of the society of fishermen and salt workers.

The Lombards did not pursue the fleeing population to Venice, but continued to spread in other directions. Pavia, capital of the Ostrogoths who had occupied northern Italy in the fifth century, resisted for three years, but fell in 572. The provinces of Liguria, Emilia, and Tuscany were overrun, until most of inland Italy was in Lombard hands. Rome, sacked three times in the fifth century, fought over by Goths and Byzantine Greeks, found itself in the front line of the new struggle between Lombards and Greeks; by 600, the ancient capital was reduced to a vast ghost town where a few thousand papal functionaries and soldiers survived among crumbling ruins and goat pastures.

In the rest of Europe, German tribes employed as mercenaries by the Romans took over control. Paris, burned during disorders in the third century, contracted into its island in the Seine, rebuilding the Roman ramparts with the stones of ruined suburban villas. Across the Channel in England the Roman occupiers had gradually withdrawn, leaving the Britons to fight it out against Germans originally imported as mercenaries; these Germans, or "Anglo-Saxons," or "English," won a major victory against the British natives just three years after the Lombards crossed the Alps. The old Roman towns decayed; only York and London kept any substantial population, though the "English" kept a trickle of commerce going with Germanic settlements in France and the Low Countries. Along the Rhine and the North Sea coast, a few stockaded forts remained.

One place unaffected, perhaps even favorably affected, by the massive dislocations was the city that stood on the straits between the Sea of Marmara and the Black Sea. Constantinople, capital of the eastern half of the Roman Empire, was a wholly Greek city that gloried in the title of the "New Rome." It carried on many of the old traditions of empire and started new ones. Byzantine craftsmen produced fine textiles, leather, armor, metalwork, porcelain, mosaics, ivories. They imported silks and spices from China, paid for with their own goldpiece, the bezant.* Just before the Lombards overran Italy, two Orthodox monks from Constantinople executed a historic coup of industrial espionage by bringing silkworm eggs, concealed in recesses hollowed in their staves, home with them from China. Byzantine factories began turning out fine silk cloth, guarding the secret of the caterpillars and eggs as tightly as had the Chinese. The Byzantines were advanced in business methods, as they were in technology, and alone among Europeans made use of banking and credit.

To the south, another migration changed the face of the Western world in the early years of the seventh century. Muhammad, a successful young businessman of the Arabian caravan-crossroads town of Mecca, began to preach a new religion; within a generation of his death in 632, Islam, a military force as well as a creed, had spread over Arabia, Persia, and Egypt; within a century, it extended from the Atlantic to the Indus. In the immense area overrun by the Muslims, commerce flourished under the unifying religion, law, and culture, enriching cities old and new: in Spain, Cordova, Seville, and Granada experienced a new flowering; Fez, Tunis, and Kairouan rose in western North Africa; in the Near and Middle East, Alexan-

* See appendix 1, "Medieval Money."

dria, Damascus, and Baghdad prospered, as did the Silk-Road cities of Isfahan, Rayy, Bukhara, and Samarkand; in the ninth century, ancient Palermo was reborn as the capital of Arab Sicily; in the tenth, Cairo began a brilliant career as chief city of Egypt under the Fatimid dynasty (909–1171). In handicrafts, shipbuilding, navigation, agriculture, business techniques, the Muslims, assimilating technology and science from the people they conquered, forged far ahead of western Europe. Muslim ships and caravans brought rubies and emeralds from Persia and Arabia, pearls from the Persian Gulf, silk and porcelain, camphor, musk, and spices from China, fur, skins, and amber from Russia, sandalwood, ebony, and coconuts from India, linen from Egypt, carpets from Persia and Armenia, gold and slaves from Africa.

Muslim merchants sailed to China. In 851 Suleiman, one of the models for Sindbad the Sailor, reported that in the Chinese port of Canfu there was a Muslim colony, headed by its own consul, where Persian ships called regularly, sailing from Basra and Oman along the coasts of India and Sumatra. "The Chinese are dressed in silk both winter and summer," recorded Suleiman. "Their common food is rice, which they often eat with a broth, like what the Arabs make of meat or fish, which they pour upon the rice. . . . Their drink is a kind of wine made of rice. . . . They are not very nice in point of cleanliness, and wash not with water when they ease nature, but only wipe themselves with paper. . . . They have an excellent kind of earth wherewith they make a ware of equal fineness with glass, and equally transparent. When merchants arrive here, the Chinese seize on their cargoes . . . take thirty percent of each commodity, and return the rest to the merchant."

The Muslims fought the Byzantines for domination of the Mediterranean, and were especially successful in the West. In the ninth century, according to the later Arab historian Ibn-Khaldun, "not a Christian plank floated" on the Mediterranean. The ports of Provence and Languedoc—Marseille, Nice, Arles, Avignon, and Narbonne—suffered at the hands of Arab corsairs operating from Spain, the Balearics, Corsica, and Sardinia, and even from a nest in the Provençal mountains at Garde-Frainet, whence they descended

Arab caravans crisscrossed Asia long before A.D. 1000 when Europe began
to emerge from the economic slowdown called the Dark Ages. Here,
Arab traders rest in the court of a caravansary, or inn, where they have
stopped for the night. (Bibliothèque Nationale)

to raid the coasts. Genoa and its sister city Pisa, old Roman ports
now under Lombard domination, suffered repeated depredations.
Once-flourishing Genoa was reduced to a subsistence economy,
farming, fishing, shepherding. Its feudal princes had their residence
across the mountains, leaving administration of the city to their representatives, the viscounts, and to the bishops and abbots, who lived
outside town off their lands and taxes paid in farm produce.

Elsewhere in Europe, commerce barely survived. In the West
Charles Martel, perfecting the new military technique of fighting

from horseback, made possible by the importation of the stirrup from the East, confiscated Church lands and distributed them to his vassals to help them pay the enormous costs of their horses and armor. Other areas quickly copied the new regime of feudalism, with its manorial economy of small, self-contained units, estates which produced only for their own consumption and consumed only what they produced. Yet a scattering of merchants continued to function: in the country, peddlers to castle and monastery; in the town, artisan shopkeepers, and even more substantial businessmen who sustained a slender volume of long-distance commerce. Many were foreigners, especially Syrians, Greeks, and Jews. The Syrians imported wines, pistachio nuts, papyrus, and glass from the Near East via Marseille, Narbonne, and other Provençal ports. The Jews traveled and traded over even greater distances; one group, the Radanites, was described by the Muslim geographer Ibn-Khurdadbih, a provincial postmaster of Persia:

"These merchants speak Arabic, Persian, Roman, the languages of the Franks, Andalusians, and Slavs. They journey from west to east, from east to west, partly on land, partly by sea. They transport from the West eunuchs, female and male slaves, silk, castor, marten and other furs, and swords. They take ship in the land of the Franks, on the Western Sea [Mediterranean] and steer for Farama [Egypt]. There they load their goods on the backs of camels and go by land to Kolzum. . . . They embark in the East [Red] Sea and sail to al-Jar and Joddah [in Arabia], they go to Sind [between Persia and India], India, and China. On their return they carry musk, aloes, camphor, cinnamon and other products of the Eastern countries. Some make sail for Constantinople to sell their goods to the Romans; others go to the palace of the King of the Franks. . . ." Other itineraries of the Radanites included the Tigris and Euphrates route to the Persian Gulf, the land route across North Africa from Spain, and the Silk Road through Central Asia from Balkh to China.

Some native merchants were active in Europe, too. In the depths of the ninth century, when the economic slowdown called the Dark Ages reached its darkest, textiles were manufactured in France and the Low Countries. Frisian merchants sold their cloth in

Worms and Mainz. Breton ships carried salt and fish from the Bay of Biscay to Ireland and to the Loire valley. Merchants operated in Verdun, Paris, Rouen, Chappes, Meaux. Even the Vikings who descended on Europe from Scandinavia often turned from brigands to merchants to sell their loot; they also exchanged furs and wax from the East for German iron and Rhine wine and even sailed down the Russian rivers to trade with Constantinople. In Italy, the Lombard cities, Pavia, Milan, Ferrara, managed to carry on some business across the Alps with Germany.

The Italians also traded with Byzantium and Syria through the mediation of the new community on the Adriatic coast founded by the sixth-century refugees from the Po Valley. The base of the fishermen and salt panners became a commercial center, as the newcomers began to transport goods by sea and river. By the ninth century, inhabitants of the Venetian islands were trafficking with Sicily, Greece, and Egypt, and had developed a busy shipbuilding industry. Sailing up the Po and the Adige to Cremona and Pavia, they sold the salt of their own lagoons and a variety of luxury goods purchased in the East—furs, hides, dyes, silk, velvet, and spices. They took in exchange timber, grain, oil, wine, silver, and copper, and, most valuable merchandise of all, slaves brought across the mountains from Slavonia. A Lombard writer commented that the Venetians "do not till the soil, do not sow, do not gather vintage," but depended on Pavia for grain and wine, paying for it with salt and Oriental goods.

The leading families, many descended from the sixth-century refugees, invested their wealth in land and commerce. In the ninth century, Venice produced medieval Europe's first "patricians," families who combined wealth acquired in business with leadership in public affairs: for example, the Partecipazio family, representatives of a class which was to dominate Venice for a thousand years. Between 811 and 887, seven Partecipazios were elected doge (duke). Simultaneously other members of the family, often brothers of the doge, either sat as bishops or occupied the highest local Church position, the patriarchate of Grado, northernmost island in the Venetian archipelago.

The Partecipazios established the government on the island of Rialto, which henceforth assumed the name of Venice. A landless empire of islands, channels, ports, and wharves, Venice was an anomaly in a world of fiefs and demesnes. Instead of the arts of soil-turning, crop rotating, and sheep shearing, a Venetian knew sailing, bookkeeping, and bartering in strange languages. His eye was equally practiced at recognizing a promontory and a grade of cloth; he knew the coasts, islands, and ports of the Adriatic and the markets and bazaars of Constantinople and Syria.

Lacking Venice's intimate connection with the Byzantine Empire and its defensively valuable isolation from mainland Italy, the ancient ports of Genoa, Pisa, Bari, and Naples were slower to awaken; behind them lingered northwest Europe. But in the tenth and eleventh centuries a better organized resistance slowly drove the Viking and Muslim marauders back to their homelands. New life stirred everywhere. Just as population had declined in the latter days of the Western Roman Empire, now it rose significantly.

As either a cause or an effect of this population growth, or perhaps both, an agricultural revolution was taking place; land was cleared, better technology and better crops were introduced. New developments in mining played their part, as did stouter ships, galleys built on Byzantine models, stronger and more capacious than the swift but light Viking ships, and sailing vessels equipped with the triangular lateen (fore and aft) sail borrowed from the Arabs.

The records of this earliest renaissance are scanty; we know far less than we could wish of the men who made it. Only tantalizing shadowy glimpses reveal the silhouettes of these pioneers of the West's great surge into history.

I

Pantaleone di Mauro, a Merchant from the Amalfitan Eagle's Nest

In 968, Liutprand, Bishop of Cremona, spent an uncomfortable six months at the Byzantine court as ambassador of the German emperor Otto I. He was subjected to a campaign of slights and insults by the xenophobe emperor Nicephorus, whom he described to Otto with understandable bias as "a monstrosity of a man, a pygmy, fatheaded and like a mole as to the smallness of his eyes; disgusting . . . bristly . . . ; in color an Ethiopian; one whom it would not be pleasant to meet in the middle of the night; with extensive belly . . . short stature . . . bold of tongue, a fox by nature, in perjury and lying a Ulysses." Before he left Constantinople, Liutprand bought five handsome purple silk ceremonial robes, but court officials confiscated them. Such garments, they said, were too good for Italians, a plebeian and mongrel race, product of miscegenation of Roman dregs with barbarians. Proud Liutprand retorted with icy sarcasm; such ceremonial robes, he asserted, were so common in Italy that "with us, prostitutes and carnival performers wear them." Where did such people buy the robes? "From Venetian and Amalfitan traders who, by bringing them to us, support themselves from the food we give them."

These "Amalfitan traders" played a role in the Tyrrhenian Sea analogous to that of the Venetians in the Adriatic. Like the Venetians, they were indispensable to Byzantium as transporters of grain; after the Muslims overran Egypt, Constantinople depended heavily upon Apulia and the Po Valley for its food supply, and Venice and Amalfi provided the carriers. In return, Amalfitan trading privileges in Constantinople gave them a monopoly in the import to western Italy of the silks and spices of Byzantium. In 1062 when the abbot of Montecassino wanted to buy presents for the German emperor Henry IV, he went to Amalfi for silks and metalwork. Amalfitans sold Byzantine silks in Rome to princes and prelates from northwest Europe; they sold spices and other Oriental luxuries in Genoa and at the annual fair of Pavia, where they bid against and bought from the Venetians.

The setting which produced these ambitious entrepreneurs was at first glimpse an unlikely one: a tiny fishing village clinging to the Sorrentine cliffs on the rugged coast south of Naples. Cut off from the world on three sides by mountains and on the fourth by the sea, with no hinterland to feed its population or provide raw materials for industry, Amalfi turned to the sea, first to fish, then to trade. Its near neighbors, Beneventum and Salerno, were overrun by the Lombards in the seventh century, but Amalfi remained under Byzantine protection. By the ninth century it was virtually autonomous; it coined money, made alliances, and fought wars.

Amalfi's prosperity depended partly on Byzantium; but even more important were its relations with Islamic North Africa. The city's first commercial treaties with the Saracens probably go back to the eighth century. Secure between its cliffs and fortifications, Amalfi was free to pursue its own policy, which it did with a consummate diplomacy that was part of its stock in trade. While wars raged on every side, among the Lombards of Salerno, the Lombards of Beneventum, the Greeks, Franks, Saracens, the Amalfitans steered a neutral course with the open-mindedness of businessmen willing to accept anyone's money. From the Arabs of North Africa they obtained gold, ivory, and wax; in exchange they brought timber, linen, wine, fruit, and grain. African gold permitted Amalfi to buy luxury

Isolated from the world by the rugged cliffs that protected their village on three sides, the inhabitants of Amalfi, home of the eleventh-century merchant-diplomat Pantaleone di Mauro, turned naturally to the sea for their livelihood, first as fishermen, then as traders. (Azienda di Soggiorno e Turismo, Amalfi)

items in Constantinople, which were exchanged in Italy for, as Liutprand put it, "the food we give them." Trading with the infidel brought censure from the Church. In 875 a commercial treaty with the Saracens caused the Pope to threaten excommunication and at the same time to offer a bribe in the form of a large annual subsidy. The Amalfitans, devout Christians though they were, ignored both threat and bribe.

They thrived; Amalfi's harbor was one of the busiest in the western Mediterranean. A kind of continual fair went on in the city. In the steep and narrow streets, Pisans, Genoese, and Venetians jabbered and bargained with Arabs, Africans, and Greeks. In 972 Ibn-Hawqal, a visiting Baghdad merchant, described Amalfi as "the most prosperous city of Lombardy [Italy], the noblest, the most illustrious for its conditions, the richest and most opulent." A century later William of Apulia, Norman poet and historian, wrote: "There was no other richer than this city in gold, silver, and precious stuffs; this nation was spread everywhere; its pilots were the most expert in the ways of the ocean and the signs of the heavens; they sailed for Alexandria and other distant shores; they visited Africa and brought back riches from the Indians, Arabs, Africans and Sicilians eager for merchandise to buy and sell."

While silver coins circulated almost exclusively in the empire of Charlemagne, which temporarily pinned northwest Europe together, the far richer Byzantine world used gold. The Greek gold bezant was common currency in Amalfi, and along with it the Muslim mancuso, also of gold. In the middle of the tenth century, Amalfi opened its own mint, to coin a gold piece called the tareno or tare, modeled after the gold quarter-dinar struck by the Arabs of Sicily.

Thanks to their Byzantine connections, the Amalfitans shared with Venice the privilege of having their own self-governed quarter in Constantinople, the crossroads of the world. There they founded churches and monasteries. By the middle of the eleventh century, merchants from Amalfi occupied a street in Antioch. Amalfitans lived in towns all along the coast of Asia Minor, in the islands of the Aegean, and in the cities of Sicily—Catania, Cefalù, and Syracuse. In Palermo there was a Street of the Amalfitans. Amalfitans had colonies in the principal coastal towns of Apulia, and across the Adriatic at Durazzo, they marketed the products of Sicily in Ravenna, once the capital of the Western Roman Empire, now occupied by the Lombards. In Rome itself Amalfi had its biggest settlement, where pilgrims and other tourists shopped for Greek and Arab luxuries.

While Venice traded almost exclusively in the eastern Mediterranean, Amalfitan ships sailed in both directions: they competed with Venetians in the Aegean, and with Pisans and Genoese in the Balearic islands and Spain. They outstripped all rivals in sailing to nearby Sicily and North Africa. In the last half of the tenth century, there was a large community of Amalfitans in Cairo. Amalfi provided North Africa with ship timber and slaves, grain, linen cloth, wines, fruits, and nuts. Of all these products, grain was probably the most important. Amalfitan middlemen were scattered throughout the agricultural centers of Apulia and Arab Sicily. The ports of Tunisia, especially Mahdia, were the usual destination of Amalfitan ships; here they were welcomed by local emirs who gave them protection and privileges—reduced duties, a place to live, a church. Wherever they did business, their role was that of carriers, transporting other people's goods; their only native products were ships and fish. They traded for oil, wax, and spices, but most of all for Arab gold, from which they struck the gold coins that improved their bargaining position with Byzantium, where the balance of trade was such that a ship paying two solidi customs when it entered the port left with a cargo assessed at fifteen solidi, indicating the differential in value between Western and Eastern products that had to be made up in gold. In the late ninth century, when Arab marauders attacked Salerno, Naples, Pisa, Genoa, and even Rome, they left friendly Amalfi alone. Enlisted under pressure in an anti-Saracen League in 903, Amalfi refused to join a second in 915. The Byzantine commander in Italy enrolled Salerno, Naples, and Gaeta, but Amalfi held out, the first city to maintain a political and commercial neutrality in the divided Mediterranean world.

It is not surprising that the first Italian businessman of whom we have personal knowledge is an Amalfitan. Our scanty information about this man, born when Amalfi's prosperity was at its pinnacle, comes from chronicles and diplomatic documents. Pantaleone di Mauro was one of six sons born early in the eleventh century to an old patrician family. A Costantino di Pantaleone di Mauro, whose four-year voyage to an unknown destination in 990 is recorded in Amalfitan contracts, was probably his grandfather. His father, Mauro, was a wealthy merchant known for his philanthropies, not only in Amalfi but in pre-Crusade Muslim Jerusalem. In 1048 Mauro had negotiated with the Egyptian caliph, Mustansir, for permission to restore the ancient Benedictine monastery and church of Santa Maria di Latina, and to found a hostel adjoining it for the men and women of Amalfi as well as a hospital which was to be the cradle of the famous Order of the Hospital of St. John of Jerusalem, rival of

The great bronze doors of the cathedral at Amalfi, first of their kind in Italy, were donated by Pantaleone di Mauro, who ordered them made in Constantinople by the artist Simeon of Syria. (Azienda di Soggiorno e Turismo, Amalfi)

the Knights Templar. In Antioch, too, he founded a hospital. These projects were financed by alms and donations collected in Amalfi.

Pantaleone's Amalfi had none of the Roman relics possessed by many Italian towns; its glory was new, and many of its monuments date from Pantaleone's lifetime. The great bronze doors of the cathedral, first of their kind in Italy, were the gift of Pantaleone, ordered by him in Constantinople from the artist Simeon of Syria, and subsequently copied for the abbey of Montecassino. At Rome, he contributed bronze doors to St. Paul-Outside-the-Walls. He built the church of St. Michael on Monte Gargano, in Apulia, where the Archangel Michael was supposed to have appeared, and Monte Gargano became one of the principal places of pilgrimage for Amalfitans.

For many years Pantaleone lived in Constantinople, where he presided over an Amalfitan colony which was Venice's only rival in that city. We know nothing of his commercial activity, which nevertheless was his principal function, but have a record of his diplomatic career. Amalfi's prudent peace-keeping policy, which had prevailed for four centuries, had begun to fail, perhaps unavoidably. Over the years, class strife and family rivalry had developed, an augury of the future of other medieval towns. In 958 the government ceased to be administered by elected prefects and became a duchy; the office of duke, at first elective, became hereditary, and was soon a touchstone for intrigue and insurrection. Several violent overturns engineered by rival patrician families gave an ambitious prince of Salerno, Guaimario V, an opportunity to move in and seize control in 1039.

Guaimario's rule lasted only thirteen years, ending in 1052 with a revolution in Salerno in which he was assassinated, with more than a suspicion of Amalfitan complicity. But his expansionist ambitions already had other consequences. A set of mercenary adventurers had recently arrived in southern Italy from Normandy, and had won an immediate reputation as fighters. Prominent among them were the Hauteville brothers, two of whom, William Iron-Arm and Drogo, after gaining experience and reputation fighting the Byzantines, took service with Guaimario. Soon the Hautevilles were a political-military power on their own, forcing Guaimario to marry one of his daughters to Drogo in an effort to keep him loyal.

In the confusion of temporary alliances and hostilities that ensued among Normans, Lombards, and Byzantines, Amalfi decided to strike a diplomatic blow at the Hautevilles. Pantaleone di Mauro, in Constantinople, sought to negotiate an anti-Norman alliance between the Byzantine emperor and the pope. Despite the common interest of conservatism in halting the depredations of the Hautevilles, Pantaleone was unable to bring about the entente. Turning to arms, the Amalfitans were even less successful; their contingent, fighting side by side with the Pope's German mercenaries, was badly defeated by the Hautevilles.

Pantaleone next appears as a mediator a few years later when the death of Pope Nicholas II was followed by an election scandal which left Christendom with two popes. The Normans were backing the "legitimate" pope, Alexander II; Pantaleone countered by supporting his rival, Honorius II. He made an attempt to bring Honorius, the young German emperor Henry IV, and the Byzantine emperor Constantine Duca together in a triple alliance; again he failed. Events took a turn for the worse when Gisulfo, Guaimario's son and successor as Prince of Salerno, began a fierce piratical war against Amalfi. One of Pantaleone's nephews was killed at sea; another, named Mauro after his father and grandfather, was taken prisoner and tortured. At the consecration of the great abbey church of Montecassino in 1071, Gisulfo, old Mauro, now a member of the abbey's community, and Pantaleone's brother Mauro were present. Pope Alexander and Abbot Desiderio attempted to use the occasion to promote peace between the two cities; but Gisulfo's only concession was to release Mauro's son without ransom.

The strenuous diplomatic efforts of Pantaleone were doomed to failure because of the growing disparity in military power between Amalfi and its enemies. It was no longer possible to survive as a lamb among wolves. When the reigning duke died—of heartbreak, according to a chronicler—leaving a son who was a minor, a delegation of Amalfitans, doubtless including either Pantaleone or his son, approached the new pope, Gregory VII, offering to place their city under his suzerainty. But Gregory was already allied with Salerno, and not only refused the offer, but urged his visitors to submit to Gisulfo.

It was a moment for desperate measures, and in 1073 the Amalfitan merchants took one. They sent a diplomatic mission to Robert Guiscard—Robert the Sly—a younger brother of Drogo and Iron-Arm. Robert had followed Drogo's example by marrying a Salernitan princess, and had won such spectacular battlefield successes against the Byzantines that the Pope had recognized him as Duke of Apulia and Calabria, a title Guaimario had claimed in vain. Robert capped his triumph by seizing Bari, the last Byzantine stronghold in Italy, while still another Hauteville brother, Roger, crossed the Straits of Messina and took over Sicily from its Muslim rulers.

Robert Guiscard readily accepted the Amalfitan merchants' overtures. He sent garrisons to man the fortresses, giving him effective control of the city, and followed up with a vigorous offensive against his brother-in-law Gisulfo. Salerno resisted heroically, but finally had to surrender. By 1076 the two old rivals, Salerno and Amalfi, were both relegated to the status of Norman vassals.

Amalfi's reduction and the Norman conquest of Sicily were felt at once in North Africa. A Jewish judge in Mahdia wrote a letter to Egypt: "Most of Sicily is already conquered. We are very much disturbed because this country relies for its grain supply on it." Grain export soon became a royal monopoly in Sicily, a valuable source of revenue to the Norman kings. The Amalfitans were reduced to the role of middlemen for grain exporters licensed by the Sicilian state.

Amalfi made several attempts to liberate itself, against Robert and later his brother Roger. Roger's son, who assumed the title of Roger II, King of the Two Sicilies, put an end to Amalfitan pretensions by incorporating the city directly into his royal domain.

What was perhaps most painful for the Amalfitan merchants, their submission to the Normans cost them their privileges at Constantinople, leaving the Venetians without a rival. As Byzantium's last Italian satellite, Venice was accorded freedom from customs duties while all the possessions of Amalfitans in the Empire were taxed, the tribute to be paid to the Church of St. Mark in Venice.

Much as its position had deteriorated, Amalfi did not disappear immediately from the commercial and political scene. An Amalfitan flotilla joined the galleys of Pisa, Genoa, Gaeta, and Salerno in the victorious assault on Mahdia in 1087. One of the leading captains, according to the chronicles, was a "Pantaleo Amalphitanus," probably a nephew or a grandson of Pantaleone di Mauro.

The tenth century, Amalfi's hour of glory, corresponded with the period in which Arab power reached its height in the western Mediterranean, and Amalfi's decline coincided with the decline of Muslim power in the eleventh. Pantaleone, businessman and statesman, arrived on the scene at the moment when his city's fortunes reached their apogee and began their downward trend. He treated with dukes, popes, and emperors, placing Amalfi's commercial interests in the diplomatic arena beside those of powerful dynasties.

In the eleventh century, such business interests could not yet hold their own in competition with military adventurers like the Hautevilles. But the future lay with the businessmen; Pantaleone, rather than Robert Guiscard, was the precursor of a rising European class.

2

The Rozos of Milan,
Masters of the Mint

While the family of Pantaleone di Mauro was directing the diplomatic policies of Amalfi, moneymen of another kind were achieving prestige in northern Italy. The Rozos, descendants of a line of coiners, became masters, or managers, of the Milan mint.

Milan, in the fourth century a capital of the Western Roman Empire, stood in the center of the finest farming region in Italy. From a commercial point of view, its situation was strategic, a few miles up the River Olona from the Po, close to the Lombard capital of Pavia, at the meeting of main roads to France and Germany. The Po brought ships from Comacchio and Venice, with salt, spices, luxury goods; the Alpine passes brought horses, slaves, swords, cloth. Under the Lombard kings and, after a crisis and period of adjustment, during the period of Charlemagne's rule, Milan recovered and then surpassed its old size and prosperity. The merchant class, growing in wealth and stature, allied itself with the powerful bishops and abbots, who became its protectors and sponsors.

As a Roman capital, Milan undoubtedly supported a mint, which is known to have existed later under Ostrogoth rule; it almost surely disappeared during the period of anarchy following the Lombard invasions. In the seventh century, the Lombard king Rothari reorganized the coinage in his domain, establishing mints at Pavia and Lucca, hiring Greek coiners, and introducing Byzantine methods and statutes (including a law that prescribed the severing of a counterfeiter's hand). Lombard mints multiplied, with new establishments at Milan, Pisa, Mantua, Piacenza, Verona, and Treviso. They issued gold as well as silver coins, and went on minting in gold while a constricting economy caused contemporary (Merovingian) France to limit itself to silver. Lombard gold pieces were copied from traditional Roman gold solidi and tremisses (a third of a solidus), bearing the inscription and later the likeness of the king. Under Charlemagne, who conquered the Lombard kingdom late in the eighth century, the coining of gold ceased, although gold ingots or gold dust were still occasionally used for large transactions, or transactions with foreigners. Some Byzantine and Arab gold coins circulated in Italy, and Sicily and southern Italy still produced gold solidi and tremisses well into the ninth century. At the same time, the number of mints in Lombardy decreased, until those of Pavia, Milan, and Lucca dominated. A money economy continued to operate, however, and the chaotic feudal multiplicity of coinage that occurred in France and Germany never took place in Italy.

Milan's mint was established near the marketplace, in the area where the old Roman forum had stood. There, in 936, Benedetto Rozo, son of Giovanni Rozo, was a coiner; in all probability his father Giovanni and his grandfather had practiced the profession; the family may, in fact, have been descended from the Lombard coiners, or from Byzantines hired by King Rothari. Crafts were typically passed from father to son. Among Byzantine coiners this hereditary tendency had been elevated to legal status, and only the sons and nephews of coiners could ordinarily become coiners; such probably was also the case in Milan. Like the jewelers, painters, coppersmiths, shoemakers, tailors, soapmakers, and masons of Milan, the coiners were skilled craftsmen and freemen; they were also well paid. They belonged to a guild, a prestigious, tightly closed corporation; acceptance in it qualified a man to strike coins "anywhere in the world." Its origins went back to Roman times, when the slave gangs who

St. Eligius, a seventh-century master of the Paris mint, later bishop of Noyon and patron saint of mint workers, is shown striking a coin in this window from the Milan cathedral. His apprentice is punching coin blanks. (Strada, *La zecca di Milano e le sue monete*)

operated the imperial mints won their freedom, formed corpora-
tions, and made profits.

In 941 Benedetto Rozo was promoted to become one of the
four masters, or foremen, of the mint. Late in the same century his
nephew Remedio, a coiner, or moneyer, also became a mint master.
Early in the eleventh, Remedio's son Benedetto repeated the pattern,
rising from the ranks of the moneyers to become master of the
mint; he was also apparently the first Rozo to learn to read and
write.

Like many crafts, the art of coining had changed little since
Roman times. The silver denarius, the coin mainly produced by the
mint, was made by melting and assaying metal in a carefully mea-
sured proportion of silver and alloy, for which the mint master was
strictly responsible, since the coin's value depended on the amount
of silver. The metal was molded into ingots, which were hammered
into sheets of the desired thickness. Blanks were punched out with a
cylindrical die, placing the sheet over a shallow round; irregularities
were removed with metal shears. The lower die ended in a spike
which was driven into a block of wood to hold it in place. The
blank was positioned on the lower die; the moneyer held the upper
die against the face of the block with a tool or with his hand, and
struck it one or more sharp blows with a hammer, impressing the
design from the die onto the coin.

The Rozos' income came principally from seigniorage, the difference between the cost of the metal and the face value of coins, a
percentage which mints have necessarily exacted from time imme-
morial (and still do). The seigniorage which masters of the Milan
mint retained for the guild amounted to one-sixth, or two denarii in
every twelve, out of which they had to pay an annual rent to the
Crown of twelve pounds of coin, to which was apparently added
four pounds to the archbishop.

The Rozos and their compatriots had other ways of making
money. As guardians of the currency, they were supposed to appre-
hend and punish forgers, in the process of which they doubtless acquired part of the forfeited goods. Moneyers were also, by a natural

The monastery of San Ambrogio in Milan, with which the Rozo family
had close connections. Not only did the Rozos make bequests of property to San Ambrogio, but the monks created titles for other parcels of
land by forging the family name to charters, attributing to the Rozos as
gifts what the monastery already owned.

transformation, money changers, earning a commission of just over eight percent for that service. They probably also loaned money. In the tenth and eleventh centuries, moneyers, with their steady revenue in coin, were among the few people who had cash to lend. They may even have accepted money for deposit, to keep in the strongboxes of the mint.

Like other moneyers of Milan, the Rozos invested in real estate. The first Benedetto Rozo owned land in the suburbs near the river Olona; in 936 he traded it with the abbot of the monastery of San Ambrogio for other lands near the Vepra River. The family had a country villa on the western edge of the city. Later, Remedio rented a fine house from San Ambrogio, somewhere in the vicinity of the mint, where land was most expensive, with an oven and a well in a small courtyard which gave the surname Corticella to one branch of Remedio's descendants. By the time of Remedio's son, the second Benedetto, the family had increased in wealth and status to the point where he was able to found a church, Santa Trinità, near the Rozos' town house. Just before the death of the second Benedetto in 1036, he appointed three of his nephews (one of them also named Benedetto) priests and patrons of the church, with the privilege of choosing their successors from the Rozo family.

Benedetto's son Nanterio climaxed the rise of the Rozo family over a century and a half; in 1051, on his deathbed, he had his wife Guida buy for the sum of 180 pounds a fourth share in a castle with moat, chapel, and surrounding land northwest of Pavia. After his death, his widow went on buying land. When she died, leaving no heirs, the monastery of S. Ambrogio was her principal legatee. Guida and Nanterio also benefited S. Ambrogio in unforeseen ways; their names were used in charters which the monks skillfully forged, attributing to the gift of the Rozos land for which the title had been lost, or which the monastery may have obtained by illegal means. In honor of these two, an inscription was installed in the monastery, and services were held in their memory at regular intervals.

Nanterio and Guida were childless; but sixty years after the death of the second Benedetto Rozo, a namesake described by the chronicler as "of illustrious origin," was one of four patricians who commanded a Milanese contingent in the First Crusade. Returning to Milan in 1100, this descendant of the sponsor rebuilt the family church, modeling it after the Holy Sepulchre in Jerusalem. Before he himself left on Crusade, the archbishop of Milan consecrated the remodeled church, making it the seat of a new parish in the heart of the wealthiest district of the city and granting it the privilege of holding an annual market, exempt from sales tax, in the church square.

The Rozos illustrate an important recurring aspect of medieval moneymen: the family dynasty. As in the case of the Rozos, this tendency grew out of the passing of crafts from father to son, but the dynastic theme remained long after families had ceased to practice crafts.

The Rozos' skill, moneying, was a branch of a larger Milan specialty, metallurgy. From the nearby hills Milan drew metal ores, especially iron; by the time of the Crusading Benedetto Rozo the city was already renowned for its production of arms and armor. Not surprisingly, Milan supplied the leadership for north Italian towns when Frederick Barbarossa marched on Lombardy in 1158. The besieged city had to surrender in 1162 and was burned to the ground, and salt spread on its smoking ruins; the population was scattered, and the city ceased officially to exist. But six years later Milan rose from its ashes to head the Lombard League, sending a seismic tremor through Europe in 1176 by defeating Frederick Barbarossa's army and establishing the principle of the free, independent city.

3

An English Peddler-Saint: Godric of Finchale

While eleventh-century Italian entrepreneurs were setting the stage for the Commercial Revolution, backward northwest Europe too was feeling the winds of change. Great merchants in the style of Pantaleone of Amalfi were not to be found in this region, but in at least one recorded case a poor boy made good with pluck, determination, initiative, and above all the help of God: Godric of Finchale, a true Horatio Alger hero of the eleventh century, who rose from rags not merely to riches but to sainthood. He had the distinction, exceptional in the Middle Ages, of having not only a biographer, but several. His claim to fame in his own time was piety; in the twentieth century he gained new luster because Henri Pirenne, the Belgian scholar whose theories revolutionized medieval history, saw him as the archetype of the emergent merchant class, "new men," who were adventurers, *déracinés*, vagabond younger sons, or runaway serfs, landless men "who lived, so to speak, on the margin of a society where land alone was the basis of existence. . . . The story of Godric was certainly that of many others. . . . Speculation . . . largely contributed to the foundation of the first commercial fortunes. The savings of a little peddler, a sailor, a boatman or a docker furnished him with quite enough capital, if only he knew how to use it."

Godric was born in the decade after the Norman conquest into an England of small towns and local markets. His father Aeilward was a Saxon peasant living on the Lincolnshire coast; the family—the mother Aedwen, the first-born Godric (God's reign), a brother William, a sister Burcwen—lived a marginal existence, never far from starvation.

Godric's authorized biography was written by Reginald, a monk of Durham, who visited the saint at Finchale in his last years and recorded his life story at the dictation of Godric, who corrected the copy, according to Reginald, on his deathbed. The book was popular, and has survived in several versions. One gives a physical description of the subject, rare in medieval biographical works. Godric was thickset and sturdy; of medium height, with muscular arms and broad chest, a long face, clear sparkling gray eyes, bushy eyebrows, a broad forehead, flaring nostrils, a fine aquiline nose, a heavy black beard (white in old age), full lips, a sinewy neck, and knees calloused from kneeling.

The first seven of the book's fifty-two chapters deal with Godric's business career, the rest with pilgrimages, visions, and pious works. Godric began as a boy scavenging on the seashore along with other young peasants, walking far out on the sands when the tide was low in search of salvage. Once his boldness nearly cost him his life. He found three dolphins stranded by the tide, two alive, the third dying. Sparing the living, he killed the dying fish, cut off a large fillet of the meat, prized for its fat, slung it on his shoulders, and started for shore. The tide had turned and soon the water covered his ankles, legs, chest; finally it was over his head. Crossing himself, he swam ashore, a thousand paces. Home safe with his booty, he regaled his parents with the narrow escape.

Sometimes scavenging was rewarded with marketable flotsam. Saving the money from such sales, Godric acquired a hoard with which he bought a stock of cheap merchandise. For two years he roamed the countryside near Lindsey, in northern Lincolnshire, with a pack full of pins and needles, scissors, knives, religious amu-

Godric of Finchale began his highly successful business career as a peddler, packing his wares on foot from farm to village; later, he embarked on international ventures and, in his retirement, became a saint. This woodcarving of a medieval peddler is from Swaffham Parish Church. (National Monuments Record)

lets, and ribbons. His customers were country people on the farms
and in the hamlets. Often he must have traded rather than sold, for
cash was scarce. As he trudged the roads in all kinds of weather, he
meditated on God. "Christ and St. Mary supported me," in the
words of a hymn he wrote long after, "that I on this earth should
not with my bare foot tread."

In a few years he was able to undertake longer journeys, with
more valuable merchandise, from which he drew greater profits:
cloth, medicines, silver cups. He visited the towns on market day,
usually Sunday, when booths were set up in the market squares or
in the widest street in town. Most of these urban nuclei were small;
only London and York had populations in excess of seven or eight
thousand; the other English towns were merely large villages. In
company with other merchants, Godric called at the castles of the
new French lords who had displaced the old English thanes and
taken over most of the land. He visited rich monasteries whose
long-wooled flocks provided the abbot with a handsome revenue,
and where a peddler with metalware or fine finished cloth could
make a sale. He appeared at the fairs held by abbeys and churches,
like the famous one at Winchester, which occupied three days during which all buying and selling for miles around was forbidden except at the fair. The fairs were visited by foreign merchants; here
great lords and members of the royal court came to buy furs, cloth,
spices, wine. Godric bought wholesale, to sell to his customers on
the road. From fair to monastery to town, he and his fellow merchants traveled in armed bands, on the alert as they passed through
forests, taking care to find safe lodgings for the night.

Already Godric had passed through two stages of merchant activity: first as a poor dusty-foot peddler going from farm to village;
second as a market trader, working with other merchants, very possibly in some form of mutual protection society. Now he took a
third step. From St. Andrew's, north of Edinburgh in Scotland, he
made a pilgrimage to Rome. Taking ship for France, he followed
the arduous overland route to the Mediterranean, then took ship
again from Marseille. When he returned from Rome, he entered the
final stage of his career, perhaps stimulated by this first taste of

travel. Joining in an association with other merchants, he became a seafaring businessman.

In his new role Godric visited the North Sea ports. His biographer Reginald recorded that he bought goods "of many kinds" where they were plentiful and cheap, and sold them in places where they were rare and "seemed more desirable to the natives than gold." Boston, Lynn, and the other ports of the English east coast traded mainly with Norway, supplying that country with foodstuffs, linen, flax, wax, and iron. Godric visited Flanders, the center of a fast-growing cloth industry; since Lincolnshire and Scotland produced fine wool, we can speculate that Godric was an early wool merchant, bringing raw wool from England and buying finished cloth and perhaps French wine to sell at home. He may have carried other English products too—tin, lead, skins, and leather. Probably he frequented the Flemish fairs, which flourished by this time at Ypres, Lille, Bruges, Thourout, and Messines, where a merchant could buy not only cloth but butter and cheese, Spanish shoe leather, fine skins, dyes, condiments, spices, metal objects, perfumes.

Godric was not a mere passenger on the ships that carried his merchandise; he took part in the operation of the vessel, and became an expert mariner, serving sometimes as navigator, sometimes as pilot. Eventually he became ship's master. He studied winds, currents, and weather as carefully as merchandise and market conditions. "From the sequence and strength of the winds and from the changing course of the streams of air," said Reginald, "he reckoned the coming storms with clever art." Without the aid of compass or astrolabe, he found his course by the sun and stars.

When he had acquired enough capital, Godric became a shipowning partner. First he owned a half share in a ship with several others, then he bought a fourth part by himself.

On his travels Godric visited many holy places, and collected prayers which he taught his associates to use in time of danger. They were efficacious; he survived many storms without shipwreck, escaped the traps of highwaymen and attacks of pirates, and even the intrigues of his fellow merchants. Several times he stopped to visit the Isle of Lindisfarne, to meditate at the shrine where St.

Cuthbert had lived as an anchorite. He began to think about retiring from his strenuous business life.

Godric's career as a merchant lasted for sixteen peril-laden but profitable years, toward the end of which he sailed the Mediterranean to make pilgrimages to Jerusalem, Rome, and St. Gilles. After his last voyage he settled briefly ashore as steward to a great lord. He soon found himself joining in banquets of servants at which the master's beef and mutton were consumed under the pretext that the meat was game. When strait-laced Godric discovered that the servitors were butchering their master's sheep and cattle, he reported at once to the lord, who refused to believe it. Godric resigned and went on another pilgrimage to Jerusalem and Rome in penance for having innocently taken part in the feasts.

Not long after, in the early years of the twelfth century, Godric made his decision to quit the world and devote himself to Christ. First he took his mother on a barefoot pilgrimage to Rome. On the long journey he sometimes carried the aged woman on his shoulders. Returning, he gave away all his money and property to the poor. Setting out through northern England, he began looking for a likely spot for his hermitage. He found it in the forest of Finchale, a peninsula on the River Wear in Northumberland. There he spent the remaining years of his life. According to the calculations of his biographers, these amounted to no fewer than sixty, though he was forty when he retired. In his long life as a holy man, he became celebrated for his prophetic visions, the most famous of which was the martyrdom of St. Thomas à Becket, an event that took place in 1170, the year of Godric's own death.

The question of how typical was this white-bearded saint, progressing from peasant's son to beachcomber, to peddler, to market trader, to seafaring merchant, has inspired lively debate among scholars since Pirenne. Were eleventh-century businessmen, in the words of a modern French scholar, *"fils de riches ou nouveaux riches"* (born rich or self made)? Were the harbingers of the commercial revival parvenus or were they more typically the descendants of merchants? The answer differed from place to place. In regions where an exchange economy had continued to operate, such

as parts of Italy, eleventh-century merchants and moneymen followed the profession of their fathers and grandfathers, and town-re-
siding nobles went into business. In more backward regions, the rising merchant was more likely to come from the ranks of such
dusty-foot peddlers as St. Godric. The economic tide was rising,
carrying with it the urban aristocrat like Pantaleone, the father-to-
son craftsman like Benedetto Rozo, and the plebeian adventurer like
Godric.

II

ADVENTURERS AND PROFITEERS

Businessmen of the Time of the Crusades

It was about the year of the millennium, 1000, that the men of Genoa and Pisa began the counterraids against the Saracens that grew into the European counteroffensive against Islam. At first the Italians fought from their fishing boats; later they used boats captured from the Saracens. In the eleventh century, they rapidly expanded their shipbuilding activity and began constructing warships. As ship design progressed and shipbuilding volume grew, shipyards were required, and Sicily, Pisa, Venice, and Genoa all established them. These new workshops employed skilled workers; a master builder directed a crew of carpenters, caulkers, and laborers in building two principal types of vessel, fighting ships and cargo boats. War galleys, light and of shallow draft, were usually about 130 feet long and 18 feet wide. On the poop rose the castellum, a two-level structure on the lower deck of which the officers slept; above was a balcony from which archers could fire. The prow terminated in a battering ram fashioned as a dragon's or lion's head. Down the center line of the ship ran a planked corridor where crew and passengers gathered for religious services or disciplinary hearings; on either side were the rowers' benches, each occupied by two oarsmen who shared an oar and slept by their benches. The oarsmen were free men, hired for the voyage, and capable of fighting. Oars lent speed and maneuverability, but most galleys were also equipped with sails for long-distance runs. All ships steered with side rudders, two great lateral oars toward the rear. Layers of leather protected the ship from shock and from incendiary projectiles; her own armament included missile-hurling catapults, mangonels, and trebuchets.

As time went on the counteroffensive expanded from improvised raids, undertaken by private merchants for protection and pillage, into genuine naval expeditions. In 1015 when an Arab adventurer named Mugiahid seized Corsica and Sardinia and threatened Liguria and the Tuscan coast, Genoa's feudal lord, the Marquis Obertenghi, led a papal-supported attack against the islands; the ships were commanded by the viscounts of Genoa and Pisa, nominal governors of those cities. The Italians won a decisive victory, marking the beginning of commercial penetration of Sardinia and Corsica by Pisa and Genoa. Thus the two cities passed from self-defense to counterpillage to a third stage: overseas trade. So profitable were these commercial operations that landowners began to sell property and invest the proceeds in ships and cargoes. Farmers deserted their back-breaking scratch plows to become sailors. Though galleys were too small to carry bulky merchandise, they were pressed into merchant service to transport spices, jewels, gold, luxury products small in volume and high in price, needing protection against pirates. Larger sailing ships, traveling in convoy with galley escort, carried timber, iron, grain, and other heavy goods.

Genoese and Pisans began to trade with the Arabs instead of fighting them. In 1088 when a North African king violated commercial treaties, Genoa and Pisa organized a punitive expedition against Mahdia (that in which a Pantaleone of Amalfi took part). Following an impressive victory that forced Muslim King Temim to pay a large indemnity and sign a landmark commercial agreement, the two Italian cities continued to grow and prosper, trading in the eleventh century in the Tyrrhenian and in western North Africa, though not as yet in any volume with the East.

At this time, probably during a military undertaking when

unity was indispensable, the armed companies of the parishes of Genoa came together to form a sworn association for mutual defense. At first temporary, renewed every three years, this arrangement assumed the name of "Commune." Many of the consuls who were its officials in the eleventh century were descendants of the viscounts; the rest were members of the lesser nobility. Similar aristocratic "consular" communes appeared in Pisa and other cities.

On the other side of the Italian peninsula, Venice's wealth and prestige grew as the city extended its commercial and political hegemony over the rivers of the Po Valley and over the upper Adriatic from Ancona, down the Italian coast, into northern Dalmatia, on the opposite shore. By the eleventh century, Venice was the regular port of embarkation for merchants and pilgrims from Germany and the Po Valley traveling to the Levant. Settled in Constantinople, thousands of Venetians did business with Greece, Asia Minor, Syria, and Egypt.

Signs of revival also multiplied in the north. In Flanders, a cloth industry had grown up in the Scheldt Valley, where fuller's earth, valuable in wool manufacture, was abundant and where the soil was suited to the growing of dyeplants. Now the industry spread along the rivers into Artois, Hainaut, and Brabant. In the last half of the eleventh century, a small social-economic revolution took place; within a generation the industry moved out of its rural cottages into town, and out of the hands of women into an intensive putting-out industry operated by male weavers, fullers, and dyers. The workers were in the employ of wholesale merchants operating on an international scale, importing fine wool from England (paradoxically, Flanders was not a wool-raising district), and selling their choice cloth in Amiens and Soissons as well as at the fairs of the Flemish cloth towns. Already these Flemish entrepreneurs enjoyed positions of wealth and power.

At the end of this century of transition and rapid social development came an event which accelerated the rate of change: the First Crusade. The Italian cities, especially Genoa and Pisa, furnished ships and money, food and equipment, arms, siege machinery, and men. In return, they won a powerful commercial bridgehead which gave them places beside Venice in the crucial Eastern trade.

Finally, in the twelfth century, the two geographic extremes of the Commercial Revolution, the cloth merchants of the north and the Italian businessmen who sailed to the eastern Mediterranean, found a historic meeting ground in the Champagne Fairs, where they exchanged Flemish wool cloth for the spices and silks of the Orient.

To underwrite the bursting commercial activity, new forms of investment were devised, methods of sharing the expenses and risks of undertakings, credit instruments, ways of carrying on business at a distance. Finance labored under a handicap: the Church's condemnation of usury, inherited from a less dynamic economic era in which borrowing was mostly by the needy, and lenders extorted high interest from the poor. The Church's censure of such usurers was energetically righteous. Abbot Guibert of Nogent tells the story of a usurer of Laon who on his deathbed "demanded interest from a certain poor woman who had already paid the debt itself. She begged him to remit the interest, calling upon his approaching end, but he obstinately refused to do so. She then brought in and placed on the chest all the agreed-upon interest of that miserable loan except one penny. And when she begged him to remit that alone, he swore he would never do it. . . . She sought for a penny, which she was scarcely able to find, and brought it to him when in the last conflict between flesh and spirit the death rattle was in his throat. Taking it in the moment of death, he placed it in his mouth; while he was swallowing it as though it were the viaticum [the Communion wafer] he breathed his last and under that protection went to the Devil. Consequently, his body was deservedly buried in banishment from holy ground."

This moral attitude, appropriate when credit was mostly for consumption, carried over into a period when credit was needed for production. Any kind of interest, receiving more in payment than one had lent, whether in money or goods, was categorized as usury; only money earned through work was considered legitimate. The pressure of economic growth demanded a relaxation of these moral pronouncements; shipowners, merchants, bankers all needed capital, and no one was willing to lend money and undertake risk without compensation. The theologians refusing to budge, businessmen had to invent ways of concealing interest, as a gift, or as damages suffered for delayed repayment, or in a difference in rates of exchange. Various forms of sleeping partnership were devised, in which one partner furnished capital and the other undertook the travel. But the exuberant demands of commercial growth continued an uneasy coexistence with the rigid moral tradition throughout the Middle Ages.

After a spectacular initial triumph, the Crusades failed in their advertised purpose of ousting the Muslims from the Holy Land. Far more significant than their political-religious failure was their resounding commercial success. By the middle of the twelfth century, the Italian maritime cities dominated Mediterranean commerce from Gibraltar to Asia Minor. At the beginning of the thirteenth century, the Fourth Crusade, led by Venice against Constantinople in the teeth of the Pope's excommunication, opened a vast new theater of operations: the Black Sea, with access to Russia, central Asia, and the Far East.

4

A Genoese Crusader:
Guglielmo Embriaco

"At this time news of the anchoring of six of our ships at Jaffa came to us as well as demands from the sailors that we send a garrison to protect the towers of Jaffa and their ships in the port," wrote the chronicler Raymond d'Aguilers, chaplain of Count Raymond of Toulouse. "The Crusaders gladly sent knights and foot soldiers. . . . By God's grace the enemy was routed and put to flight and around two hundred were killed and great booty was captured. . . . Following the fight and the collection and division of the booty, our knights went to Jaffa where the sailors joyously received them with bread, wine and fish. Now heedless of danger they posted no seaward lookouts. . . . The sailors found themselves surrounded from the sea by their enemies. . . . At daybreak they saw they had no chance to fight the superior forces, so they left their ships and bore only the spoils. . . .

"The Count of Toulouse . . . received aid from William Embriacus and his Genoese sailors, who, as I related earlier, lost their ships at Jaffa, but had salvaged ropes, hammers, nails, axes, mattocks and hatchets, all indispensable tools. . . ."

Building siege machinery with their "indispensable tools," the technically proficient Genoese helped the French knights of the First Crusade press the siege of Jerusalem (1099) to its successful conclusion. "The day of the assault dawned. . . . We pushed our towers against their walls and all the hellish din of battle broke loose; from all parts stones flew and arrows pelted like hail. . . ." It took two days, but finally the valor, prayers, and especially the siege machinery of the Christians won over the courage, prayers, and defensive skill of their adversaries, and, "In the Temple of Solomon," recorded the devout Raymond in an unforgettable phrase borrowed from the Book of Revelation, "the Crusaders rode in blood to the knees and bridles of their horses."

The Genoese who had played so conspicuous a role in the Crusade (though oddly inconspicuous in the innumerable latter-day accounts of it) were commanded by a pair of brothers, Primo di Castello and Guglielmo (William) Embriaco, also known as Capo di Martello (Hammerhead). Descendants of the viscounts who had governed Genoa in the Dark Ages, they were cadets of a large family and had joined the Crusade to seek their fortune, arming two galleys and undertaking to carry supplies to the army besieging Jerusalem.

The brothers were part of a second wave of Genoese Crusaders; the first had sailed two years before, in 1097, to reinforce the army

The siege of Antioch in 1097. The Genoese, participating for the first time in the Crusades, provided valuable logistical and engineering support during the siege, and were rewarded with commercial concessions after the city was taken. (Bibliothèque Nationale)

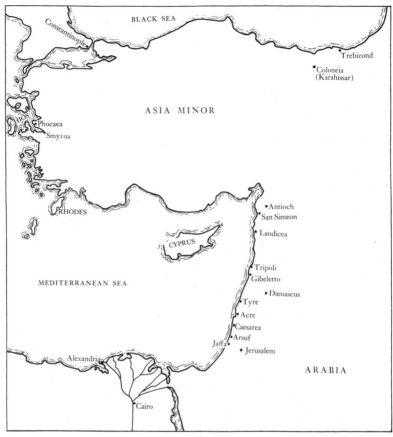

Asia Minor and the Crusader States of Syria

of Bohemund d'Hauteville at the siege of Antioch. The Genoese were inspired by the same mixture of religious zeal and love of plunder that motivated the French knights, but while the feudal French sought to acquire land, the Italians had a different goal: the acquisition of commercial footholds in the cities of Syria and Palestine. At the very outset they had scored a sensational success; their logistics and engineering support had gained them the privilege of a square in Antioch with thirty houses, a warehouse, a well, their own church, and perpetual exemption from all taxes. The agreement between the Genoese and Bohemund became a model for all future concessions to the Italian seafarer-adventurers in the Crusading states. The collaboration between the land-hungry French barons and the more sophisticated Italians was a congenial one; the Franks needed the Italian ships and engineers, the Italians needed the powerful French cavalry, and their goals of conquest were not conflicting but complementary.

Guglielmo Embriaco and his brother left Jerusalem with the Crusaders, spreading out to subdue the other strongholds of the Holy Land. Defeating an Egyptian army near Ramleh, the Genoese took possession of gold, silver, and jewels abandoned by the Muslims. With this booty they bought a new ship and sailed back to Genoa, carrying letters from Godfrey of Bouillon, king of Jerusalem, and Daibert, archbishop of Pisa who had been made patriarch of Jerusalem, urging reinforcements for Palestine. These letters, the stories of the treasure to be won in the Holy Land, and the fear of losing it to the Pisans and Venetians, had a healing effect on internal discords which had been plaguing Genoa. A huge armada of twenty-six galleys and four sailing ships, carrying 8,000 men, both Ligurians and Lombards, left Genoa on August 1, 1100, under the command of Guglielmo Embriaco, who was given the title of Consul of the Genoese Army.

When the ships put in to port at Laodicea, south of Antioch, in the dead of winter, Embriaco and his followers found the Holy Land in a state of crisis. Godfrey of Bouillon, the king of Jerusalem, was dead. Bohemund was prisoner of the Saracens, and the European-occupied coastal area, essential to the line of communications with the kingdom of Jerusalem, was in peril. Even worse, Pisans and Venetians had won important privileges in Syrian and Palestinian cities. But the Venetian fleet had gone home, and the Pisans served only as suppliers to the combatants. Embriaco seized the opportunity to reassert Genoese leadership. Taking over the defense of Laodicea, he backed Tancred d'Hauteville, grandson of Robert Guiscard, as regent of Antioch, and Baldwin of Flanders as king of Jerusalem, promising the latter to help him conquer at least two cities before summer. While he waited for favorable campaigning weather, Embriaco took his fleet on a pillaging expedition along the coast, shipping plunder home to Genoa. In May of 1101, the Genoese sailors joined the French knights in assailing Arsuf, ten miles south of Jaffa, capturing it after three days' siege. Then they turned their attention to the important city of Caesarea.

The Genoese historian Caffaro, an eyewitness and combatant, recorded the impassioned harangues addressed by the leaders to the gathering of Crusaders before the battle. First Daibert, the Patriarch of Jerusalem, spoke to the army: "God sends me to you and through my mouth commands that on Friday morning after receiving the Host, you will begin to scale the walls of the city, not with castles and siege machines, but only with ladders taken from your galleys. So that you may understand that you win the city not by your own valor but by the will of God, I prophesy that He will give it into our power before the sixth hour, and along with it the men, the women, the wealth that lie inside its walls." To this combination of appeals, the Crusaders responded with cries of "Fiat! Fiat!" (So be it!) Then Guglielmo Embriaco arose. "On, on, brave citizens and warriors of God, to fulfil the commands which the Lord has given us through the mouth of the Patriarch! These are God's orders, and we will swear to them: tomorrow after Mass, you are to gather without castles or siege machines, but only with the ladders from the galleys, following me to the walls of the city, which I, God willing, will climb, and you will surely not delay in imitating me."

At dawn the next day the Genoese, Guglielmo Embriaco at their head, entrusting themselves to Divine Aid and the advantages of a surprise attack, spearheaded the assault. It was successful, the city fell, the men and women of whom the Patriarch had spoken were massacred and raped, the wealth plundered, the city razed. The battle over, the Genoese withdrew to San Simeon, where they divided the booty according to the established arrangement: fifteen percent of the whole to the shipowners; gifts to officials and ship officers; and forty-eight solidi and two pounds of pepper each to the 8,000 soldiers and sailors. Only one item was set aside from the common spoils: the supposed Holy Grail, from which Jesus drank at the Last Supper. Carved from a single great emerald (much later discovered to be green glass), it was dedicated to the cathedral of San Lorenzo in Genoa. After the distribution of the booty, Guglielmo Embriaco and his men departed for home, where he remained for several years, serving a term as consul.

The Genoese joined the princes of the Holy Land in many further conquests, each conquest bringing them concessions and privileges like those of Antioch. When they helped capture a city, they were usually awarded a third of its area, with tax exemptions and administrative and judicial autonomy. In 1104 Baldwin, king of Jerusalem, gave them a section in Jerusalem, a street in Jaffa, and in Arsuf, Caesarea, and Acre a third of the city area and a third of the customs revenues. Gibeletto, just north of Beirut, was awarded to Genoa in its entirety; two-thirds of this town was ceded to the Embriaco family as a hereditary fief.

These privileges and others the Genoese proudly commemorated in a long and costly inscription in letters of gold on the pulpit of the Church of the Holy Sepulchre in Jerusalem. Sixty years later a jealous king of Jerusalem had the inscription removed, but by that time the Genoese had such deep roots in the Holy Land that inscriptions, even in gold, were beside the point.

The colonies established in the First Crusade became bridgeheads of Genoese commerce in the East. At first they dealt more in booty than in trade. Jerusalem, Arsuf, Caesarea, Acre, Gibeletto, Tripoli, Gebel, Beirut, Mamistra: almost the whole coastal strip of Syria and Palestine fell into European hands. The territory was small but its economic value was tremendous. Italian merchants could set foot in Asia in ground that belonged to their own city, under protection of European garrisons. In particular for the Genoese, who had never enjoyed the privileged position in Constantinople of Venice and Amalfi, the First Crusade was a historic turning point.

Along the narrow winding main street (*ruga*) of each Genoese colony, running down to the sea, intersected with little dead-end alleys, low wooden houses and narrow shops were crowded into every available inch of space. Large colonies sometimes had more than one ruga and a reserved section of the harbor, which could be closed off by a chain. At the harbor's edge stood the warehouses, for storage and sale of merchandise, and the customs house.

Ibn-Jubayr, a Spanish Muslim traveler, visited an Italian customs house at Acre in 1183, the kind of establishment from which Guglielmo Embriaco and his sons and grandsons took their wealth: "We were taken to the customs house, which is a khan [inn] to accommodate the caravan. Before the door are stone benches spread with rugs, where are Christian clerks of the customs, with their ebony inkstands, ornamented with gold. They write Arabic, which they also speak. Their chief is the Chief of the Customs, to farm the customs. He is known as al-Sahib, a title bestowed on him by reason of his office. . . . All the dues collected go to the contractor for the customs, who pays a vast sum [to the government]. The merchants deposited their baggage there, and lodged in the upper story. The baggage of any who had no merchandise was also examined, in case it contained concealed [and dutiable] merchandise, after which the owner was permitted to go his way and seek lodging where he would. All this was done with civility and respect, and without harshness and unfairness."

Following the principal ruga inland from the customs house, the traveler arrived at an open area surrounded by public buildings of stone and brick. One was the administration building of the colonial government, where government representatives lived, where the tribunal met, and where notaries drew up their deeds. Next to it was the church, dedicated to the patron saint of Genoa, San Lorenzo. Sometimes there was also a mint, which manufactured not Genoese coins but imitations of the Arab and Greek money which circulated locally. Some colonies had a slaughterhouse and a mill, all had a well and an oven; often there was a bathhouse. Rarely were there inns; visitors were expected either to stay in the customs house, find lodgings with fellow-countrymen, or rent houses for themselves. At the season when merchant ships arrived from the West, rents rose sharply.

Usually the colony owned orchards and farms in the country, which supplied it with food; sometimes it also had cotton and sugar-cane plantations. Silk, glass, and dyestuffs—indigo, madder, and

Tyrian purple—were local products in which they traded. But their chief source of income, and reason for being, was the commerce with the Far East. From China by sea, through the Indian Ocean to the Persian Gulf, then by the Tigris and Euphrates, or from Aden and the Red Sea, or by caravan through central Asia and Persia, silk and porcelain arrived in Syria, pearls from the Persian Gulf, brocades from Persia, spices and ivory from India, musk from Tibet, incense and dates from Arabia.

In the twelfth century, Europe had only inferior wares to offer in exchange—raw wool, hemp, linen, wood, iron, pitch, slaves—and had to redress the balance of trade with gold and silver. Much precious metal was looted in the Crusades, more was earned by trading with North Africa. Italians like the Embriaci grew rich on middlemen's profits. Two flotillas left Genoa every year: one around Easter, the other in August or September. Clinging to the coasts, with stops to pick up merchandise and merchants at Motrone, at Porto Pisano, and on down the Italian peninsula, they put in at Messina. Then they headed east across the Ionian Sea, pausing at Candia, halfway between Sicily and the Holy Land, then at Rhodes, finally at Cyprus. Under favorable conditions the crossing from Messina to Acre took about a month. Usually the ships that left Genoa in September arrived in the Holy Land in October and remained there for the winter, sailing the following spring and arriving in Genoa toward the end of June.

Before the Crusades, the Syrian trade was in the hands of Jews, Syrians, Arabs, and Byzantines. In the middle of the twelfth century, a few Levantines remained involved in trade with the Holy Land, notably a Syrian, Ribaldo di Saraphia, and a Jew, Blancardo; but the field was now dominated by five noble Genoese families, most of them descendants of the viscounts. In the forefront of these was Ingo della Volta, son or grandson of one of Guglielmo Embriaco's companions in the First Crusade, head of an autocratic faction which for many years controlled not only trade with the Crusading States but the government of Genoa, which they committed to a costly expansionist policy. That and corruption brought opposition and the downfall of the faction. In Syria, where the Embriaci had steadily improved their grip on the commercial life of the colonies, Guglielmo's grandson and namesake successfully exploited the financial straits of the home government. In 1134, when war with Pisa left Genoese coffers empty, the Embriaci obtained the remaining third of Gibeletto in rent, and the Genoese colonies of Laodicea, Solinum, and Antioch. After a costly Genoese expedition to Spain in 1147, the Embriaci obtained release from their Gibeletto rent for a fraction of what they owed. Seven years later they acquired the Genoese quarter of Acre at a disproportionately small rent. Such was their self-esteem that they coolly violated Genoese regulations limiting the height of buildings in the interests of public safety to build a splendid tower that dominates the old quarter of Genoa to this day.

When in 1189 Richard Lionheart and his fellow sovereigns, Philip Augustus of France and Frederick Barbarossa of Germany, organized a new (Third) Crusade, the Genoese were again active participants. An Embriaco, a della Volta, and a Doria joined the warriors, while other merchants supplied the army and initiated an important new Italian financial activity: loans to kings.

But beneath the surface, a change was taking place in Genoese affairs. Men of more modest resources were elbowing their way into business life. With the Eastern trade monopolized by the old patrician families of the First Crusade, the new merchants turned their ships toward Spain and North Africa to market the products of Europe's burgeoning industries. In Bugia, Ceuta, and Tunis they traded wool cloth and arms, brought from Flanders, Champagne, Germany, and Lombardy, for slaves, alum, and gold dust. Egypt offered its own alum, cotton, and hemp, the spices of the Orient and the ivory and incense of Africa—all at lower prices than Syria, thanks to the faster route via the Red Sea and the Nile from India and the Orient. Furthermore, here Genoese merchants did not have to pay in gold or silver, as in the Holy Land, because Egypt was hungry for wood, iron, pitch, oakum, and ships, as well as slaves. Unfortunately, the products that the Genoese furnished to the Egyptians

The Embriaci Tower in Genoa, built by the descendants of the Crusader Guglielmo Embriaco. The family had become so powerful from its colonial holdings that they could afford to ignore the city's height regulations when they built this tower, which still dominates Genoa's old quarter. (Ente Provinciale per il Turismo, Genoa)

were used principally against the Christian Holy Land. Popes and emperors vainly forbade the lucrative trade.

By the end of the twelfth century, the new men had effectively supplanted the old Embriaci–della Volta patrician class as the ruling group in Genoa. In Syria the Embriaci's ties with the mother country became increasingly attenuated. Their allegiance was rather to the princes of Antioch, descendants of Bohemund d'Hauteville, who had given Genoa its first colony. In the opening years of the thirteenth century, Plaisance Embriaco, the great-great-grandaughter of the first Guglielmo Embriaco, married Bohemund IV (Bohemund the One-Eyed); their son Bohemund V succeeded to the throne of Antioch in 1233. The Embriaci renounced their Genoese citizenship and ceased to pay rent or swear fidelity to the Commune of Genoa, although they continued to welcome their former fellow-countrymen to their ports free from all imposts. When later in the century the Holy Land fell, the Embriaci withdrew not to Genoa but to Cyprus, where they continued to live until the fifteenth century. In 1488, Tristan of Gibeletto, the last of the Embriaci, suspected of plotting against Venetian dominion of the island, was seized and taken to Venice; on the voyage, he committed suicide.

5

A Merchant of Venice: Romano Mairano

By the twelfth century Venice had undergone a profound alteration from the primitive scattering of huts of fishermen and salt workers described by Cassiodorus. Dikes and canals had transformed marshland into solid ground. Timber bridges crossed many of the tree-lined canals. On the banks stood great stone salt pans and mills that operated with the tides. The wooden houses of the poor rose from the mud, their foundations laid on platforms or piles, their roofs thatched or covered with wooden slats; rich people brought stone or brick from the mainland to build palaces. The town still had a partly rural look; there were vineyards, cattle-grazing meadows, and orchards. To house the relics of St. Mark which three enterprising Venetians had stolen and smuggled out of Alexandria in a basket of pork, the basilica of St. Mark had been completed in 1063. Pigeons strutted in the piazza; legend asserted that they had followed the last wave of fugitives from the mainland in the sixth century. Ferries plied between the islands, along with single-oared skiffs adapted for the canals and given a new name, gondola.

Venice was a mature maritime power. The prowess of her galleys, fighting alongside the Byzantine fleet, won from the Greek em-

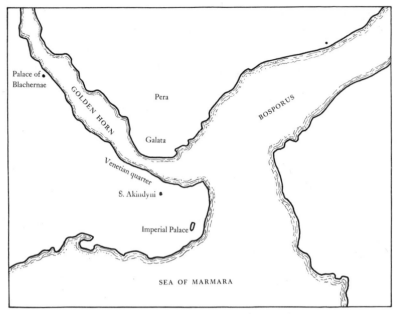

Constantinople in the Twelfth and Thirteenth Centuries

peror a Golden Bull, or decree, giving Venetian merchants a substantial reduction in tolls at Constantinople. Not all Venice's and Byzantium's fighting was against the Muslims. In 1081 when Norman chief Robert Guiscard attacked Byzantine Durazzo (in modern Albania), sixty Venetian war galleys routed his fleet. Emperor Alexius I rewarded them by issuing another Golden Bull, enlarging their concessions to give them an overwhelming advantage over all other foreign merchants.

Among the Italian colonies that lined the entire western shoreline of the Golden Horn, Constantinople's incomparable harbor, the Venetians had the most advantageous location: a strip of land a third of a mile long between two gates of the maritime wall of the city. Extending along the coast of the Golden Horn at its narrowest point, where the ferry crossed to Galata, a street on the seaward side of the wall ran the entire length of the quarter, one line of houses backing on the city wall, another facing them and running back to the water. A second street ran along the inside of the wall. Three wharves interrupted the shoreline; from the easternmost of these, the

Great Wharf, a street passed through the Jew's Gate into the inner city. Just inside the gate was the headquarters of the colony, in the shadow of the tower of the Monastery of St. George. Farther up on the slope of the hill stood St. Akindyni, the principal church of the quarter, belonging to the patriarch of Grado, highest church official of Venice. St. Akindyni's sphere of influence included the business community. The communal oven abutted on the church wall, ringed by shops owned by the church. St. Akindyni had a monopoly of the weights and measures for wine and oil used by the colony; sometimes the Patriarch of Grado leased this for cash.

To the east along the waterfront clustered the colonies of the other Italian maritime cities: first the Amalfitans, then the Pisans. In the early 1100s the Genoese were dispersed through the city, not establishing a colony until 1160, in the suburbs across the Golden Horn. Rivalry among the Italian colonies bred chronic feuds, turning into little wars; in the 1160s a conflict drove the Genoese colony out of Constantinople for more than ten years.

The population of the Latin colonies was mostly youthful, made up of sons of merchants sent from Italy to learn the arts of commerce. Young patricians commonly began their careers by sailing off in the spring on the family ships, each apprentice merchant in charge of a small stock which he marketed abroad, returning in the fall to winter in Venice. Gradually he gained knowledge of markets and goods; he married and invested his wife's dowry in trade; he was promoted to larger cargoes and finally sent to represent the family in Alexandria, or Beirut, or at Constantinople.

But the young businessmen were not all members of the patrician class. Among the Venetians who trod the streets of the colony on the Golden Horn in the middle of the twelfth century was Romano Mairano, a "new man" whose family's name had never appeared in either Venetian annals or business records. Mairano himself never held public office or attained great fortune; but through the accidents of history, which cast him in a hero's role, and through the chance that his business records survived him, he has become the most famous Venetian merchant of his century.

Born in the 1120s or 1130s, Romano Mairano was first mentioned in commercial documents in 1150, in association with his brother Samuel. The Mairani, with headquarters in Constantinople, made short voyages to Macedonia, to Thessaly and to Smyrna. The scope of Romano's affairs in these years was limited, as is shown by the smallness of the loans by which he financed them. He spent the year 1152 in Venice, marrying the daughter of Corrado Mangiacaccio, who brought him a modest dowry consisting of household articles. After 1160 his activities broadened. Still maintaining his base of operations at Constantinople, he sailed to Acre and Alexandria, trading with the kingdom of Jerusalem and with Egypt, and borrowing larger sums to finance his enlarged operations.

Most commonly, Mairano employed the straight sea loan, by which the lender assumed the risk of shipwreck or piracy and the borrower paid for this protection in a high rate of interest— Romano paid as much as 45 percent—which included a heavy premium for insurance. Occasionally he used a sleeping-partnership arrangement called in Venice the *collegantia*—elsewhere it went by other names: *societas maris* in Pisa, *societas* or *commenda* in Genoa. The origin of this device may have been Arab, Jewish, or Greek; the Venetians acquired it from Byzantium. In this popular arrangement one partner contributed all or the greater part of the capital and the other man undertook the voyage, the profits of which were divided according to a prearranged formula. If the capitalist contributed all the backing, he usually got back three-fourths of the profit. But if he contributed two-thirds of the money and the active partner one-third, the profits were divided equally. Both arrangements were ways of broadening the base of investments, evading the prohibition against usury, and, in the absence of marine insurance, spreading the risks. Often the capitalist was an older man who had retired from active trade; but a man might be capitalist for one contract and active partner for another, often at the same time. Sometimes Romano Mairano borrowed money by another form of contract, the *cambium maritimum* (maritime exchange), repaying the loan in another currency, with interest concealed in the rate of exchange.

These contracts, which allocated capital and profits, usually listed the merchandise to be transported, but the destination was frequently designated only as "overseas," "to Barbary," "wherever God wills it," "where he wishes," or other indeterminate phrases. The traveling partner had a certain liberty of itinerary and merchandise, although the stay-at-home had the right to recall him at any time and oblige him to return his capital. The traveler was also required to render an accounting on his return.

In 1158 Romano's business association with his brother was interrupted by their father's death; but four years later he and Samuel renewed their partnership, undertaking to furnish 50,000 pounds of iron to the military order of Knights Templar in Syria. July 1167 found him sailing from Constantinople to Salonika and on to Alexandria with two of his own ships, commanding one himself, the other captained by a fellow Venetian, Bartolomeo Zulian. This venture was financed by eight sea loans, the lenders being, with one exception, Italians rather than Greeks. At least four of the backers went along on the trip and collected principal and interest in November when they arrived in Alexandria; the rest were repaid in February and March of 1168 when the ships returned to Constantinople. On the return trip, Romano Mairano also entered into a collegantia contract with Domenico Giacobbe, a merchant traveling on Bartolomeo Zulian's ship, investing two shares to one of Giacobbe's in the cargo. Giacobbe was to sell it in Thessaly and render accounts to Romano fifteen days after Zulian's ship arrived in Constantinople, profits to be divided equally between the two partners and losses shared proportionately to the investment.

The following year, 1169, political trouble overtook Mairano. The wealth and numbers of Venetians operating virtually tax-free in Constantinople had for some time been an irritant to the native Greeks, while Manuel Comnenus, the emperor, nourishing dreams of reconquering long-lost Italy and reestablishing the Western Roman Empire, saw his hopes of Venetian assistance fading; more and more Venice showed signs of developing into a rival rather than an ally.

The crisis came to a head in 1166 when Venetian Doge Vitale Michiel refused to pay a subsidy to defend the Empire against the

Normans, on the grounds that Venice did not want to risk its trade in Apulia. At the same time, foreseeing trouble, the doge ordered all Venetian merchants to quit Constantinople. Forced to give up his business when the outlook was most promising, Romano Mairano returned home. His first wife had died, and he now married a comparatively wealthy woman who brought him 300 pounds in dowry. With the aid of this money, and in anticipation of returning to Constantinople, he undertook his biggest venture, building a three-masted ship, the *Kosmos,* and raising more capital by negotiating eleven sea loans. He signed a contract to farm the revenues in Constantinople of the patriarch of Grado, including the monopoly of weights and measures in the imperial city. He paid 500 pounds in advance for the privilege of collecting the patriarch's taxes and fees, speculating on the assumption that the Venetians would soon return to the Greek city.

This time Mairano's principal backer was a wealthy patrician, Sebastiano Ziani, who apparently helped negotiate the concession of the patriarch's revenues. Perhaps partly to protect his own investment, Ziani undertook an embassy to Constantinople with another Venetian, Orio Mastropiero. Unfortunately the solution became part of the problem; the size and magnificence of the convoy which escorted the delegation added to the Greeks' resentment of Venice.

But as a result of the diplomatic representations, normal relations were uneasily resumed; and Romano Mairano and his fellow merchants returned to Constantinople. Soon after, Sebastiano Ziani and Orio Mastropiero received disquieting intelligence; the emperor was secretly moving soldiers into the city. The Venetian ambassadors demanded an audience. The emperor coolly denied that he had any hostile intentions, and broadcast a proclamation threatening to hang anyone who molested a Venetian. But troops continued to concentrate, manning the walls as if for a siege.

On March 12, 1172, the emperor suddenly dropped the mask, ordering the arrest of all Venetians and confiscation of their goods. Troops invaded the Venetian quarter, arresting merchants and their families wholesale and killing all who resisted. Romano Mairano's *Kosmos* lay anchored in the Golden Horn. That night, a number of

Venetians who had managed to escape arrest and death stole on board. Romano gave the command to weigh anchor, the *Kosmos* hoisted sail and headed for the open sea. As day dawned, Byzantine galleys rowed out in pursuit, drawing close enough to fire their catapults loaded with projectiles charged with the famous incendiary Greek fire. But Romano had ordered hides soaked in vinegar hung around the bulwarks, and the flaming projectiles were extinguished. The breeze was favorable and, according to a chronicler, the *Kosmos*, seeming "to fly rather than sail," outran the galleys to safety in Latin-held Acre.

The *Kosmos* and other Venetian ships that had escaped from Thessaly brought Venice news of the outrage; they reported that ten thousand Venetians (doubtless an exaggeration) had been imprisoned, so many that the prisons could not hold them, and monasteries were pressed into service as detention camps; property worth

The waterfront of Venice, busy with boats of all sizes and kinds, including multi-oared galleys as well as sailing ships, in a detail from a map by Jacopo de' Barbari. (Ente Provinciale per il Turismo, Venice)

two million pounds was seized. The Venetian public was enraged and demanded war. Against his better judgment, the doge gave in and an expedition was organized. Ravaged by pestilence, it had to return to Venice, a frustrating military failure that resulted in the assassination of the doge. His successor was Sebastiano Ziani, Romano Mairano's patron. Diplomacy was substituted for arms, and for several years ambassadors from both sides shuttled between Constantinople and Venice without being able to reach any agreement, the chief obstacle being the Venetian demand for indemnities. Meanwhile, the Venetians, looking for other footholds, made a commercial treaty with William II of Sicily, the first such compact of Venice with the Norman kingdom.

Romano Mairano had returned home a hero, but bankrupt. His contract with the patriarch of Grado was void, his property and goods in Constantinople had been seized, he was in debt, all the opportunities which had opened before him had evaporated, yet he did not give himself up to despair. With Constantinople closed off, he looked for a new field of operations, using Venice as his base. He began to sail to Egypt, still acting as captain, unable to send a younger man or to replace his aging ship.

In 1173 he undertook a voyage to Alexandria underwritten by Pietro Ziani, the son of his old backer Sebastiano. Not only did Pietro Ziani lend Mairano the large sum of 1000 pounds outright, to be invested in pepper, but one of his agents brought a cargo of timber from Verona and consigned it to Mairano, to be exchanged for alum. In Alexandria, Mairano turned over some shares of pepper to two fellow Venetians who had anticipated the price in the form of a maritime loan.

In the spring of 1177, Mairano was back in Venice, busy with preparations for his boldest naval undertaking: a trip to Barbary, an unusual destination for Venetians at that time. A new ship was built for the voyage. For the first time, Mairano did not make the journey himself, but entrusted the command to one Giovanni da Ponte, who also purchased a fifth share of the enterprise, financed by four other large loans. Departure was delayed until the spring of 1178, when the ship left for Zara, reaching Alexandria in July, and continuing to Bugia and Ceuta. Da Ponte was back in Venice in February of 1179 to collect the 1,333 pounds he had invested, plus 200 for his services, plus another 100 pounds bonus. The voyage had been completed, but the venture was not a success; to satisfy his creditors, Mairano had to sell the ship.

The trip to Barbary was not repeated, and the next year Mairano resumed trade with the Holy Land and Egypt, again commanding in person ships nominally his own, but actually belonging to the investors. In 1184 he built a new ship and financed a voyage by a new kind of contract, obtaining maritime loans in Venice which he repaid by delivering alum and pepper from Alexandria when he returned.

In 1182 Constantinople was shaken by another violent xenophobic storm, following the death of Emperor Manuel Comnenus. Mob action escalated into a general massacre of all Latins. Forty-four galleys loaded with refugees escaped; the remaining Italians, including many women and children as well as the aged and infirm, were slaughtered. The Latin houses and shops were burned, monks and priests tortured and killed, tombs violated, the sick in the hospital of St. John put to the sword, men sold into slavery with the Turks.

For three years the ruined foreign quarter of Constantinople lay deserted. Then in 1185 the Norman fleet seized Salonika and threatened Constantinople. The new emperor Isaac Angelos ousted them; but he also undertook to end Byzantine isolation and invite the Latins back to the imperial city. The marriage of Constance, daughter of Roger II of Sicily, to Henry VI, son of Frederick Barbarossa, presaging a Norman-Hohenstaufen alliance, heightened Byzantine alarm. Peace was concluded in 1189; not only was Venice promised the indemnity it had demanded, but an offensive-defensive alliance made the Venetian navy Byzantium's chief protector. Significantly, the Golden Bull which embodied these provisions was not a unilateral edict, like those of 992 and 1082, but a pact in which Venice was a contracting party, on an equal plane with Byzantium.

The year the treaty was signed, Romano Mairano established himself at Tyre, sailing from there to the Dardanelles. Finally, after twenty years' absence, he set foot once more in Constantinople. He had never recovered the ground lost during the rift. Sixty years old, after more than forty years at sea, long past the age when more fortunate merchants quit the rigors of commerce for the dignity of public service, or confided their capital to younger men on the ships and in the colonies, Romano Mairano was still at the helm of his own ship. Not till 1190 did he retire, turning over the command of his last two voyages, to Apulia in 1192 and to Alexandria in 1199, to his son Giovanni. He was in financial straits in 1201; he had to borrow fifty pounds from a cousin, who loaned the old man the money without interest. Apparently Romano's son died at about this time, for at Romano's own death not long after 1201, his property passed to his daughter, a nun whose convent preserved the documents which tell the story of his career.

In contrast to the fate of this courageous and able man of modest means, so hard hit by the political upheavals of his time, was the story of his financial backers, the Ziani. Patricians, although not among the old "tribunal" families descended from the sixth century refugees, the Ziani had gradually risen through commerce to become the richest family in Venice. "L'haver de cha Ziani," "the wealth of the Ziani," was proverbial. Sebastiano Ziani, who had a distinguished career as a judge and ambassador before he became doge at the age of seventy, owned whole blocks of the city, including all the houses that surrounded the piazza of St. Mark. He was one of twelve capitalists who farmed the revenues of the market of Rialto for eleven years, from 1164 to 1175. His son Pietro, captain and administrator, was a landowner on a large scale. He possessed vineyards and farmlands bought by himself or by his father, on the Venetian islands, in the Po delta, and around Padua, saltworks and mills, property in Constantinople, houses, shops, whole streets in Venice, all highly profitable speculations on Venice's rapid expansion.

The Ziani, with ample capital behind them, weathered the storms of the last quarter of the twelfth century with little difficulty. Sebastiano, the doge who built the first crossing over the Grand Canal, a pontoon bridge at the site of the later Rialto Bridge, and who played an influential role in the victory of the pope in his struggle against Frederick Barbarossa, was architect of an even more important innovation, significant for his own patrician class and for the middle-class Mairani: "reforms" which intensified the oligarchic tendencies of the Venetian government and weakened the position of the smaller businessmen, the sailors, and the traveling merchants. Elsewhere, the end of the twelfth century was the era when the *popolo*, the organization of the lesser merchants and "new men," was beginning to stir, forming itself into guilds and armed societies which succeeded in gaining control of the government of many cities, including Milan, Florence, Lucca, Orvieto, Volterra, Siena, Bologna, Faenza, Pisa, and Genoa. Nothing like this happened in Venice; the strong, exclusive rule of the patricians frustrated the development of popular government. The merchant company, so influential in other Italian cities where government was weak and unstable and the economic power of individuals and families strong, never appeared in Venice. Venice had its bankers, some very wealthy and important; but they were forced by law to limit their activities to deposit banking and exchange, while credit was monopolized by foreign bankers, mainly Paduans, Veronese, or Tuscans, and pawnbroking by Jews. Never in Venice did there appear the combination of merchant, banker, and industrialist which was the rule in Florence. The State dominated business and exercised firm control over its merchants. This autocratic system minimized the family feuds, factional wars, and anarchic individualism that raged chronically in Pisa and Genoa.

A short time after Romano Mairano's death (1202 or 1203), another patrician, Doge Enrico Dandolo, nephew of the patriarch of Grado whose privileges in Constantinople Mairano had contracted to farm, only slightly less wealthy than the Ziani, was responsible for the adventure that brought Venice its greatest triumph. The Doge, over ninety and totally blind, weeping sentimentally on public occasions, talked the leaders of the Fourth Crusade into an expedition against Constantinople. On April 12, 1204, Venetian sailors and French knights leaped into the waters of the Golden Horn and stormed the walls that had stood for nine hundred years. "There followed a scene of massacre and pillage," wrote Geoffrey de Villehardouin. "On every hand the Greeks were cut down, their horses, palfreys, mules and other possessions snatched as booty. So great was the number of killed and wounded that no man could count them. A great part of the Greek nobles fled towards the gate of Blachernae; but by this time it was past six o'clock, and our men had grown weary of fighting and slaughtering. . . ."

The revolution in Venetian-Byzantine relations was complete: the apprentice had overthrown the master, and did not delay in despoiling him. The establishment of the Latin Empire in Constantinople, opening up the Black Sea region to commercial exploitation, was the beginning of Venice's golden age in the East, an age that Romano Mairano did not live to share.

Pietro Ziani became doge in 1205, contracting in 1213 an almost royal marriage with Constance d'Hauteville, cousin of Holy Roman Emperor Frederick II, and granddaughter of King Roger of Sicily. In 1229, fabulously wealthy and covered with honors, he retired to the monastery of San Giorgio Maggiore to live out the remainder of a life unmarred by the uncertainties and misfortunes which had plagued Romano Mairano.

6

The Royal Milch Cow:
Isaac of Norwich

Jewish moneymen of the Middle Ages formed a group apart. Their special status as Jews gave them special characteristics, and too often a special fate. Though their situation was basically similar throughout Europe, like other customs and institutions it varied from the advanced Mediterranean to the lagging northwest. Nowhere was the Jewish moneyman's tragedy more brutally played out than in feudal, backward England.

Isaac fil' Jurnet of Norwich grew up in the last quarter of the twelfth century and died about 1235. Norwich, where coins were minted in Saxon times, and which was prosperous enough to invite a Viking attack in 1004, was one of the largest towns in England, with perhaps 3,000 inhabitants, when the Normans took over. Until 1066 there were no Jews in England; the first to arrive followed in the wake of Hastings, settling in London. In the next two generations they spread to other towns; their presence in Norwich by 1144 is known from the record of the martyrdom of St. William, a murder mystery with ominous overtones for European Jews. St. William was an adolescent boy whose half-naked body was found in a wood outside Norwich, the victim, modern scholars speculate, of a sexual attack. The Jews were blamed because of minor circumstantial evidence, and because a local prior saw an opportunity to create a saint to the profit of the diocese. But despite the threats of the bishop, the Jews received protection from the sheriff, who as the king's representative would not permit them to be tried by ecclesiastical court; the Jews belonged to the king and were always tried in the royal court, where the revenue went to the king. This first European ritual-murder case ended inconclusively, but the anti-Jewish feelings among the Anglo Saxon populace were aroused and continued to smolder dangerously, in Norwich and elsewhere. Similar accusations were made across the island in Gloucester in 1168, at neighboring Bury St. Edmunds in 1181, and at Bristol in 1183. None of these cases had serious consequences, but all heightened the anti-Jewish atmosphere in England.

At the time of Isaac fil' Jurnet's birth in about 1175, Norwich had grown to 5,000, probably the third or fourth city in England. Isaac's grandfather seems to have been a Jewish immigrant named Deodatus, from either Normandy or the lower Rhineland. His father was Jurnet, by the time of Isaac's birth a leading member of the Norwich Jewish community. The city's economic life had three aspects, as a market center for a prosperous farming region, as an industrial center for leather manufacture, and finally as an important center of foreign trade, exporting woad, the source of blue dye, and importing timber, iron, olive oil, alum, and other commodities from Scandinavia, Germany, France, and Spain. In all these activities the hundred and fifty Jews of Norwich took no part. Their few craftsmen—a fish seller, a cheesemonger, a vintner, a doctor—supplied the needs of the Jewish community only. The role of the Norwich Jews in the economic life of the city was restricted to a single function: moneylending. The Church's prohibition of usury was taken far more seriously in England than in Italy; the Jews, barred from holding land and encumbered with handicaps as merchants, were forced into moneylending. Nearly all their lending was pawnbroking. From rich and poor Christians they accepted pledges —clothes, pots and pans, farm produce, jewelry, wagonloads of hay, monastic manuscripts, furs, carpets, saddles, cows, coats of mail.

Jurnet, father of Isaac, was one of the few Norwich Jews who operated on a large scale. In the 1160s he lent money to the Countess of Brittany, and from 1175 on, in partnership with other Jews, to King Henry II. In that initial year he and a London Jew paid the king four gold marks for the privilege of forming a consortium.

The Jewish quarter of Norwich, like those of many western European cities, was not strictly a ghetto; Christians lived there too, and Jews were not restricted to it. It consisted of a number of small streets clustered around the marketplace, just southwest of the castle, bordered on the north by Saddlegate, now White Lion Street, and on the south by Horsemarket, the present Rampant Horse Street. The houses of the Judeismus or Jewry were the same tall narrow timber-and-plaster dwellings with shops on the ground floor, crowded together cheek-by-jowl, as those of their Christian neighbors. Half a mile away on the bank of the River Wensum stood the Jurnet house, built at about the time of Isaac's birth, where he grew up. Located in the southeastern quarter of town, on Conesford Street, today King Street, it was one of the very few houses in town built of stone. Rectangular in plan, with a twenty-foot frontage on Conesford Street by a depth of slightly over fifty feet, it had no door on the street but a stone porch and entranceway on the side and a small court behind. The ground floor consisted of two large rooms, the shop and the storeroom. Both were arched and vaulted, illuminated only by a few narrow windows. Upstairs were the family's living quarters, the solar and sleeping area. A small fortress, the house was designed to give protection to its owners and their possessions, including the pledges of their clients. The elder Jurnet built his miniature castle between 1175 and 1190; by the latter date there was good reason for a rich Jew to look to his defenses.

During the reign of Henry II (1154–1189) English Jews were relatively well off, though they may not have thought so themselves. When one of his partnerships failed in 1177, Isaac's father had to pay £1,333 (2,000 marks) as his share of a terrific £4,000 fine. Yet he paid it off in four years. In shifting partnerships with other Norwich Jews and with Isaac fil' Rabbi of London and Aaron of Lincoln, reputed the two wealthiest Jews in the kingdom, Isaac's fa-

ther was a regular lender to the Crown. Jewish advances to the Exchequer were commonly made on the security of the "farm of the shire," that is, the local share of the tax. Ecclesiastics were also large borrowers. The steward of the abbey of Bury St. Edmunds ran up a debt of £60 without letting his superiors know; when the elder Jurnet dunned the abbey the steward was sacked.

In the mid-1180s Jurnet sojourned abroad, probably in Normandy, we do not know why, or whether Isaac went with him. In 1186 he paid 2,000 marks for the privilege of returning to Norwich. That December he was assessed no less than £6,000 in the tallage, the feudal tax levied on the royal towns, a sum he succeeded in getting reduced to £1,221, no doubt by appropriate bribes.

That year the wealthy Aaron of Lincoln died, setting in train events of sinister significance to his fellow Jews. Normally the king's succession duty (inheritance tax) from a Jew was a third of all assets, but if the Jew could be found guilty of a crime, the king's right of escheat—the reversion of property to the Crown in default of legal heirs—gave him the whole estate. Henry II needed money for the war he was waging against his sons in France. A pretext was found; all the property of the dead usurer was declared escheated, and all the cash and bullion sent straight to France. Unluckily the ship carrying it sank. That still left very substantial assets, for Aaron had outstanding credits amounting to £15,000, which equaled three-fourths of the normal royal income. Collecting it for the Crown was a problem; there were 430 debtors, scattered all over Britain—earls, bishops, the king of Scotland, the archbishop of Canterbury. A special Exchequer task force was organized, the *Scaccarium Aaronis*, with two treasurers and two clerks at its head.

While the Scaccarium Aaronis was pursuing Aaron's far-flung debtors, old King Henry was succeeded by his rebellious son Richard, who immediately announced his intention of taking over the Crusade his father had planned. Henry had already levied the "Saladin tithe," a special tax on personal property by which the English Jews were relieved of a fourth of their goods rather than a tenth like their Christian fellow countrymen. On the basis of the Exchequer's

Entrance to the shop on the ground floor of the house Jurnet the Jew built in Norwich sometime between 1175 and 1190. One of the few buildings in the town constructed of stone, the house was virtually a small castle, designed as much for protection of the owner and his belongings as for shelter. (Hallam Ashley) calculation of the Saladin tax, the Jews were credited with possessing more than a quarter of the nonlanded wealth of the nation, for their fourth was expected to amount to £60,000 as against £70,000 for the tithe of the Christians. That was doubtless an exaggeration, but it is a graphic reflection of the economic situation created by the money-lending monopoly enjoyed by, or more precisely, forced on the Jews.

The Saladin tithe was not the only bad news the Third Crusade brought English Jews. Richard's coronation in London triggered the first of a series of violent pogroms. Early in 1190 there was an outbreak in Lynn, a port forty-five miles west of Norwich on the Wash, in which sailors killed a number of Jews. A little later (February 6), "all the [Norwich] Jews who were found in their homes," according to chronicler Ralph de Diceto, "were butchered; some had taken refuge in the castle." Jurnet, his wife Muriel, Isaac and his sister Margaret remained unscathed in their stone house; that poorer Jews perished we know from the record of the Constable of the Tower of London who rendered account of £28 7s 2d of their chattels which escheated to the Crown.

The most serious anti-Jewish riot took place at York, where a hundred and fifty men, women, and children anticipated their fate by committing mass suicide, setting themselves on fire in the castle while a mob, whose members included the sheriff's posse, raged outside. The royal government was aroused, especially as it was observed that the mobs sacking the houses of rich Jews took care to destroy moneylending records, causing the Crown to lose the value of the escheated loans.

Unmistakably, Jewish fortunes in England had taken a turn for the worse by the day, sometime before Michaelmas 1197, that Jurnet of Norwich died peacefully in his bed. No charges were leveled against the dead moneylender, and no attempt made to seize his assets. Son Isaac bought the royal restraint by paying a thousand marks for the right to collect debts owed his father.

That, it turned out, was barely the beginning. The lesson learned from the destruction of Jewish records by the Crusade mobs, and the precedent set by the Scaccarium Aaronis, alerted the government first to the danger, and then to the opportunity. A Scaccarium Judeorum, or Exchequer of the Jews, was set up. Unlike the Scaccarium Aaronis, the new department did not wait for Jews to die before looking into their accounts, but instead kept the Jews' records while they were living. "*Archae,*" or recording bureaus, were established in all the principal towns, and all moneylending transactions officially recorded. If a Jew lent money, the government knew about it, and when a Jew died the government could not be cheated. The Exchequer of the Jews had a further value; it provided the government with accurate knowledge of Jewish revenues, and so tempted royal exactions. Richard Lionheart, back from the Crusade and pressed for cash by his war with Philip Augustus, king of France, did not overlook the possibilities; Jewish money helped build Chateau Gaillard, the strong castle guarding Normandy. Richard's successor John, even more pressed because of his military reverses, overlooked them even less. Under Richard and John the traditional royal policy of benevolent rapacity began to be distorted into confiscation.

It started with the idea that taxing rich Jews was simpler than borrowing from them, and more convenient than waiting for them to die. If the kings had stopped there they might have arrived at a rational arrangement. They could not, or at least did not. Richard's administrators worked out the tax machinery which their successors under John improved, and which those of John's successor Henry pushed to grotesque perfection.

To make possible the payment of the new large taxes, Jewish moneymen had to be given strong protection by royal authority. The economic process that resulted was described by a picturesque metaphor: the Jewry was a sponge, which the king periodically picked up, squeezed into the Exchequer, then set back in the stream of economic life. In another metaphor, English Jewry was dubbed "the Royal Milch Cow."

Isaac fil' Jurnet was an outstanding example of how the system worked. His inheritance from Jurnet made him the richest man in Norwich. Already active for several years in the business (together with his mother, Muriel, and his Uncle Benedict), Isaac demonstrated energy and capacity. His transactions extended all over eastern England and into London. He bought a house in London, on Lothbury Street in Old Jewry, where the Bank of England now stands, and six houses in Lynn. Within a few years his reputation had succeeded Aaron of Lincoln's as the wealthiest Jew, which meant the richest man in liquid assets, in England. He came to be known as "Isaac of Norwich" and even as "Isaac le Grand"—a lesser Norwich Isaac was known as Isaac Parvus.

Isaac's financial intake was steady and large; his output to the government was intermittent and enormous. In the tallage of 1199 he paid over £400, an eighth of the entire tax levied in Norwich. When in 1210 the Bristol tallage of £44,000, to pay for King John's renewed preparations for war, fell as usual most severely on the Jews, Isaac of Norwich was among a large number seized and imprisoned, evidently for failure to meet the limit of the exaction. Another Isaac, of Canterbury, was hanged; Isaac of Norwich succeeded in escaping with a fine of 10,000 marks (£6,667). His bonds, his house, and his chattels were all confiscated, including the stone house on Conesford Street.

Either Isaac remained in prison or he was later reincarcerated; in 1213 the Constable of Bristol Castle was ordered to send him to the Tower of London.

A year later King John's military fortunes reached their low point with the battles of Bouvines and La-Roche-aux-Moines, forcing him to renounce his hope of recovering Normandy, and largely shutting off English Jews from their coreligionists on the Continent. The defeat also brought the Magna Carta, two clauses of which related to the Jews. The clauses (tenth and eleventh) stipulated that debts due Jews and other usurers should bear no interest during the minority of the heir of a deceased debtor, and that if such debts fell into the king's hands (through the death of the Jew) the capital only, without interest, should be paid. Also, a widow's dowry and support of minor children should come out of an estate before debts were paid. In these clauses may be read the bitter resentment of the barons at the Jews and their relationship to the king.

The following year (1216) John died. The accession of Henry

III at first brought a respite for English Jews, as the new administration sought to restore their financial position. Imprisoned Jews were released and some of their confiscated bonds even restored. Isaac of Norwich was set at liberty and the sheriffs of Norfolk and Suffolk, Essex, Hertford, Cambridge, and Huntingdonshire were ordered to help him collect a list of debts bearing the king's seal. The Constable of Norwich Castle was instructed to aid Isaac "and all his people and all his goods and all other Jews of Norwich. You are to protect them; Isaac himself and his people you are to receive into our castle." That the sheriff was instructed to take Isaac into the castle implies that his confiscated house was not yet returned; however, we know that he recovered it presently, doubtless at a price. The Prior of Norwich, into whose safekeeping Isaac's papers had been given, was directed to restore them to their owner. By the 1220s Isaac's status was largely if not fully recovered; his transactions in one surviving list amount to £1,647, compared with £258 for the next highest creditor. There are other indications of his recovery: a suit he filed against the abbot of Winchester over a debt, and a complaint brought against him by a Christian named Peter de Nereford, alleging that Isaac's squire Hugh and twenty other retainers broke into Peter's property and "evilly beat and entreat" Peter and his men, inflicting "much loss beside and mischief to the great detriment of their bodies and chattels." The surprising aggression was probably part of a royal sheriff's seizure.

Another mark of Isaac's position with the king, a royal grant of 1231 of freedom from tallage for the remainder of his life, was more form than substance; in the first place, Isaac was old, and in the second he still paid. In 1234 the king wrote: "If Isaac of Norwich pays to the Treasury what he ought to pay . . . order the Sheriff of Norfolk not to compel Isaac to come in person to London but without hindrance let him return to his own," implying that the sheriff had Isaac in custody.

In actual fact, in spite of the appearance of Isaac's continuing prestige, the era of Jewish prosperity in England was over. The sponge policy was back, more merciless than ever. Simultaneously, popular animosity, guided and inflamed by the Church, became

Isaac fil' Jurnet, richest Jew in England at the beginning of the twelfth century, is the central figure in this caricature sketched on a contemporary document. At left is Mosse Mokke, one of three Jews hanged on the charge of having circumcised a Christian boy in Norwich. (Public Record Office)

more and more threatening. The anti-Jewish decrees of the Fourth Lateran Council were reinforced with canons issued by Archbishop Langton which were directed primarily against the Jews of Norwich, Oxford, and Lincoln, where the Church organized the townspeople to boycott Jews and even to refuse to sell food to them. The Crown stepped in to order anyone arrested who refused to sell food to Jews.

In the 1230s a strange legal case further exacerbated relations between Norwich Jews and Christians. It was an accusation not of murder but of circumcision. The allegation was that the Jews had taken a Christian boy named Odard, circumcised him, and renamed him Jurnepin. One Jew, Senioret fil' Josce, was outlawed; later Senioret and twelve other Jews were brought to trial on the complaint of Benedict, the boy's father (who may have been a converted Jew). Several were imprisoned, various fines were levied, appeals made, and ultimately three—Mosse Mokke, Isaac Parvus, and Diaia le Cat—were hanged, their property escheating to the Crown. The long-drawn-out case was doubtless a contributing factor to an outbreak against the Jews in 1235, when several houses were set fire and looted.

In that incident as in all others, the king's sheriff acted to protect the Jews, which only further inflamed popular feeling. From the king's point of view, his sheriffs were upholding law and order while preserving a priceless fiscal asset; from the people's point of view, the Jews were robbing them by usury and receiving protection from a corrupt government. From the Jews' point of view they were being despoiled by the Christian king and murdered by the Christian populace.

In 1235, the year of the anti-Jewish riot in Norwich, Isaac fil' Jurnet died, whether at home or in prison we do not know. Though his sons Moses and Samuel continued inevitably in the moneylending business, their transactions were on a reduced scale. They and their compatriots were being systematically and legally plundered. Between 1227 and 1259 over 250,000 marks were collected from English Jews. In 1244 the ritual-murder charge was suddenly revived in London and the Jewish community fined 60,000 marks. The royal authorities had at last awakened to the financial possibilities of this charge, now well-established in popular credulity. The most celebrated example of all occurred in the case of little St. Hugh of Lincoln, along with Norwich one of the most notoriously anti-Jewish towns in England. The legend of St. Hugh, a schoolboy said to have been ritually slain by the Jews, entered at once into English folklore and literature.

The officials of the Scaccarium did not overlook their own interests while serving the king in the Jewries. On one occasion, the Jews having been taxed £500, the officials collected £700, and turned over to the king £462.

The fact that the royal government was itself increasingly unpopular during these years was of no help to the Jews, now cordially hated by all classes. During the rebellion led by Simon de Montfort against Henry III, pogroms were freely sanctioned by the rebels against these appanages of the king.

The last act of the tragedy of English Jewry was played out between 1275 and 1290. The new king, Edward I, inherited a Jewry hardly recognizable from the days of Richard Lionheart. Greatly diminished in numbers, shorn of their wealth, England's Jews were now a powerless minority, universally despised and of little value to anybody. Edward's government perceived the Jews not as an object of exploitation but simply as a problem to get rid of. Their approach had some statesmanlike merits. The *Statutum de Judeismo*

(Statute Concerning the Jewry) of 1275 canceled the traditional role of moneylenders and sought to convert the Jews into merchants, craftsmen, and farmers. They were prohibited from lending money at interest. All outstanding loans were to be immediately liquidated, all pawns redeemed, interest was canceled, the seizure of property for unpaid interest forbidden. At the same time, they were allowed to enter trade, to become artisans, and to lease land for farming.

Unfortunately the provisions of the new decree were far more effective in prohibiting Jewish moneylending than in opening the doors of commerce and agriculture. The new freedoms were under cut by long-standing legal disabilities, many reinforced in the new law itself—for example, the ban on travel and restrictions on residence. Excluded from the guilds and from citizenship in the towns, permitted to lease land only on short terms (fifteen years), the mass of English Jews were unable to take advantage of the opportunity offered by the Statutum while suffering disastrously from its prohibitions.

The new law expressly extended the "badge of shame" to all Jews over the age of seven. The imposition of this outward symbol, specified as a piece of yellow taffeta six fingers long and three wide, cut in the shape of the tablets of the Ten Commandments, signaled increased persecution.

A few of the wealthier Jews went into the wholesale grain or wool business, some pawnbrokers became jewelers, a handful of Jews leased land for woodcutting, and inevitably some turned Christian. The rest were relentlessly squeezed out of the national economic life. The tax collector was as exacting as ever; new levies, backed by prison sentences, confiscations and deportations, impoverished the remaining well-to-do Jews, and a new head tax wrung the poor. Many helpless Jews turned to clipping coins and to clandestine moneylending; arrests and hangings followed throughout the kingdom. By 1290 when the experimental Statutum was terminated, English Jewry, which had a hundred years earlier contributed a seventh of the tax revenue of England, paid only £700, hardly more than a hundredth of the total. Italian moneymen had taken the place of Jews as lenders to the Crown and to other large borrowers; from the mainstream of English commercial life, centering about the wool trade, the Jews were for practical purposes excluded. Already Jews had been expelled from many of the towns of England—Bury St. Edmunds in 1190, Leicester in 1231, Derby in 1263, Cambridge in 1275. In 1290, no longer of any value to the Crown, object of a long tradition of popular hatred, restricted to residence in the ghettos of a shrinking number of towns, the remnant of Jews were finally expelled from England. No more than two thousand penniless survivors made their way to France and Germany.

The ritual-murder fiction did not depart with them. A hundred years later Chaucer wrote the most elegant embellishment of the St. Hugh tale; since not a Jew was alive in England he set the scene of the little boy's murder in a city in distant "Asye." But at the end the Prioress adds a stanza:

> O yonge Hugh of Lyncoln, slayn also
> With cursed Jewes, as it is notable,
> For it is but a litel while ago,
> Preye eek for us, we synful folk unstable,
> That of his mercy God so merciable
> On us his grete mercy multiplie,
> For reverence of his mooder Marie. Amen

Stone houses in Lincoln, Norwich, and other English towns survive to recall the era of the Royal Milch Cow. The dwelling of Jurnet and his son Isaac, on Conesford Street in Norwich, passed to Isaac's son Moses, who died in 1242. Moses had three sons, Abraham, Isaac, and Jurnet. Jurnet vanished from the historical record, and little is known of Abraham except his death date, 1255. But the second Isaac followed in his father's footsteps in acting out in his person the fate of English Jewry. Arrested in 1253, he was taken to the Tower of London where torture and threats had their usual consequence; Isaac foreswore the religion of his ancestors and purchased his survival by turning Christian. Such transactions depended less on theology than on property, for the converting Jew had to yield up all his possessions to the king. Among those of Isaac was the stone house on Conesford Street. Henry III bestowed it on Lord

William de Valeres "for his services," doubtless a cash contribution; the house passed through the hands of several other noble Christian families, including the Pastons and the Cokes, Sir Edward Coke acquiring it as part of the dowry of his bride Bridget Paston. Sir Edward, famous jurist and father of the idea of the supremacy of common law, reconstructed the façade and the upper story, to which he gave a characteristically sixteenth-century cross-braced raftering. The house remained in the Coke family until the eighteenth century when it experienced a succession of modifications, for a time being partitioned into shops and apartments. In the 1840s it became part of a brewery and inn, the Music House, providing offices and lodgings for the Chief Brewer and a tavern where the brewery's products were sold.

In the present century the house, now called Wensum Lodge, came into the possession of the city of Norwich, serving local cultural activities. The most recent of these is the Norwich International Club, a student group whose members include, in the proud words of the housekeeper, "all creeds and colors."

7

Symon di Gualterio, a Patron
of the Champagne Fairs

Not all the merchant-farers of the twelfth century took to the sea;
some carried their wares overland to trade at distribution points
where they could meet fellow merchants coming from the opposite
direction bearing complementary goods. The Roman trade fair, a
temporary market held at regular intervals, had been kept alive
through the Dark Ages. Many of the maritime towns continued to
hold fairs where native and foreign merchants met. In the seventh
century, these spread to inland towns in Italy and southern France,
at the intersection of principal roads; in northern France, the town
of St. Denis, near Paris, initiated its fair (later the Fair of Lendit) in
about 635. In the ninth century, under the Carolingians, these annual meetings of merchants multiplied; in the tenth, under the
Ottos, fairs appeared in northern Germany and in Flanders. When
Flemish merchants began to find a market in volume for their cloth
and Italian merchants for spices and luxury products, a new impetus
was given to the ancient institution. Of the new trade fairs that
sprouted from Flanders to the Mediterranean shore, by far the most
famous and successful were the Fairs of Champagne.

Geographic situation, though favorable, was not the chief rea-

St. Ayoul, Provins. The September–October Fair, one of the six in the annual cycle of Champagne Fairs, was held under the auspices of this church.

son for the Champagne Fairs' prosperity. In the eleventh and twelfth centuries the counts of Champagne were clear-sighted enough to perceive the immense potential of the trade fairs which had sprung up spontaneously on their territories. These enlightened feudal lords organized the Fairs into an annual cycle of six, held in four towns, and occupying the entire year, with travel time between. The counts also guaranteed safe conducts to foreign merchants and patrolled the roads to the Fairs to protect convoys from banditry. They provided facilities and officials to ensure smooth, efficient, and honest transactions, laying down regulations for the marketing of the various kinds of merchandise.

Throughout the twelfth century the Champagne Fairs grew in size. The merchants of two European cities, one northern and one southern, both advantageously sited, at first dominated the traffic. Arras, in Artois, was the nearest to Champagne of the great northern cloth towns, and Asti, in Piedmont, within striking distance of the Mont-Cenis and Little St. Bernard passes, was the nearest of the important Italian towns. The men of Asti had the longer and more difficult journey; from Arras the country was flat, the roads good, and the distance to Lagny, the nearest of the Fair towns, less than a hundred miles. The Arrageois brought their wool cloth in wagons, an almost luxurious means of transportation compared with that of the Italians, who led their pack animals up the narrow and treacherous Alpine trails to the sleet-driven, snow-covered passes, with constant danger to their persons and their precious cargoes. The arduous round trip was made once a year by young, ambitious, landlocked counterparts of Romano Mairano. At the head of the pass they could count on the shelter of an Augustinian hostel and the hospitality of the friars. Descending the western slopes, they followed the valley of the Isère and ascended the Rhone-Saone north through Burgundy. They traveled armed, and in groups; despite treaties made by the counts of Champagne with the dukes of Burgundy and the kings of France, they had to be alert against outlaw bands of the forests. They picked their way over ruined Roman roads, and paid for the privilege of fording streams. Their traffic stimulated development of ferries and hostels, and their tolls built timber and later stone-arch bridges.

The last leg of their journey lay through the hills of the Côte d'Or, bringing them to Bar-sur-Aube, the easternmost of the Fair towns. The Bar Fair was open in March-April, followed by the May Fair of Provins in May-June, the Hot Fair of Troyes in July-August, the Fair of St. Ayoul in Provins in September-October, the Cold Fair of Troyes in November-December, and finally the Fair at

Lagny, next door to Paris, in January-February. Most important were the four Fairs running successively in Provins and Troyes through the good traveling season. Once inside Champagne the caravan merchants felt fairly secure; brush was cleared well back from the roads, which were patrolled by the counts' men.

At the Fairs, they sold their packs of spices, alum, sugar, wax, silk cloth, and jewels, and bought wool cloth. The mechanics of buying and selling presented certain problems, which in the course of the twelfth century were solved by two means: first, the organization of the Fairs into periods for preparation, for marketing different classes of merchandise, and for final settlement of bills; and second, the development by the Italians of the cambium contract, a land version of the cambium maritimum, one of the sea documents which Romano Mairano used.

The first of the Fair's four stages was a week of entry, when every merchant registered with the Keeper of the Fair. This was a time of confusion, with merchants seeking out halls, stables, and lodgings for their wares, their animals, and themselves. Then came a ten-day Cloth Market during which the Italians examined, priced, and bargained over the varieties of wool cloth displayed by the men of Ghent, Ypres, Bruges, Arras, and the other cloth cities; third came a month-long "avoir de poids," during which nontextile commodities, but above all spices, were sold, as Italians and Flemings exchanged roles of salesmen and customers. The final week was reserved for the *pagamentum* or settling of accounts, not only to the jingle of silver Provins pennies, but to the scratch of quills and styluses, for credit transactions grew steadily in volume, helping shape a significant element of the commercial future. The whole six-week Fair was a noisy, lively, many-languaged Babel, with gawking peasants and knights as audience for the show, which included real show people like acrobats, jugglers, and sleight-of-hand artists, as well as cooks, taverners, and prostitutes.

The second important element, the cambium contract for land commerce, created an entirely new kind of Fair client, one who never had to risk frostbite and broken limbs in the Alpine passes, or ambush in the forests of Burgundy. The land cambium, like the seagoing version employed in the Mediterranean, provided for a loan in one place in one currency to be repaid in another place and another currency. Unlike the cambium maritimum, which made payment contingent on safe arrival of the vessel, thus introducing an element of marine insurance, the land cambium was unconditional. It was both a way to earn interest, concealed in the difference between two rates of exchange, and a means of transferring funds abroad, and it made possible the transaction of business by remote control. By using the cambium, an Italian merchant could stay home and do commodity trading through an agent stationed permanently in Champagne.

Typical of this new kind of Fair merchant who never went to the Fair was Symon di Gualterio of Genoa. In March 1253, as set down in notarial records, Symon invested over 2,800 Genoese pounds and 1,300 Provins pounds, sold merchandise worth 316 Genoese pounds, and extended credit in cambium contracts for over 2,000 Provins pounds. He not only shipped a large quantity of spices to Champagne for the May Fair, but sent silk and saffron to France by a sleeping partnership commenda contract, bought and sold raw wool and English cloth, and invested in trade in the western Mediterranean.

All this Symon accomplished without stirring from Genoa, where he lived the year round in the bosom of a large family, including a wife, four daughters, and four sons. He was able to do so by means of the cambium contract, which he used to transfer funds to his agents abroad, and to borrow money in Genoa to finance shipments by carrier to the Fairs, repaying the loans in local currency in Champagne after the goods had been sold. Using the credit institutions and paper transaction techniques which had grown up around the money changers' tables at the Fairs, he could buy goods at one Fair and pay for them at the next.

In one cycle of commerce at the Fairs, in 1253, Symon purchased thirty pieces of English wool cloth on March 17 from Bernardo Camorerio of Parma on credit, payment specified for mid-July, when he would have in hand his profits from the sale of spices at the May Fair of Provins. Meanwhile twelve bales of ginger had been shipped to Lagny by Lanfranco di Gualterio, his cousin and traveling partner; Symon commissioned two Piacenzan merchants bound for the Fairs to collect the ginger from his agent at Lagny and take it to Provins to sell at the May Fair, the profits to be invested in wool cloth for return shipment to Genoa, completing the circle.

Later, after borrowing 1,319 Provins pounds and investing 1,000 in cambium agreements at the May Fair through associates in Champagne, he signed a contract naming Giovanni the Tuscan his general agent in France and Champagne, with authority to send merchandise to him in Genoa by land or sea; bulky cloth shipments could be transported to Genoa more economically by ship from Marseille than over the passes by pack animals. On March 27 he loaned more money in cambium to a Sienese banker for payment at the Fairs, and on March 20 he sent saffron and silk worth over 770 Genoese pounds in a commenda contract to "France," perhaps partly for marketing in Champagne.

This is in striking contrast to the arduous activities of the Asti caravan merchants of two generations before. Symon di Gualterio not only saved himself the struggle over the Alpine passes to the hospice of St. Bernard, and the laborious unloading of pack animals in the crowded Fair towns of Champagne, he also widened his horizons. At home in Genoa he was able to direct his attention to other markets besides Champagne. In April, following his month-long preoccupation with the northern Fairs, he turned his attention to the Mediterranean, and in the following month committed over 6,-500 pounds to commenda-financed ventures to Sicily, Sardinia, Tunis, Bugia, Acre, and to a still more exotic port than any of these, investing 900 pounds in a voyage bound for Safi, on the Atlantic coast of Africa, 400 miles south from the Straits of Gibraltar. Genoese galleys braved the open Atlantic to this distant point to trade for gold from the African interior for the banking city's expanding gold coinage. The variety of Symon's investments included another dimension; he bought a three-quarter interest in the ship *St. Francis* for 390 pounds, later investing his share in a commenda with the ship's skipper for a voyage to Bugia.

Mediterranean trade complemented the Champagne Fair activity in Symon di Gualterio's extensive and remarkably well-organized business empire. The principal commodity carried to Syria, Tunisia, and elsewhere by his commenda partners was Flemish, French, and English cloth purchased at the Champagne Fairs and borne to Marseille by pack-ass and barge, and thence to Genoa by ship. Except for gold from Safi, most of the merchandise the traveling partners brought to Genoa from the Mediterranean was shipped north to the Fairs.

Following the crescendo in April and May, when most of the sailing departures took place, Symon's business activities gradually slackened to a period of summer doldrums, then picked up again in August with a different emphasis; now the contracts were receipts for quittance of commenda obligations; in other words, his ships were coming in. As autumn wore on, and a new departure season began, he once more plunged into a round of commenda ventures.

In his younger days Symon di Gualterio doubtless sailed as the traveling partner in a commenda arrangement himself to all the ports of the Mediterranean, and probably made more than one trip to the Champagne Fairs. He may even have occasionally sailed with one of his ventures in middle age. The significant fact about him, however, is his basically sedentary position, amounting to much more than a matter of attaining the age and status in which he could remain at home while younger men underwent the hardships and took the risks. His own comfort aside, it was best for the business for Symon to stay home; if he had taken the first ship in spring bound for Bugia or Syria he would have missed, or had to leave in others' hands, the opportunities of the next several months. Business life in Italy had reached the point where it became indispensable for the head of the firm to remain in the home office.

The notarial record book which records Symon di Gualterio's humming activities of 1253 also includes his will, a document which gives the touch of humanity to his portrait. Leaving the bulk of his estate, consisting of commenda contracts, cambium contracts, goods in transit, and accounts receivable, to be divided among his four minor sons, he set aside 2,000 pounds to supply dowries for his four

daughters, and made a number of other cash bequests. For his funeral expenses, including masses and alms, he left 100 pounds, and
two other bequests totaling 275 pounds for the Church's charitable
works, a generosity which at least set him apart from a fellow Genoese magnate who a few years later found the sum of three pounds
sufficient for the requirements of his soul. To his faithful wife
Symon left the house, for as long as she remained unmarried (in
which case, presumably, she would move to her new husband's
house), her dower, 100 pounds in cash, all her clothes and jewels
(gifts which he thus bestowed on her twice), and finally, for her
comfort, his own "fancy" bed.

III

AFFLUENCE

In the thirteenth century, the cloth cities of Flanders and Artois—Ghent, Bruges, Ypres, Douai, Lille, Arras—formed a pocket of industrial capitalism in a precapitalist world. The profits of industry paid for palatial cloth markets, imposing town halls, handsome guild houses, cathedrals, walls, paved streets, reservoirs, warehouses, wharves, bridges, and canals. Not surprisingly, the towns also experienced the problems of industrial society, class conflict, violent market fluctuations, labor unrest, and splendor jostling misery.

The men who manufactured cloth and their families formed the bulk of the population. Though indispensable to industry, they led a precarious existence, at the mercy of every economic crisis. Set apart by their dress, speech, and manners, they formed a new class: the urban proletariat. They roamed from town to town in search of employment, living in rented hovels on the outskirts and owning little more than the clothes on their backs. Every Monday morning they could be seen in the marketplaces waiting to be hired for the week. Their hours were long and their pay small, and despite town regulations not even always in cash. Wholesale merchants often cheated them on the quantity and quality of raw materials. Super-

vised by industrial police, their wages set by a municipal government in the hands of the very merchants who employed them, they
were without political power or recourse.

The first, inevitable eruption was sparked by a bizarre episode
in 1225 when a man appeared in Flanders claiming to be Count
Baldwin, the father of the countess of Flanders and the first Latin
emperor of Constantinople. Instead of being killed in 1205 at Adri-
anople as reported, the pseudo-Baldwin claimed to have been captured by the Bulgarians, from whom he escaped with the aid of a
Bulgarian princess, whom he later murdered. Subsequently, he said,
he had been sold into slavery, escaped again, and had now returned
incognito to Flanders and become a hermit to atone for his sins. The
weavers and the fullers (cloth finishers) seized on this romantic
figure, who had suffered even more than they, as a kind of King of
the Plebs. They rose in revolt against his supposed daughter, Countess Jeanne, driving the patricians out of power in Valenciennes. The
Countess fled to Tournai, collected troops, then returned and took
the town by siege; Baldwin was exposed as an imposter and hanged
in chains at Lille. But the incident was only the first of a series of
uprisings that went on for two centuries. Twenty years later, in
1245, Douai was the scene of the first strike recorded in labor history. It was suppressed with dispatch by the outraged cloth merchants. Further strikes or even assemblies of the weavers were forbidden by the town council, itself an assembly of the town's
patricians.

Flemish cloth manufactured in the northern cities was imported
by Italian merchants both to sell in the Mediterranean area and for
their own luxury wool-finishing industry. These businessmen enlarged their horizons and developed sophisticated business techniques, as new markets opened to them. In 1204 the Fourth Crusade
had made the Black Sea accessible to Venice; the recovery of the
Byzantine throne a half century later by the old Greek dynasty,
with Genoese help, opened it to Genoa. In Asia Minor and the
Black Sea area the Zaccarias of Genoa created a commercial empire;
from Soldaia, in the Crimea, the Polos of Venice traveled across

central Asia to China. At the same time Genoa intensified its overland trade with Lombardy and with Flanders and France.

The Polos' fabulous adventure notwithstanding, the principal
trend in business life in the thirteenth and early fourteenth centuries
was the tendency for merchants to stay at home, conducting business
from the counting house. The Champagne Fairs reached their apogee around the middle of the century; after that the new commercial techniques developed at the Fairs rendered the Fairs themselves obsolete. Instead of traveling thither or sending agents, merchants established permanent branches in the great commercial centers: in Bruges, Paris, and London; in Avignon, where the papal
court was located during the greater part of the fourteenth century;
in Italian cities other than their own, and in Constantinople.

New methods of business organization were evolved to meet
the new conditions. Where merchants of the twelfth and early thirteenth century had organized partnerships for a single venture, like
the societas, collegantia, and commenda, businessmen now began to
enter into longer-term associations, called *compagnie*. These were at
first merely family partnerships among father and sons, or among
brothers—people who lived in the same house and broke bread
together—whence the term (*cum pane*). Each of the partners supplied capital and helped direct the firm, and each was responsible to
third parties for debts contracted by the others. The partners were
not salaried, but shared in the profits. Later, companies came to include members outside the family, but control usually remained
with the family.

Between company headquarters and the branch offices, a courier service operated, partly paid for by carrying mail for outsiders.
In the second half of the fourteenth century, a dozen Florentine
companies organized the *scarsella*, a postal combine with regular
weekly departures for Avignon by way of Genoa. The scarsella delivered the letters of its own members first, then several hours later
letters of the general public, in other words, those of business competitors. This practice was in accordance with self-interest, as fourteenth-century merchant Paolo di Messer Pace da Certaldo wrote,

so that a merchant could first read his own dispatches and act on them; "you should not serve another and thereby suffer in your own affairs." Courier services also furnished information to member companies about political events, market prices, exchange rates, and any other news affecting business.

The great companies were primarily dealers in wool cloth; but they also sold many other kinds of merchandise: silks from Persia and China; pearls from the Persian Gulf and Ceylon; tin from Cornwall; Polish and Scandinavian copper, imported from Bruges; lead from Sardinia; armor from Milan and Germany. Most also became bankers, dealing extensively in credit.

To satisfy the need of ever-increasing complexity, new methods of record-keeping had to be devised. The Italian merchants were diligent scribes, not only in account books, but in private notebooks and diaries where they wrote down household expenditures, family events, and reports of public affairs. The pages of mercantile manuals were full of advice to businessmen on bookkeeping: "I must urge you to write down your affairs carefully, and do it immediately before they slip your mind"; "The lazy man who is remiss in writing down his dealings cannot live long without damage or mistake"; "Never spare pen and ink"; "Keep your accounts carefully and make no mistakes." Paolo di Messer Pace da Certaldo wrote: "Every time that you enter into a contract, have a book at hand, and write down the date, the names of the notary who drafted the deed, and of the witnesses, the reason why you made the contract and the name of the party with whom you dealt, so that if you or your children need to look up the record you will find it easily; and in order to forestall any possibility of deceit by men of bad faith, have the contract drafted in due form and put away in a safe place."

During the thirteenth century, accounting methods underwent a significant evolution. In the earliest surviving Italian account book, dating from 1211, memoranda were arranged in chronological order, with no separation of debit and credit. Soon merchants learned to enter debts in one part of the book and credits in another; special records were kept for foreign customers, for dyeing and finishing establishments, and for associates, plus a petty cash book, a rough copybook in which receipts were entered from day to day, a "great book" summing up this information in more orderly fashion, and finally a "secret book" containing the accounts of the partners and staff.

The thirteenth century saw the new class of cloth-trade capitalists come into sharp competition with the old viscontal families, men like the Embriaci and the della Voltas who had in the eleventh and twelfth centuries controlled both commerce and city government. A revolution in Genoa in 1256 raised the new middle class to power. Pisa also fell into the hands of a "popular" regime. In the 1250s Florence adopted a similar government, which was overthrown in 1260 and restored in 1282 with the institution of "Ordinances of Justice," giving the craft guilds a share in the government and legislating against the "magnates," the noble families who had formerly controlled the council. These new governments of the "people" (*popolo*) did not include the working classes. Suppressed and exploited by both old and the new capitalists, this proletariat, the *popolo minuto*, like the Flemish weavers, contained the seeds of social troubles.

The rival class factions tended to polarize into the Guelf (papal) and Ghibelline (imperial) parties that divided the entire Italian peninsula. Generally, though not always, the *popolo* was Guelf, the magnate faction Ghibelline. This internal division played an important—and no less violent—part in the external politics of the Italian cities. In Italy and in the Holy Land, war was a chronic condition. Pisa was allied with Holy Roman Emperor Frederick II against the pope; Venice backed the pope, Genoa joined in. Frederick commented ruefully, "While I was playing chess with the Pope, I was checkmating him . . . and then the Genoese arrived and seized the chessmen and upset the whole game." The seal of the Genoese commune, a griffin rending an eagle (the emperor) and a wolf (Pisa) bore the impudent and prophetic inscription: "*Griphus ut has angit, sic hostes Janua frangit*"—"As the griffin strangles these, thus Genoa crushes its enemies."

The businessmen of the thirteenth century stand out from the shadows more clearly than their forerunners. Individual personalities can be discerned. These vary, like the personalities of any class in any period, but a few characteristics are common to all and reinforce our picture of earlier medieval businessmen. Among these are courage, prudence, organizational skill, and unabashed materialism.

8

A Flemish Merchant Prince: Sire Jehan Boinebroke

Reclamation against the Estate of Sire Jehan Boinebroke, Deceased, Patrician of Douai, 1285–86

Item: "Jehan Dou Mares, of the New Town, declares under oath that he bought a sack of wool from Sire Jehan Boinebroke for 60 shillings [sous]. When he opened it, he found only six stones weight, which would sell for no more than 6 shillings. And he demands 60 shillings. . . .

"Awarded 40 shillings."

Item: "Donnet Casee, son of Margot, declares under oath that Sire Jehan rented two houses from them for twenty-two years or more, in Copee Street, at 40 pounds. . . . And he demands this 40 pounds for his mother and himself, and heritage to the amount of 30 pounds. . . .

"Jakemes de Cambray, sworn witness, says that he several times heard Belin, father of said Donnet, say, 'Sire Jehan Boinebroke owes me money, but, God's death, he never pays!' . . .

"Pieronne Casee, sworn witness, says . . . that she spoke of it to Sire Jehan and said, 'Sire, you should pay my uncle,' and he said, 'Get out, leave me in peace!' . . .

"Awarded: 100 shillings."

Item: "Angnies li Patiniere, daughter of Druion le Patinier, wife of Jehan Dou Hoc, declares under oath . . . that after her father's death, Sire Jehan Boinebroke made a claim on Mariien, wife of Druion le Patinier, for a debt she owed him; and seized a vat of dye, which was worth 20 pounds more than she owed: which 20 pounds she demands. . . .

"Jehane As Cles . . . says that she heard her mother demand 20 pounds over the amount of the debt from Sire Jehan. And Sire Jehan said, 'Goody, I don't know what I owe you, but I'll remember you in my will.'

"Sainte Caperous swears that . . . Sire Jehan said to Mariien: 'Goody, go and work in the tannery—I hate to see you suffer like this.' And she said . . . 'Sire, if you want to do justice, you will give me alms, for I am in need.' And Sire Jehan replied that he would think about it . . . and thereupon, he departed.

"Awarded: 100 shillings."

Item: "Maroie Des Lices declares under oath that her late mother, Sare Des Lices, served as a stretcher [of woven cloth] for Sire Jehan for twelve years or more; and when she came to an accounting with him, he forced her to take her pay in wool, and she had to accept for fear she would lose her employ, and every year she lost on this wool 60 shillings or more. And she demands 8 pounds . . .

"Angnies Des Lices, sworn witness . . . sister of Sare, says that she heard her several times ask Sire Jehan for 2 shillings and a half he owed her; and Sire Jehan said, 'Goody, if you ask for a lien on my property, I'll have you fined 60 pounds!'

"Awarded: 12 pounds."

Item: "Robert le Kos demands under oath 38 shillings for 38 stone of wool which he bought from the said Jehan . . .

"Maroie de le Gherende, sworn witness of Robert le Kos, says that one day the said Robert bought wool from Sire Jehan . . . and the best wool was on top. And when he went to take out the wool, what was underneath was inferior. Robert said to Sire Jehan, 'Sire, I don't want this wool and I won't take it, for it isn't what it should be.' And Sire Jehan said, 'Whatever it is, you bought it and you'll take it!' and he said to his servant, 'Go and get the sergeant, and I will make a claim against him.' And Robert, weeping, took the wool out of fear . . .

"Awarded: 38 shillings."

Item: "Jou Sare, wife of Jehan le Jahier, of Aubi, testifies that Jehan le Jahier had a field between Oscre and the Abbey des Pres of Douai, which he rented from Sire Jehan Boinebroke, God rest his soul, and that he planted with madder |red-dye plant| the field, which belonged to him . . . because he duly paid his rent to Sire Jehan Boinebroke, God rest his soul . . . The goodman sold it for 30 shillings a measure, which was too cheap, for he did not know that the price of madder had gone up . . . And when Sire Jehan Boinebroke, God rest his soul, heard that the goodman had sold the madder, he said that he wanted it; and the price of madder was going up, and it was worth at least 100 shillings a measure. And then Sire Jehan Boinebroke, God rest his soul, went and took two laborers with him and had them dig up the madder and take it to his house . . . And several times Sire Jehan Boinebroke, God rest his soul, said that he would make amends to Jehan le Jahier, but he did nothing. . . ."

The above testimony is drawn from an extraordinary document consisting of eleven sheets of parchment sewed together end to end making a roll five and a half meters long and fifteen centimeters wide. The minutes of legal proceedings against the estate of a deceased patrician of Douai, Sire Jehan Boinebroke, it was taken down jointly from forty-five plaintiffs, all members of the working class of Douai and vicinity. Twenty-nine of the forty-five were weavers or widows of weavers, the remaining sixteen mostly sellers of hay, fruit, construction materials, and other commodities. Not only the testimony of the plaintiffs is recorded but that of sworn witnesses who gave many details, including conversations in which the patrician heaped sarcasm, invective, and threats on those who complained of his mistreatment. The same accusations are repeated again and again: wages underpaid or not paid at all; goods overpriced and sold, or underpriced and bought; property seized; tenants unjustly evicted.

The largest claim was that of a widow of one of Boinebroke's agents, who had died at the Champagne Fairs. Before leaving home, this man had assured his wife, "Margot, I'm leaving you well-fixed." He had settled accounts with "my lord Jehan Boinebroke" and owed him only 12 pounds plus 32 pounds for wool he had in hand for sale at the Fair. But on news of the agent's death, Boinebroke summoned the widow, took her into his office, told her that her husband was heavily in debt to him, and presented her with a bill for 131 pounds, attested by the town council. The widow wept, but the merchant swore that his accounting was "good and loyal" (although the documents were all of his own creation), and in the end the widow had to sell her little estate and borrow from relatives to pay the 131 pounds.

At the other end of the scale, a farm laborer asserted that he had done the harvesting on one of the lord Boinebroke's farms the year before last and had never received a farthing of the four shillings due him for the week's work.

Some of the complaints dated back many years. Often the plaintiff had received a promise to pay which the merchant had gone to his grave without honoring. Weavers charged that he had tried to pay the rate for "medium" work when the weaving was properly classified as "great." Others swore that he tried to pay two days' wages for three days' work. All expressed varying degrees of fear of the consequences of his anger.

The picture that emerges from the Reclamation document is that of a strong-willed, rapacious despot, a pitiless exploiter of labor, and a cunning and unscrupulous businessman.

Boinebroke's personality was his own, but the source of his power lay in his class. The patriciate of Douai, as of other Flemish cities, controlled the city government, forming a closed ruling class to which entry could be effected only by invitation. Every fourteen months the outgoing council of Douai elected its own successors, a process known as co-optation. At the end of its own term the members of the new council were likely to recall to office many of the same men who had elected them fourteen months before. Sire Jehan Boinebroke served on the town council at least nine times between 1243 and 1280.

Each councilman was elected subject to the approval of the count of Flanders, but this was formality. Mutual self-interest between count and patricians dictated close collaboration. The counts and countesses of Flanders during Jehan Boinebroke's lifetime repeatedly needed money and their chief reliance was on their towns. Between 1244 and 1268 Douai was called on by her thriftless sovereigns on no fewer than seventeen occasions—"the accession of Countess Margaret," "to recruit crossbowmen," "to outfit Count William for the Crusade," "dispensation of the townsmen from military service," "to ransom the Countess Margaret's son Guy"—for a total of 32,600 pounds. Boinebroke and his colleagues were obliged to raise the money by apportionment among themselves and their fellow citizens. These apportionments led to rebellious murmurings, despite the solemn oath taken on the relics that the assessments were "honest and loyal."

Douai was one of the cloth-producing cities which had long since made Flanders the wealthiest country in northwest Europe. Wool cloth was the cornerstone of Flemish prosperity, and the principal business of nine out of ten Flemish patricians. Sire Jehan Boinebroke belonged to this majority. His family origins are obscure, though Boinebrokes are known to have sold cloth in England and at the court of the counts of Artois before he was born, and it is virtually certain that he inherited a prosperous business. The name itself is a curious example of one type of medieval nomenclature, the sobriquet or descriptive nickname that becomes a surname—often humorous. "Boine-broke" may be literally translated as "good penis."

However and whenever he came into possession of his cloth business, Boinebroke was its sole proprietor in 1260 when it first appears in written records. His large house-office stood near the Porte Olivet, in the upper town of Douai, where most of the wealthy patricians lived. He employed three clerks, hiring the services of a copyist when he needed one. His two sons, Jehan Boinebroke the Younger and Simon Boinebroke, entered actively into the business as soon as they were old enough, and two relatives, Philip and Hugh Boinebroke, sold cloth in England and Scotland. Behind the house stood a dyeing establishment, owned by Boinebroke, in which five or six dyers soaked cloth in mixtures of alum, a dye fixative, with madder, woad, and other colorings combined with water from a stream that flowed into the Scarpe.

Boinebroke's economic role was technically that of a middle-man, but he was a middleman who controlled all aspects of production and marketing. Although he owned a few sheep pastures, his chief sources of wool supply were English Cistercian monasteries in Cumberland, Lincolnshire, and Northumberland. Boinebroke contracted for wool in advance, making down payments of about three percent. It was delivered by the abbeys to Boinebroke's agents in England and shipped to Flanders from either Newcastle-on-Tyne or Tynemouth, ascending the Scheldt and the Scarpe to Douai. The raw wool was graded as "good," "medium," and "inferior," priced accordingly, and sold either by the stone (fourteen pounds) or by the sack. Good Newminster wool was worth ten and a half marks per sack (seven pounds, or 1,680 silver pennies), the lesser grades eight and six marks.

Alum and dyes for the Boinebroke establishment also arrived at the wharves on the Scarpe. Alum was imported from as far off as Castile, dyes from various places near and far. Madder, source of red coloring, Boinebroke grew on his own farms.

The wool in hand, Boinebroke proceeded to the next step, putting out. Weavers bought wool from him, taking it home to sort, card, spin, and weave, with the help of their wives and children. They then sold the unfinished cloth back to Boinebroke, who put it out to a fuller for cleaning and treating, and finally either put it out to a dyer or sent it to his own dye shop. Dyeing might be done at an earlier stage, in the yarn or even in the raw ("dyed in the wool"), but typically it was an end process.

In form, putting out was a sale by Boinebroke to the master weaver, the master fuller, or the dyer; in actuality, it was an employer-employee manufacturing operation carried on by remote control and with greatly diminished risks for the employer. In the absence of a factory where labor could be supervised, Boinebroke and his fellow merchants resorted to putting out as a means of protecting themselves against bad or inefficient labor. When the weaver paid for the raw wool, Boinebroke made a profit on the transaction, even if he never saw the wool again. The system also protected the merchant-manufacturer against market fluctuations. If war interrupted traffic to the Champagne Fairs, Boinebroke could decline to buy back the wool cloth, or buy it back at a low price. When such disasters to commerce occurred, the roads of Flanders were filled with vagabond weavers and their starving families.

The relationship between Boinebroke and the weavers is clearly revealed by repetitions of such phrases as "he sent," "he ordered," and "he directed," in the testimony of the plaintiffs in the Reclamation suit. The weavers were as effectively at the mercy of the cloth merchants as if they were directly employed by them. Guaranteeing Boinebroke and his friends absolute power in the cloth trade, the law forbade sale of cloth except under specified circumstances—at the Douai cloth market, or at either the Flemish or the Champagne Fairs. The bulk of the cloth was sold at the latter. An agent, such as the husband of the widow in the Reclamation suit, took Boinebroke's cloth there on consignment, promising to pay a certain price on return. Thus Boinebroke bought and sold wool four times; he bought it raw from the Cistercians, sold it to the weavers, bought it from the weavers, sold it to the fullers, bought it from the fullers, sold it to the dyers, bought it from the dyers, sold it to the agent going to the Fair. A sack that cost seven pounds in Lincolnshire might sell as cloth for forty pounds in Champagne, with a sizeable proportion of the thirty-three-pound markup going into the strongbox of Boinebroke, who, it may be noted, followed the same rule with his agents as with his weavers and fullers, paying, in the words of the modern scholar Georges Espinas, "little, badly or not at all."

The profits that found their way into his strongbox did not rest there. Boinebroke invested his money, principally in real estate. He acquired many houses and shops in Douai, both in the upper town and in the proletarian lower town. He owned several houses in the Rue des Foulons (Fullers' Street), frequently renting to the weavers and fullers who worked his cloth. Sometimes he guaranteed a weaver sufficient work for a year provided he rented a house from Boinebroke.

Besides this city property, Boinebroke owned a country retreat just outside the city gates, and farther out a number of farms which he rented to tenant farmers. A few of these raised sheep or madder, supplying raw materials for his putting-out factory, but most were wheat farms, exporting their produce via the Scarpe. Boinebroke also owned more distant properties, including a farm as far away as Amiens, which may have been a halfway house on the way to Paris or the Champagne Fairs.

Although we do not know the date of Boinebroke's birth, we may assume from his first election as town councillor in 1243 that it was no later than 1213. By 1270 he was probably in his sixties, and at the height of his career. Continuing to carry on wool cloth manufacture, with all its ramifications of import and export, he began to devote more of his attention to real estate and moneylending. He purchased a number of houses and farms, including an evidently splendid manor for his son Jehan the Younger at Helesmes, twelve miles (twenty kilometers) from Douai, for 777 pounds. In 1275 he made some alterations on his own house, in the course of which he petitioned the Council to let him convert a public street into a private road; the Council granted him permission on condition that he dig a new well for other citizens cut off from their customary source of water by this move.

In 1280 violence broke out in Douai, part of a wave of revolution that spread throughout Flanders in that year, uniting the craft guilds and the small merchants against the patrician oligarchies which controlled the towns. In defiance of the law against strikes and assembly, the cloth workers flocked into the streets and battled patricians and police. Boinebroke, a prominent target of the weavers' resentment, was one of the most vigorous organizers of the suppression of the riot.

The same year, though not for the first time, Jehan Boinebroke participated in a loan to the count of Flanders—entirely separate from the "aids" which the count so often exacted from his towns. A few years later the count gave proof of his appreciation. The king of England had taken advantage of friction between England and Flanders to confiscate the goods of a number of Flemish merchants, including Boinebroke. The count of Flanders intervened and the merchandise was restored to its owner. The volume of Boinebroke's business is indicated by the quantity of wool involved—two batches of 93 and 120 sacks respectively, the total worth about a thousand pounds.

At about this time the patriarchal tyrant, advanced in years, turned over his business to his sons. In the winter of 1284, when a feud between the merchants of Douai and those of Lille threatened the Douai wagon train returning from the Champagne Fairs, the two younger Boinebrokes were prominent among the patricians who armed themselves and met the train near Péronne to escort it home. Some time the following winter Sire Jehan Boinebroke the Elder received the last sacraments.

His sons inherited his cloth establishment, his wide-flung properties, and his seat on the town council. When another insurrection forced the patricians to flee the city, the two Boinebrokes left Douai, but eventually returned and took up their cloth business and their political roles once more. Simon died in 1301; Jehan the Younger was a member of the town council as late as 1308.

The intimate portrait that the Reclamation of 1286 presents should perhaps be softened somewhat in favor of its despotic subject. The suit's executors did not wholly credit the claims, awarding only about a third of the total (218 pounds 5s 8d). Some of the demands may have represented no more than the normal claims on a businessman's estate. Nevertheless, the personality that emerges from the outraged protests of forty-five men and women of the less privileged classes is hardly that of a public benefactor.

It would be a mistake, however, to attribute Boinebroke's personality to the patrician class as a whole, either in Flanders or elsewhere. It is worth noting that the court, undoubtedly patrician, did some justice to Boinebroke's victims. A family related to Boinebroke, the Hucquedieus of Arras, presents a very different picture, gaining a reputation for philanthropy in founding hospitals and doing other good works. Businessmen were drawn to emulate the Hucquedieus by piety, and to emulate Boinebroke by cupidity. Perhaps a fair summation would be that business conditions of the thirteenth century, placing few restrictions on the exploitation of labor, and giving the employing class powerful political weapons, encouraged, for good or ill, what a much later age called "rugged individualism."

9

Benedetto Zaccaria,
Genoa's Merchant-Admiral

At the end of the thirteenth century, the buildings of Genoa crowded down toward the sea, "all of stone," wrote an Arab geographer, "and made so that every man can anchor his ship before his own house." Solid masonry towers loomed where wooden shacks had huddled two centuries before, and imposing public buildings were so embellished with spoils from the Levant that a German pilgrim exaggerated, "There is not a marble column or a construction of well-cut stone which was not taken from Athens, and the whole city is built from Athens."

In the eastern suburbs, near where the River Bisagno met the sea, stood a splendid house, fine enough so that the commune later used it to lodge the Empress Marguerite, wife of Henry VII. It belonged to one of the outstanding figures of the Middle Ages, Benedetto Zaccaria, hero of the most important naval engagement of the thirteenth century, the battle of Meloria. Yet while many a professional admiral longs all his life for the glory of a Meloria, to Benedetto Zaccaria the victory was a mere incident in a life filled with struggle and adventure, usually involving politics and frequently war, but basically rooted in business. Merchant and industrialist as well as diplomat and admiral (and very successful pirate), Zaccaria left his native Genoa in his youth and returned only at intervals, pausing on his way from Asia Minor, the Black Sea, or Constantinople to Seville or Rouen, to renew business contacts and breathe the air of home.

Benedetto was one of ten children born to Fulcone Zaccaria and his wife Giulietta some time before the middle of the thirteenth century. The family was of noble descent; his father's name bore the predicate "di Castello," which indicated either that he came from the quarter of the citadel of Genoa, the most aristocratic area, or that he derived from the di Castello family, descended from the viscounts who ruled Genoa in the Dark Ages. Fulcone was active in business, as was his wife, whose name occurred more than once in commercial contracts. Benedetto's name appeared in public records for the first time in 1256, as a councillor of the commune, signing a treaty by which Genoa acquired territory in Sardinia.

Three years later he was one of two commanders of a fleet of twenty galleys dispatched to fight the Pisans and Venetians in the Holy Land, during a renewal of the seemingly endless warfare of the Italian Levantine colonies. This Genoese force was anchored in the harbor of Tyre when a Venetian flotilla of twenty-four ships attacked. Zaccaria, at the head of ten of the Genoese galleys, made a daring sortie into the roadstead, and was taken prisoner. While he languished in a Venetian jail, Genoese and Venetians fought for Acre street by street, the Genoese finally yielding to superior force. Venetians and Pisans razed the great tower that protected the Genoese colony of Acre; letting the sea flood in, they rowed up to the wreckage, jeering, "The Genoese tower is afloat!" Two pilasters with marble reliefs were captured and taken to Venice, where they stand today between St. Mark's and the Doge's Palace.

The defeated Genoese opened secret talks with the exiled Byzantine emperor Michael Paleologus, descendant of the emperor deposed in the Fourth Crusade. These culminated in 1261 in an alliance between the Genoese and the Greeks against Venice and its puppet Latin Empire. The treaty bore immediate fruit. Two weeks after it was ratified at Genoa, a Greek army marched into Constantinople to put an end to the enfeebled Latin Empire, while the Genoese fleet guarded the sea approach. The chagrined Venetians, away on a minor naval expedition, returned to rescue Latin Emperor Baldwin and the Venetian colonists of the city. With the Genoese on guard, they could do little more. In revenge for the destruction of their colony at Acre, the Genoese organized an orchestra with trumpets, horns, and string instruments to play while they wrecked the Venetian quarter. The best stones of the podestà's palace were shipped off to be incorporated into the new headquarters of the commune in Genoa, the Palazzo San Giorgio, with several lions' heads, the symbol of Venice's St. Mark, being hoisted to decorate the windows of the first floor.

But a breach soon opened between Genoa and Paleologus, who banished the Genoese colony to Heraclea, on the Sea of Marmara, and began to negotiate a treaty with Venice. Benedetto Zaccaria, home again in Genoa (escaped, exchanged, or ransomed, we do not know) was sent as an ambassador to the Greek emperor to prevent the alliance. In the end Venice itself blundered away the opportunity by accepting an alliance with Paleologus' enemy, Charles of Anjou, a star whose rise proved temporary. The Genoese colony was reestablished at Constantinople, though in the suburbs, in the old ghetto at Pera.

Benedetto Zaccaria took advantage of his embassy to Constantinople to lay the foundations of his fortune by adroitly winning the favor of the splenetic Paleologus. A few years later, the emperor bestowed on Benedetto and his brother Manuele the town of Phocaea, north of Smyrna, as an hereditary fief. The Zaccarias readily accepted the obligation of defending the strategic outpost, in return for the right to exploit a valuable mineral deposit, a fine-quality alum. Used by pharmacists and tanners, this chemical was in greatest demand by dyers who used it to fix colors in fabric; the rapid growth of the textile industry created a constantly expanding market. Alum mined in Italy did not begin to satisfy the demand; North Africa's was monopolized by the Pisans, who also dominated the Egyptian market. A rare partnership of a Genoese and a Venetian merchant had acquired a monopoly of Turkish alum in the territory of the sultan of Iconium, and had been able to peg prices at an exorbitant level. How much the Phocaean mines were worked before the Zaccarias is unknown; probably there was limited production, which they expanded. A visitor to the Phocaean mines in the following century described the refining process: "Lumps put in the fire, then plunged in water, became like sand. This sand was thrown into a kettle with water, and when it boiled, it liquefied. . . . The broth, poured into basins, remained there for four days; then it hardened around the rims of the vessels, shining like crystal; the bottoms of the basins were full of similar fragments and pieces. The liquid . . . was poured off and the crystals were mixed with fresh water, boiled once more and poured into basins, as already described."

The first problem that confronted the Zaccarias in Phocaea was not the mining or processing of alum, but its transport to Italy in the face of a swarm of pirates—Turkish, Venetian, and Frankish—which had long infested the Aegean. The newcomers proved equal to the task, manning and arming their galleys so effectively that they not only defended themselves against the corsairs, but assailed the assailants, capturing ships, putting crews to the sword, and seizing their piratical plunder. Likening the brothers to birds of prey, a Venetian chronicler stated that they gained more riches from their raids than from their alum mines. "They kept armed galleys in this place, and . . . seized many vessels of Latin corsairs; these they either killed or blinded; thus by piracy against pirates . . . they loaded their own ships with booty and returned home very wealthy."

To carry on their warlike and commercial activities, the Zaccarias built up a large fleet. Their flagship was the galley *Divizia* (Wealth), which doubled as a merchant vessel and man-of-war. They had ships built for them, bought others, and leased some for a season. Occasionally they bought or leased a share in a ship; sometimes they leased their ships to other merchants.

In an attempt to diminish the risks of shipping, Benedetto and his son Paleologus participated in one of the first recorded schemes of marine insurance. In form this was a loan concealed behind a fictitious sale. By a contract of October 29, 1298, the Zaccarias sold for 3,000 Genoese pounds a cargo of alum loaded on their own ship in Aigues Mortes, Provence, bound for Bruges, and agreed to repurchase the alum in Bruges. Payment, however, was not to be made until the galley reached Genoa with its return cargo, when the lenders were to receive 3,780 Genoese pounds. In effect, the Zaccarias borrowed 3,000 pounds and promised to repay 3,780 on safe return of the galley. Interest on the loan and premium for the risks was slightly more than twenty-six percent. Within fifty years this technique had been converted into simple premium payments.

For the colony at Phocaea, the Zaccarias imported from Genoa sailors, soldiers, and specialized workmen, including a shoemaker and a doctor. The doctor contracted to practice his profession according to the dictates of law and his conscience, to keep the necessary medicaments ready, to treat free of charge the Zaccarias and members of their household, and when there was no work for him as a physician, to be employed at the will of his patrons.

One source in the East produced better alum than that of Phocaea: the city of Coloneia (now Karahissar), some forty miles (sixty-five kilometers) south of the Black Sea, near Trebizond. Phocaea was far more accessible, but as the textile industry improved its dyeing methods, alum from Coloneia began to be in demand; to obtain it, Genoese ships sailed to the Black Sea. The Zaccarias, aroused by the threat of competition, persuaded the emperor to issue a Golden Bull forbidding their fellow Genoese to export alum from the Black Sea. The Genoese in Pera, the suburb of Constantinople, did not dare disobey the edict; but not long after, two galleys from Genoa defiantly sailed through the Bosporus without giving the customary salute to the emperor as they passed the Imperial Palace, and in the Black Sea seized a ship loaded with alum. Michael Paleologus appealed to the Genoese of Pera, who urged the pirates at least to make the gesture of tribute on their return journey. But the rebellious Genoese, loading men and booty on a cargo ship, passed the Palace once more without salute. The enraged emperor sent galleys in pursuit, and had the pleasure of watching the chase, battle, and capture from his terrace. Ship and cargo were seized, and the prisoners were blinded.

In retaliation, Genoa declared a boycott against the ports of the Empire. Michael Paleologus, who needed his Genoese allies, sent an embassy to Genoa, but it took two years to patch up the quarrel. In 1281 alum began once more to flow to Genoa from the Black Sea, but the expansion of the cloth industry made competition no longer a threat. By the end of the thirteenth century the mines at Phocaea were producing about 14,000 cantars (700 tons) of alum per year, which the Zaccarias were able to sell at high prices because of the excellent quality. In 1289 Paolino Doria, Benedetto Zaccaria's son-in-law, bought up fifty tons of Coloneia alum, moving once more in the direction of monopoly. Not content with expanding horizontally, Benedetto Zaccaria set himself up in the dyeing business in Genoa, where he built a factory near the River Bisagno.

The Zaccarias' ships traded in Alexandria and in North Africa, in Corsica and Sardinia, in Spain, at Aigues Mortes in France, at Bruges. Their representatives went by land to the Champagne Fairs. They traded in the Black Sea: at Trebizond, where roads from the Mediterranean and from Persia intersected, and in the Crimea, at Caffa, where the commerce of the Mediterranean world mingled with that of Russia and the Far East. For centuries the Black Sea had been closed to the maritime nations of the West by Byzantium. Opened to Italian merchants after the Fourth Crusade, it had become a special area of Genoese penetration during the Latin Empire, in spite of the hostile relations between that government and Genoa. The Genoese-Greek alliance consolidated Genoa's position. A Genoese colony was established at Caffa, which grew from a minor Greek port into a city full of warehouses, shops, and banks. The Zaccarias operated an active branch there; the names of the brothers, or of their sons-in-law or nephews or their representatives appear again and again in notarial contracts of Caffa. Italian merchants were such frequent visitors in the Black Sea that Marco Polo felt the city was not worth describing, because "it seems futile and dull to speak of these places where people go every day."

Caffa was a cosmopolitan port where besides Genoese could be found Italians from Ancona, Brescia, Cremona, Florence, Sicily, Corsica (among these a Bonaparte), as well as Spaniards, Frenchmen, Greeks, Armenians, and Turks. The slaves sold in the markets of the city added to this conglomeration a mixture of all the peoples of the Near East: tall blond Circassians and Ziks; stocky, high-cheekboned Tartars; red-haired Caucasians; Bulgarians; Georgians; Alans, and Laks. Many of these were destined for Egypt where they became Mamelukes in the sultan's army.

At Caffa ships unloaded wines from Greece, Crete, Italy; figs from the Riviera; cloth from Champagne and Flanders; swords and knives from Lombardy. They took on cargoes of silk from Central Asia, leather from Russia, white wax from Khazaria, salted fish from the Don, cowhides, and caviar sold with a portion of fish. The largest exports were salt and cereals, principally to Constantinople, though when famine threatened Italy and southern France in 1276, the Zaccarias obtained permission to ship grain to Genoa.

For some reason the Zaccarias' ships never carried slaves. Of all the many contracts concluded in Pera and Caffa having to do with the sale of slaves, the name of Zaccaria, recurring so frequently in other documents, never appears. Whether because of the Church's condemnation of the slave trade, or whether to avoid supplying the Saracens with soldiers to be used against the Holy Land, or from a personal antipathy to the trade can only be conjectured.

Almost two decades after his diplomatic mission to Michael Paleologus on behalf of his own city, Benedetto Zaccaria returned to political life with an embassy for his adopted country. The occasion was the threat of war against Byzantium by an alliance headed by Charles of Anjou, king of Sicily. Early in 1282, the emperor sent Benedetto Zaccaria and another envoy to Spain to negotiate a marriage between Paleologus' heir and a Spanish princess. Civil war in Castile impeded the mission, and by the time the ambassadors arrived in Aragon to make representations to Peter II, their enterprise was no longer necessary. The rebellion called the "Sicilian Vespers," in which the French occupiers were massacred by the Sicilian population, had broken out in Palermo, and Peter II's ships were already anchored off Palermo in the wake of the revolution. On September 4 Peter was acclaimed king of Sicily.

No sooner was Zaccaria freed from diplomacy than his services were importuned for war. The long simmering struggle between Pisa and Genoa for dominance in the western Mediterranean was reaching a climax, and Zaccaria was summoned home to take command. In the spring of 1284 he led a fleet of thirty galleys out of the harbor of Genoa and blockaded the Porto Pisano, Pisa's ocean harbor. The Pisans tried to evade the blockade by loading passengers and merchandise on the ships of neutral nations, including Venice, but Zaccaria took a special pleasure in foiling this maneuver. Four years before, anchored at Zara, he had accepted an invitation to dinner from the Venetian count of Zara, only to be seized and carried off a prisoner to Venice on the grounds that he was transporting men and cargo of Venice's enemy Ancona. Zaccaria seized the chance to get even, looking for Pisan cargoes on the neutral Venetian ships which sailed the Tyrrhenian. One Venetian ship carrying a cargo of Pisan wool that he sent to Genoa was worth 4,366 pounds; a Catalan ship brought even more, 4,960 pounds.

Pisa launched a desperate effort to break Zaccaria's blockade. After intensive secret preparations, sixty-five galleys and eleven larger warships armed with siege machines gathered in the Arno with the double intention of destroying Zaccaria's fleet and attacking Genoa itself. But a storm held the Pisan fleet at the river mouth long enough for Zaccaria to detect its presence, raise the blockade, and sail to warn Genoa. The Pisan fleet pursued, but failed to intercept him, arriving (July 31) outside the Genoese harbor to find the city fully mobilized. The Pisans withdrew; two Genoese fleets, one commanded by Zaccaria, the other by Oberto Doria, followed. On August 5, the Genoese anchored off the island of Meloria opposite the Porto Pisano, while Pisan ships took refuge behind the towers of the harbor, protected by the great chain that closed it off. Zaccaria had recourse to a ruse; taking his ships just over the horizon and lowering sails, he lured the Pisans out to attack Doria's small force.

Amid a hail of arrows, quicklime, and boiling liquid, Pisa gained an advantage; suddenly Zaccaria's squadron arrived and the

The towers and chains protecting the Porto Pisano, blockaded by Benedetto Zaccaria in 1284, are depicted in this thirteenth-century bas-relief, now in the Museum of Ligurian Sculpture, Genoa. (Department of Fine Arts and History, Commune of Genoa)

battle turned. Benedetto fastened a chain to the masts of two of his galleys and sailed them on either side of the Pisan admiral's flagship. Down went the scarlet Pisan pennon. At the same moment a ship carrying many members of the Doria family, including Benedetto's sons-in-law Paolino and Niccolo Doria, attacked another ship which flew the flag of the Pisan commune and brought down that standard. The battle became a rout. Seven Pisan ships were sunk, thirty-three captured, and many prisoners taken, including the Pisan podestà. The battle of Meloria was decisive; Pisa never recovered its old position.

Yet the Pisans gamely continued the struggle, even in the face of an alliance of Genoa, Florence, and Lucca. A large Genoese fleet under the command of one of the Captains of the People, Oberto Spinola, tried to deliver the coup de grace the following year. Benedetto Zaccaria commanded his own ship, the *Divizia*. But Florence and Lucca defected at the last moment, and Spinola abandoned the attempt. Benedetto Zaccaria attacked and demolished the Pisan lighthouse at Livorno, the only blow struck in the campaign.

In the next two years Zaccaria divided his time between pursuit of Pisan privateers in the Tyrrhenian Sea and his own business affairs. The Pisans gained a measure of revenge when a Catalan merchant ship which carried one of his alum cargoes was forced by a storm to take refuge in the Porto Pisano, where it was promptly confiscated.

But in the summer of 1287 Zaccaria arrived in the *Divizia* again before the Porto Pisano, where Niccolino di Petraccio, one of his partners in the anticorsair patrol, was awaiting him. The harbor was divided into two basins, one for warships, the other for merchant ships. Amid a shower of missiles, the *Divizia* passed between the towers of the entrance; Zaccaria was severely wounded in the leg. Petraccio meanwhile succeeded in breaking the chain that closed off the other basin and set fire to the ships and siege machines. The chains of the port were carried to Genoa and preserved in the Cathedral of San Lorenzo (in 1860 they were returned to Pisa as a gesture of Italian unity, and can now be seen in the Pisan Campo Santo).

After this defeat, Pisa accepted a peace treaty. Later, when the treaty was broken, Corrado Doria finished the work of Zaccaria and Petraccio by destroying the Porto Pisano.

While Pisa and Genoa were at war, the last act of the tragedy in the Holy Land was played out. The kingdom of Jerusalem enjoyed a brief respite when civil war broke out in Egypt and Egyptian territory was attacked by the Mongols, but the Crusading barons were too busy quarreling to make use of it. In 1287, while Benedetto Zaccaria was assailing the Porto Pisano in the *Divizia*, a Crusader prince, the count of Tripoli in Syria, died, leaving his small state to his sister Luciana de Toucy, married to an admiral of Charles of Anjou. Before she could claim her inheritance, Tripoli revolted and declared itself a free commune. One of its captains, an Embriaco from Gibeletto, descendant of Guglielmo Embriaco, persuaded Tripoli to turn to Genoa for protection. Genoa hesitated, divided between the chance of recovering a lost foothold in the Holy Land and the danger of offending Luciana's sponsors, who included Venice, Charles of Anjou, and the pope. Finally Zaccaria was dispatched to Tripoli to deal with the situation, with the title of Vicar of the Genoese Commune overseas and full freedom of action.

He sailed from Genoa on July 10, 1288, with two ships. On the way he learned that Luciana de Toucy had left Italy with a fleet of five galleys. Calling in at Phocaea, he had his own *Divizia* readied, and collected two other merchant ships which had just made port from the Black Sea. He arrived in Tripoli to find Luciana already there, with an imposing array of supporters who had sent their vessels to increase her fleet. Ignoring the ships drawn up in the harbor, Zaccaria advanced, his galleys ready for battle. The Tripolitans, who had been ready to surrender to Luciana, greeted him as a liberator.

Luciana withdrew to Acre, whereupon Benedetto Zaccaria concluded a treaty giving Genoa sovereignty over Tripoli, followed by treaties with the kings of Cyprus and Little Armenia.

Genoa, however, did not welcome Zaccaria's coup. The difficulty was not with Venice or the pope, but with Qalaun, the Egyptian sultan, with whom Genoa wanted to maintain commercial relations, and who coveted Tripoli. Ignoring his lack of support at home, Zaccaria forced Luciana de Toucy into signing an agreement, and they made a dramatic entry into Tripoli together on February 8, 1289.

That same day a powerful Egyptian army moved into the Holy Land. On March 8 it reached Damascus; a few days later it began the siege of Tripoli. The city resisted desperately, but early in April it became evident that it could not hold out. When the Venetians abandoned the city and boarded their ships, Zaccaria accepted the inevitable, taking with him as many people as he could rescue. An Arab eyewitness gave this report: "The inhabitants fled to the port, and a few were able to escape on ships. Most of the men of the city were killed; the children were carried off into captivity and the booty taken by the Muslims was immense. When they had finished killing the inhabitants and sacking the city, the Sultan ordered it razed to the ground. Nearby was an island on which rose the Church of St. Thomas. . . . After the fall of Tripoli, a crowd of Franks, men and women, fled to the island and the church. The Muslims rode their horses into the sea and swam them to the island. . . . All the men who had taken refuge there were killed, and the women and children were taken prisoner. . . ."

Zaccaria sailed for Cyprus, where he landed the refugees of Tripoli and made a fruitless attempt to persuade King Hethum II to come to the rescue; next he stopped in Armenia where he was no more successful. Meanwhile the consul of Caffa, Zaccaria's son-in-law Paolino Doria, had persuaded the Genoese merchants of that city to send three ships to Tripoli; but when these vessels arrived at Cyprus, they learned that the city had fallen and that Zaccaria was in Armenia, where they sailed to join him. These reinforcements encouraged him to a daring measure, intended to force Genoa's hand and make the city take up the defense of the Crusader states: his ships ambushed the first Egyptian ship that arrived from Alexandria, captured it, and took it to Genoa as a prize.

Sultan Qalaun retaliated at once by arresting all Genoese merchants in Egypt and confiscating their goods. In Genoa Zaccaria was denounced, and the Commune hastened to send a galley carrying his prisoners and merchandise back to Egypt. Apologies and damages were offered; Zaccaria's actions were disavowed. The outcome was a new commercial treaty between Genoa and Egypt which assured the Genoese greater privileges than before and which implied an official revocation of the pope's long-standing embargo on exporting war material to the infidel.

Zaccaria was not exiled, but may have been persuaded to leave voluntarily, because the following year, 1290, he quit Genoa to serve another foreign sovereign: Sancho IV, king of Castile. Sancho was engaged in a war with the emir of Morocco, who raided Christian Spain from Tarifa and Algeciras. In the spring of 1291, Benedetto Zaccaria was patrolling the Castilian coast, in command of a fleet of seven Genoese and five Sevillian ships. His principal mission was to prevent enemy soldiers and supplies from crossing the Straits. With a much smaller force than that of the Moroccans, and with heavier, slower ships, Zaccaria employed his ingenuity to offset his naval disadvantage; he multiplied the number of oarsmen, replacing the customary two rowers on each bench with three, thereby increasing speed. On the seventh anniversary of Meloria, August 6, 1291, Zaccaria's fleet went out to meet a Muslim squadron of twenty galleys and eight smaller ships. Zaccaria's men rowed slowly forward until the enemy ships were in range, then bent to their oars and chased the Moroccans back to the African shore. Twelve Mo-

roccan ships were captured and taken up the Guadalquivir River to
Seville.

Sancho IV rewarded Benedetto Zaccaria by giving him the
title of High Admiral of the Sea. The following year Zaccaria's
fleet, reinforced by ships from every port in the kingdom, and from
Aragon, blockaded the Straits while Castilian troops besieged Tarifa
by land. In October, the Muslim stronghold fell.

Meanwhile relations between the king and the newly vested
High Admiral had become strained; Sancho increased the Castilian
element in his navy and gave more and more authority to his commander of land forces, and in July 1294 Zaccaria decided not to
renew his contract. A Spanish historian gives Zaccaria credit for
founding Spain's naval power: "The captains of the galleys were
mostly [his] relatives, associates or countrymen. . . . People gave all
the men who operated the King's fleet the metaphorical name of
'Zaccaria. . . .'"

Zaccaria sought employment with another king. Philip IV of
France, having recruited Genoese carpenters and shipbuilders to
construct a naval arsenal at Rouen, invited Zaccaria to be his admiral for war against England. Accepting, Zaccaria wrote the king a
long memorandum outlining a plan of campaign. He proposed a series of hit-and-run raids on English ports that would minimize the
expenditure of men and money, and maximize the cost to the English, arousing discontent and revolt. A fleet of *uscieri*, horse-and-
troop carrying ships, were to be built for the campaign.

The ships were ready in April 1295; but for the first time in his
life Benedetto Zaccaria was unable to join his fleet in battle; he was
ill, and the French king had to name two French commanders in his
place. The battle plan was carried out very differently from the
way Zaccaria had planned it. Rather than a small squadron of ships
striking in surprise attacks, a large fleet sailed from Flanders in August, and landed troops near Dover, who seized and burned the city.
Then, instead of immediately boarding ship, the attackers remained
to fight on land and were decimated by English reinforcements. Another French contingent at Hythe was ambushed and wiped out.
Subsequent expeditions were equally unsuccessful.

Recovering from his illness, Benedetto Zaccaria took command in person, organizing a blockade which had the unfortunate effect of driving Flanders, whose cloth makers were cut off by the blockade from their supplies of English wool, into an alliance with England. In 1298 the war was interrupted by a truce between England and France, sealed by two royal marriages, between Edward of England and Margaret of France, and between Edward's son, the future Edward II, and Philip IV's daughter Isabella. However, the interval of peace proved brief, with French troops invading Flanders the following year, while Zaccaria's fleet sailed from Rouen to blockade the mouth of the River Zwyn, cutting off traffic from Bruges, Ypres, and Lille.

In June of 1300, in the middle of the blockade, Benedetto Zaccaria suddenly left the king's service and hurried home to Genoa, this time not because of trouble with his patron but because of exciting new events in the Holy Land. The previous fall the Mongol Ghazan-Khan of Persia had invaded Syria with a formidable army, including contingents of his vassals, the Christian kings of Armenia and Georgia. The Egyptians were routed, Damascus fell, Palestine was overrun by the Mongols. In Italy everyone talked enthusiastically of a new Crusade to take advantage of the Mongol allies. A group of highborn Genoese ladies volunteered to put on armor themselves and fight in the Holy Land. Benedetto Zaccaria agreed to accept them as auxiliaries—"valiant hearts in weak bodies."

But the pope took a cautious view of the projected Crusade. He insisted on reviewing Zaccaria's plans, and declared that Tripoli was not to be retaken and rebuilt—apparently fearing Zaccaria's ambitious designs on the city that had been the scene of his political maneuvering twelve years before. While the Pope delayed, Ghazan-Khan fell ill and returned home to Tabriz. Without his help, the Crusade had to be abandoned.

Zaccaria went home to Phocaea, which he had not visited since 1289. The old settlement had been devastated by the Venetians four years before, and a "New Phocaea" had been built to the north, protected by new walls and a fortress. The Seljuk Turks in Iconium and the rising state of the Ottoman Turks made Aegean commerce more dangerous every day; Phocaea was threatened also by Catalan pirates. The island of Chios, opposite Phocaea, suffered the depredations of both Catalans and Ottoman Turks. Zaccaria occupied the island and fortified it, restoring the walls, digging moats, and organizing defenses. Chios, in addition to its strategic value, produced many exports—wine, figs, almonds, marble, citrus fruits, silk. But the product for which the island was famous, found nowhere else in the world, was gum-mastic, a plant from which was extracted an aromatic gum used by pharmacists as an astringent, by painters in varnishes, and above all by ladies to whiten their teeth and sweeten their breath. As possessor of Chios, Zaccaria monopolized the supply.

In 1306 Zaccaria was back in Genoa; his name appeared among the two hundred prominent citizens summoned by the Captains of the People to consider a request for alliance by the neighboring town of Savona.

The following year, in the spring, the aging admiral was still in action, concluding a business deal with his brother Manuele and his son Paleologus and planning a trip to Phocaea. A short time later he was dead, in his great stone house by the sea. In the (translated) words of Robert S. Lopez: "Thus it was fitting that Benedetto Zaccaria should die: in port, but ready to depart; in his native Genoa, but with his eyes fixed on the distance." Manuele did not long outlive him.

Twenty years later, the Greek emperor repossessed first Chios and then Phocaea, but they soon returned to Genoese hands, held by a commercial company, the *maona*, a forerunner of the great colonial trading companies, which governed Phocaea for another hundred years and Chios for more than two hundred. Meanwhile the Zaccarias married a succession of French Crusading princesses, finally moving into Morea (Peloponnesus), the line coming to an end with Centurion II, prince of Achaia and baron of Arcadia, in the fifteenth century; by that time the family was more Greek than Genoese, and had been almost forgotten in Genoa.

Benedetto Zaccaria's life heralded a new age, the era of vast commercial fortunes, when great merchants had their own fleets and intervened freely in politics and war, single-handedly launching enterprises of moment.

In 1291, two cousins of Benedetto, the merchants Ugolino and Vadino Vivaldi, struck out to find a new trade route to India by sea. Rounding the African corner, their ships put in at a Moroccan port on the Atlantic, revictualed, and headed south. Nothing was ever heard of them again, though Ugolino's son Sorleone refused to believe that his father was dead, and made an expedition to Africa searching for him. Some modern geographers believe that the Vivaldi were not actually trying to round the Cape of Good Hope, but that they set out from Morocco on a more imaginative voyage, one that was undertaken for similar motives by another Genoese two hundred years later.

10

The Polos of Venice

The victories of Benedetto Zaccaria and other Genoese mariners sent a stream of prisoners, aboard their captured galleys, past the Old Mole and into the harbor of Genoa. Common sailors were shoved into the dungeons, officers were locked up in the Palazzo San Giorgio. Among the crowd in the palazzo in 1297 was a forty-two-year-old Venetian merchant named Marco Polo. Initially, he did not stand out from his fellow prisoners, Venetians, Pisans, Livornese, Greeks, but presently he gained a reputation as an entertainer. Among a crowd of men who had sailed the length and breadth of the Mediterranean, some who had ventured into the Black Sea and the Atlantic, a few whom fortune had carried as far as Persia, Marco Polo was unique; he had visited the Far East. Not only had he visited it, he had spent seventeen years there, at the court and in the service of the almost fabulous Mongol emperor of China, Kublai Khan.

Polo's reminiscences fascinated his captive audience, though they were not quite sure how seriously to take him. He claimed the cities of "Cathay" were much larger and more numerous than all the cities of Europe. Furthermore, they were infinitely richer and

more magnificent: the streets of the Khan's capital were broad, and
straight as strings, the residential districts lined with fine houses and
gardens as far as the eye could see; the crowded, jumbled cities of
Europe were dung heaps by comparison. He described the Drum
Tower which boomed out alarm signals and the Bell Tower which
every evening rang the curfew. The Great Khan's court was more
majestic than the pope's, with great lords serving as cupbearers at
banquets, their mouths and noses wrapped with silk napkins lest
their breath contaminate the vessels placed before the Khan. Anyone
entering the imperial audience chamber put on white leather slippers
in order not to soil the silk carpets. Furthermore, said the narrator,
"each baron carries with him a tiny vase while he is in the audience
chamber, in case he needs to spit, for no one would dare spit on the
floor in the Emperor's palace."

Even more impressively beautiful than the city and palace of
Cambaluc (Peking) were the summer capital and summer palace of
Xanadu (Shang Tu). In fact, the whole of Cathay, whose vast reaches
he claimed to have traversed while in the Khan's service, was far
ahead of Europe in nearly every respect. Along the roads radiating
from the capital to the provinces were post stations shaded by trees
planted for the purpose, with palatial lodges for the Khan's messengers and other official travelers. Four hundred horses were kept in
readiness at each station. It was easy to travel two stages of twenty-
five to thirty miles each in a day; messengers bearing urgent dispatches covered the long distances swiftly by galloping at full speed
with bells on their bridles to signal the relay ahead to be ready.

Did his listeners think the Po and the Danube were large rivers?
The Yangtse, varying in width from six to ten miles, was a hundred
and twenty days' journey long. "I tell you truly," he swore, "that
more boats loaded with more valuable goods pass on the Yangtse
than go by all the rivers of Christians together, and all our seas." He
described the large and small square-rigged junks that sailed the
mighty river, and how they were towed upstream by ropes made of
twisted bamboo strips.

The precision of his details lent verisimilitude, yet such descriptions could not fail to tax credulity. The city of Quinsai

(Hangchow), a Chinese Venice of rivers and canals, was not only very much larger than his native city (twelve thousand bridges over Quinsai's innumerable canals!) but all its streets were paved with hewn stone and baked brick, and kept so clean that one might walk through it without soiling one's feet.

What about the Chinese women, someone wanted to know. Ah, said the traveler, the Chinese women—delicate, angelic, the most beautiful in the world, especially those of Soochow and Hangchow. They wear silk gowns and many jewels and have most attractive manners, while their worth and dignity command such respect that no one would dare address an improper word to them. That, of course, is the respectable women; as for the others, they live in their own quarter, and are so numerous you would not believe it. They also wear rich clothes, and use fragrant perfumes, and have plenty of servants. They are educated and clever, and know how to flatter and caress with words, so that out-of-town merchants who have enjoyed their favors remain long after in a sort of ecstasy. When they get home they say they have been in Quinsai, that is, in the city of heaven, and cannot wait to see the hour when they may return there again.

The port of Zaitun (Amoy) dwarfed the waterfronts of Venice, Genoa, and Pisa combined, according to Polo; a hundred times more pepper was landed there than reached the whole of Christendom through Alexandria and the Levant. He told of tall-masted ocean junks arriving laden with spices, aloes, ebony, and sandalwood from southeast Asia, or outward bound with Chinese silks to trade in India for pearls and precious stones from Ceylon, and muslin "like tissue of spiders' webs." Some of the countries with which the Empire of Cathay traded, and which Polo claimed to have visited, his hearers, seafarers though they were, had never even heard of—Tibet, Burma, Siam, Java, and Sumatra.

Some of his listeners, merchants and men of business in peacetime, were intrigued by his account of the paper money that circulated everywhere in the Great Khan's dominion. When the notes, printed from wood blocks in several denominations, wore out, they had to be taken to the imperial mint for replacement, which was done at a charge of three percent of value, not only paying for the cost of printing and paper, but assuring the treasury a profit.

Another hard-to-believe item was the assertion that the Chinese burned "large black stones which are dug from the mountains as veins, which burn and make flames like logs . . . and cook better than wood." Europe had known coal in ancient times, but it had been so completely forgotten that neither Marco Polo nor any of his fellow prisoners had ever seen it burned.

Skepticism was routed by wonder. Even the guards were entranced, and soon, according to a chronicler, "the whole city gathered to see him and to talk to him, not treating him as a prisoner, but as a dear friend and honored gentleman, and showed him so much affection that there was never an hour of the day that he was not visited by the most noble gentlemen of Genoa and presented with everything necessary for his living."

Between his fellow prisoners and his Genoese visitors, Marco Polo must have heard a thousand variations of the listener's admiring response to the interesting traveler: "You should write a book." Marco was more of a talker than a writer, but he solved this problem in the same way as many other authors of later centuries. In the very prison with him was a well-known writer, Rustichello of Pisa, who may have been taken prisoner by Benedetto Zaccaria at Melo ria thirteen years before. As a contributor to the literature of Arthurian romance, Rustichello seemed to some a particularly suitable collaborator for the Venetian yarn spinner. Polo agreed to the project, and, privileged prisoner that he was, sent home to Venice for his travel diaries.

Thus came into being one of the world's most remarkable classics, to which its author appended the bald but expansive title, *Description of the World*. Rustichello wrote in French, the language of romance, but there is no doubt that he recorded faithfully.

There is also no reason to doubt Marco Polo's veracity on nearly everything of importance, despite occasional, easily-recognized excursions into hearsay miracles and reports of marvelous Isles of Males and Females. In fact, *Description of the World* remains to this day not only a steady seller in the book markets of Europe and

America (usually under some such title as *The Travels of Marco Polo*), but a prime (and primary) source of information for Western scholars on Kublai Khan's China and its neighbors. Its author, even if he needed a ghost writer to help him, was a truly extraordinary man on at least two counts: first, his powers of observation and memory for significant detail, and second, the personality and presence which won him dazzling success at the court of Kublai Khan.

Of all the marvels recounted by Marco Polo, that success was one of the least wondered at by his contemporary listeners and readers (the manuscript Rustichello turned out was copied over and over). The same was true of the odyssey itself. Each portion of it was a journey of incredible duration, danger, and hardship. The chief heroes were Marco's father Niccolo and his uncle Maffeo. These two indomitable travelers made the 10,000-mile round trip not once but twice. It is 5,000 miles Venice-to-Peking as the crow flies; as the Polos did it, first by land both ways, second by sea, their total mileage ran to something like 30,000. Men and women of the high Middle Ages were prodigious travelers by land and sea, flocking to the shrines and fairs by foot, pack animal, and leaky boat. Thousands risked shipwreck, pirates, and contagion every year to visit Jerusalem. Yet, even among medieval travelers, Niccolo, Maffeo, and Marco Polo are so outstanding as to defy comprehension.

One neglected member of the family deserves mention: Marco's mother, Niccolo's wife. Just as merchants were accustomed to long journeys and hardships, their wives were inured to being deserted for months or sometimes years, to bringing up their children and managing their households alone, to living in fear of the messenger who might bring news of war, shipwreck, piracy, plague, or business disaster. Often a husband settled abroad for several years at a time, leaving his wife to add jealousy to her other troubles; when he returned it was frequently to take away the sons who had grown up in his absence. Sometimes the wife did not live to see her husband's safe return; this was the case with Niccolo Polo's wife, who died some time between Marco's birth and Niccolo's return.

The unparalleled adventure began by a series of accidents. Niccolo and Maffeo sailed in convoy from Venice in 1253 for Constantinople, where the Venice-dominated Latin Empire installed by the Fourth Crusade still prevailed, and where they had an older brother in business. They remained there six years, perhaps with visits to Venice, but in 1260 decided to transfer their operations to Soldaia, in the Crimea, where the family had a branch office. Their decision may have been motivated by the political situation developing in Constantinople, where the Greeks, with Genoese aid, were preparing to overthrow the Latin Empire. Business in Soldaia was a disappointment, however, and at the same time news arrived that the Genoese and Greeks had carried out their revolution, making Constantinople unsafe for Venetians.

In this predicament the idea occurred to the two merchant-venturers to take a flyer in the Eastern trade. The conquests of Ghengis Khan in the early years of the century had had the effect of turning the vast prairie of western and central Asia into a peaceful, stable region with good communications and safe roads. The Mongols, or Tartars, who had alarmed Europe earlier, had come to be regarded as not bad fellows after all, because of their successful depredations at the expense of Islam. Saintly Louis IX of France had sent an envoy, William of Rubruck, all the way to Karakorum, north of the Gobi Desert, to talk about an alliance. The Polos had no thought at first of going that far; they meant only to visit Bolgara, far up the Volga, the capital of Barka Khan, grandson of Genghis. In their thousand-mile trek across a steppe dotted with Mongol camps, they were uniformly well-received, and taught to enjoy kumiss by smiling hosts who yanked on their ears as they drank "to make the throat open widely." Barka Khan was cordiality itself, graciously accepting the jewels they offered him and giving them in return merchandise "well worth twice as much as the jewels, and also very great and rich gifts."

The brothers remained in Bolgara a year, trading their own goods and Barka's gifts. They were on the point of returning to the Crimea and thence to Venice, when Barka declared war on his cousin Hulagu, who ruled Persia. That made the roads to the southwest unsafe. After deliberating their situation, the brothers made the hardy decision to visit Barak Khan, Hulagu's nephew, in central

Asia. Loading their goods into "arabas"—covered wagons mounted on two huge wheels for negotiating streams and mudholes—they headed east. To the southeast between the Caspian and Aral seas they crossed a desert region peopled only by Tartars on the move with their flocks, and reached their destination, the ancient city of Bukhara, astride the Silk Road. Here a further accident, the outbreak of another Mongol war, kept them blocked from going home. It was three years before the return of peace. But as they prepared to head homeward at last, an embassy returning to China from Persia stopped in Bukhara and the envoy was fascinated to find two Europeans so far east. He at once made a proposal; since they had come this distance, why not continue on, in the safe escort of the embassy, and visit the Great Khan, who, they were assured, would be delighted to meet them.

Eight years and 2,500 miles from home, the two adventurous Venetians found the offer too good to turn down. Packing up once more, they joined the ambassador's caravan.

The goal of the journey was not Karakorum, where William of Rubruck had called on the Great Khan, but a new city on an old site, Khanbaligh, the Khan's City, spelled by Europeans Cambaluc, and known to a later age as Peking. Kublai Khan had judged Karakorum too far north to be comfortable. There were two ways to reach Cambaluc—by sea from the Persian Gulf, or overland by a variety of routes. From Bukhara it took a year, and even traveling first-class with the Great Khan's ambassador, the trip was rugged. The caravan bumped along 2,500 miles through every kind of terrain and weather—mountain and desert, blizzard and heat wave, storm and drought.

True to the ambassador's word, the mighty Kublai Khan gave the visitors from Venice a royal welcome, even better than that by his relative Barka Khan. He wined and dined them and asked a thousand questions about the Byzantine emperor, the kings of France and England, and especially the pope. Kublai was dissatisfied with the Mongols' primitive Shaman religion, which centered on spirits and demons, and was toying with the idea of importing either Christianity or Islam. It occurred to him that he could employ the

Niccolo and Maffeo Polo, father and uncle, respectively, of Marco, en route to Cathay, in a detail from the Atlas Catalan. (Bibliothèque Nationale)

Polos as envoys to the pope to request a Christian mission—he proposed a hundred well-educated friars. Niccolo and Maffeo, glad of the opportunity to return home and foreseeing profit in their unique connection, accepted the commission and soon set out on the return trip—once more desert, mountains, snow, heat, floods. The trip was even longer and harder this time; it took the brothers three years to reach Acre (1269) and embark for Venice.

They had been away fifteen years; Niccolo's wife was dead, and a son born shortly after his departure was nearly grown. It is a mystery why Niccolo and Maffeo, after all they had experienced, did not find an excuse to stay home and let somebody else lead the mission to proselytize the Mongols. After all, it was more the pope's business than theirs. But on the contrary, after a delay of two years while they waited for a new pope to be elected, they set out once more for Cambaluc. The pope did not even take a very pressing interest in the mission, for instead of the hundred missionaries Kublai Khan had requested he sent two Dominicans, and not very dedicated fellows at that. When on entering Armenia the party heard that a local Muslim chief was on the war path, the friars turned tail and hastened home.

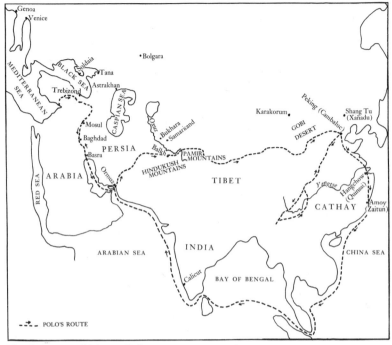

The Journey of Marco Polo

Astoundingly, the dauntless businessmen decided to go ahead anyway. If they had no missionary army to bring Kublai Khan, they had something else—Niccolo's son Marco, an adolescent who from the outset demonstrated his exceptional qualities by taking copious notes to fortify an excellent memory and capacity for observation. By way of Mosul and Baghdad the Polo caravan traveled to Ormuz, a thriving port on the Persian Gulf. Apparently they had intended to take ship there, but they found the frail Arab ships "very bad and dangerous for navigation . . . sewn together with a kind of yarn made from coconut fibers" and preferred the perils of the overland route. Organizing a caravan, they headed north, to the ancient city of Balkh, in modern Afghanistan, where Alexander the Great married Roxanne. From Balkh they journeyed northeast to Taican, famous for its salt mines ("so much of it that the whole world would have enough till doomsday"), thence through a country of almond and pistachio orchards where the natives were "great topers, in truth they are constantly getting drunk." On to the River Oxus, north of the Hindu Kush mountains, where Marco got a first glimpse of some of the wealth of the Orient—sapphire and lapis lazuli mines. But at Badakhshan young Marco fell ill and the party was delayed nearly a year. He was not too sick to record one of the first of many observations about Asian women—hereabouts, he noted, they clothed themselves in voluminous linen trousers to emphasize the breadth of their hips "because their men delight in fat women, and she who appears more stout below the waist seems to them more beautiful and more glorious."

Wending northeast, the travelers ascended the steep Pamir mountains, a "region so lofty and cold that you do not even see any birds flying." Here Marco saw the wild sheep that Western science later named after him *Ovis poli*, though William of Rubruck had seen and described them earlier. Following the ancient southern caravan route, they passed through eastern Turkestan (Sinkiang), a region where desert alternated with oases blooming with gardens, orchards, and estates, to the edge of the Gobi Desert. After a pause to rest their camels and fill their water bottles, they plunged into the wasteland, whose disagreeable reputation included evil spirits capable of spreading mirages before the exhausted travelers, calling out to them with the voices of friends, and luring them to their death. Pack animals crossing the Gobi wore bells so they could be retrieved if they wandered. The journey across the desert lasted thirty days. Arriving safely at Tangut, in extreme northern China, they proceeded toward Peking. Marco, now twenty-one, observed the Chinese with curiosity, especially the women—"the ladies have no hair except that of the head, and are white, of fair flesh, well formed in all their limbs, but very voluptuous."

For the last forty days of their interminable journey they had an escort sent by the Khan. It was spring; the escort took them not to Peking but to the summer capital of Shang Tu (Xanadu, Marco wrote it, and Coleridge six hundred years later copied), one of the most beautiful cities of that or any age. Surrounded by gardens and fountains, the summer palace with its marble facing and gilded interiors, its halls lined with paintings of exquisite landscapes with birds and beasts, trees and flowers, outshone anything any European had seen. Equally attractive and impressive was the Great Khan himself, before whom the Polos knelt "with great reverence and humbled themselves as much as they could, prostrating themselves on the ground." The Great Khan bade them stand and received them "with the greatest honor and very great rejoicing and great feasting." He conversed at length with the brothers about their adventures since leaving him, received the gifts and documents they had brought from the pope and which the cowardly friars had left in their care. Kublai then inquired about the noble young man accompanying them, and Niccolo replied, "Sire, 'tis my son and your liege man."

The Great Khan forthwith ordered Marco's name to be inscribed among the members of his household. This gesture proved to be much more than honorific; Kublai liked and trusted Niccolo and Maffeo, and apparently transferred his confidence in an augmented degree to Marco. For the next seventeen years the three Venetians dwelt at the court of the richest of the world's rulers less as honored guests than as valued aides. Marco in particular, perhaps because of his youth and vigor, and doubtless because of his intelligence, was singled out for missions to distant parts of the Empire. Why Kublai should have bestowed such confidence on foreigners is a tantalizing puzzle. It appears that their very foreignness was a factor; sovereign over a ruling warrior class of Mongols and a large subject population, he may have felt that a lone, readily identified Westerner had little potential for disloyalty.

Corroboration for this notion comes from the story of the Polos' resignation from the Khan's service. Despite their long residence, they had not accumulated great fortunes, but they had enjoyed favor for a long time, and as foreigners could not have been as popular with the Mongols and Chinese, especially those close to the throne, as they were with Kublai himself. Whatever the tensions at the court of Cambaluc, Marco passes over them in silence, attributing the Khan's stubborn refusal to permit the Venetians' departure merely to "the great love he had for them." Nevertheless, the Polos must have been concerned about what would happen to them when

Kublai died and a new Khan was proclaimed. This probably was the principal motivation for their determination to quit Cathay. Their pleas in the names of their families Kublai took with a grain of salt, as well he might in view of their history. An accident rescued them. Kublai's great-nephew, the Arghun Khan of Persia, had lost his mother, who was also, by curious Mongol dynastic custom, his wife, and was now ready to marry a younger relative. Kublai chose a comely princess named Cocacin, and sent her with his blessing off across the desert. But yet another war among the factious Mongols of central Asia blocked the caravan's path, and it returned to Cambaluc with the disappointed princess. By chance Marco Polo returned at the same moment from a long and perilous voyage in the Khan's service all the way to India. One manuscript of Marco's narrative says that his father and uncle had accompanied him, which would add still further to their record mileage. In any case the three Polos together saw the possibilities in offering their knowledge of the sea route as assistance to the Persian ambassador and the royal bride. An agreement was worked out and presented to Kublai, who was not pleased at losing his Venetians, but who did not want to annoy his great-nephew.

Thirteen four-masted junks, with many cabins and watertight bulkheads, set sail. After touching at Vietnam, tributary to Kublai, the flotilla proceeded to Sumatra, so far south that "the North Star is not seen there," and where dwelt the rhinoceros, which Marco identified with the unicorn; contrary to European fable, Marco reported, it did not allow itself to be caught in the lap of a virgin girl.

One of the curiosities of Marco's written account is its tantalizing brevity about his personal adventures. "I should have told you," he suddenly mentions, "that when they were embarked they were in number some six hundred persons, without counting the mariners, but nearly all died by the way, so that only eighteen survived." Shipwreck or pestilence? Marco supplies no basis for conjecture. But after two years' voyaging, described with frustrating dearth of detail, the eighteen survivors reached Persia. There they found that Arghun Khan had died, an incident of no great moment; his successor married the lady.

Because the hostile sultan of Egypt now held the Syrian ports (Acre's fall in 1291 came a year before the Polos quit Peking), they took the ancient northwest road which Xenophon and the Ten Thousand Greeks had traveled, to the Black Sea, and after an unexplained nine-month delay, during which they learned of the death of Kublai Khan, sailed from Trebizond to Constantinople. Venetians were no longer lording it in the Byzantine capital, but they were at least not being hunted down, so the Polos refreshed their party and continued home to Venice, sailing into the harbor in 1295, after an absence of twenty-five years. For this homecoming, Marco's book records a perfunctory thanks to God.

Legend surrounds the Polos' return: that when they arrived, travel-weary and dressed in coarse Tartar clothes, on the threshold of their house in the district of St. John Chrysostom, no one recognized them. Relatives had moved into their house, and refused to believe that these were the long-absent owners. To prove their identity, the travelers gave a banquet, donning with each course a more splendid set of robes, and each time giving the command for the satin and brocade and velvet of the clothes they had worn to be cut into pieces and distributed among the servants. Finally, with the dessert, the Polos appeared in their shabby traveling clothes and, before the eyes of their dumfounded guests, proceeded to rip open the seams and the lining, "upon which there poured forth a great quantity of precious stones, rubies, sapphires, carbuncles, diamonds, and emeralds, so that no one could have suspected that they were there. . . . And now they at once recognized these honored and venerated gentlemen in the Polo house, whom they had at first doubted, and received them with the greatest honor and reverence. And when this became known throughout Venice, straightway the whole city, the gentry as well as the common folk, flocked to their house, to embrace them and to shower them with affection. . . ."

This Arabian-Nights-cum-Odyssey tale to the contrary, the Polos do not seem to have grown measurably richer from their twenty-five-year enterprise. According to one account, not long after their return Marco undertook a trading voyage, and was captured by the Genoese; according to another, he was a commander in the fleet that attacked the Genoese and was defeated by them at Curzola, off the Dalmatian coast. All that is certain is that Marco was a Genoese prisoner of war from 1296–97 to May 1299, when a peace treaty was concluded and prisoners were released.

Back in Venice at the age of forty-five, Marco married, apparently for the first time. His wife was Donata Badoer; the marriage produced three daughters, Fantina, Bellela, and Moreta. He lived on for another quarter of a century, continuing in the family business. When he died in 1324, he divided his modest estate among his three daughters, with a settlement for his wife, and released his Tartar slave "from all bondage as I pray God may absolve my soul from all guilt and sin . . ." On his deathbed, one chronicler reports, friends suggested that he save himself in the eyes of God by removing everything in his book that was exaggerated, to which he replied indignantly that he had not told half of what he had really seen.

The entire story of the adventures of Maffeo, Niccolo, and Marco occupies only a short prologue of the *Description of the World*. What Marco sought to do as he dictated to Rustichello in the San Giorgio prison was to depict all the lands of Asia—"the World"—to his fellow Europeans, who lived on a small peninsula of it. Despite the instances of exaggerations or too readily accepted hearsay, and despite some lacunae, the book was amazingly accurate, and comprehensive beyond belief. In Marco Polo the outstanding qualities of the Italian merchant—intelligence, courage, adaptability, linguistic skill, self-reliance, social address—were exemplified in the highest degree. His book, with its precision of detail and affectionate dwelling on the wealth of the East, was technically and ideologically an expression of his class.

It was an immediate success. Louis IX's emissary, William of Rubruck, and the pope's envoy John of Pian de Carpine, had written earlier, much terser accounts of their Asian journeys, but Marco Polo's knowledgeable and authoritative book was a revelation. From it European merchants became aware of the significant transformation wrought by the successors of Genghis Khan in the pacification of central Asia. Suddenly two of the three great trade routes between industrious, ignorant, aggressive Europe and the richer, more civilized East were open to direct exploitation, as they had not been since ancient times. Instead of waiting at the Eastern gates, in Syria and Egypt, and taking what the Arabs brought from China and India, European merchants started going to the sources. Caravans began trekking across the Russian steppe and over the Silk Road to Cathay, along which the Khan's imperial postal service moved from Samarkand to Peking in six months, and which a merchant's caravan could cover in a year. At the same time, the friendly Il-Khan of Persia provided access to the sea route, by which the Polos had returned; taking ship at Ormuz, at the mouth of the Persian Gulf (which the outward-bound Polos had decided not to do), European merchants could reach India in a few weeks. By 1315 the enterprising Vivaldi of Genoa, cousins of Benedetto Zaccaria, two of whom had perished seeking the Atlantic route to India, had trading stations on the Gumerat and Malabar coasts. From there, they could sail to Indonesia, southeast Asia, and China, as some of them did. But most dealt for their spices and silks with the Chinese merchants whose tall-masted junks anchored next to Arab dhows and Indian vessels in the harbors of Calicut and Quilon; by 1329 there were enough Europeans in Quilon for Pope John XII to make the place a bishopric.

Francesco Pegolotti, factor (agent) of the Bardi of Florence, writing in 1340, gave detailed guidebook instructions for eastward-bound merchants—the stages of the journey, the proper pack animals, kinds and amounts of provisions required, estimated costs, and valuation of potential return cargoes. "First you must let your beard grow long," he advised his readers. "At Tana [on the Sea of Azov] you should furnish yourself with a dragoman, and you must not try to save money by taking a bad one; besides, it will be well to take at least two good men servants who are acquainted with the Cumanian tongue, and if the merchant wants to take a woman with him from Tana he can do so; . . . he does not have to, but if he does he will be kept much more comfortably. . . . From Tana to Astrakhan, you will need provisions for twenty-five days, that is, flour and salt fish, because sufficient meat can be found everywhere along the way. . . . The road from Tana to Cathay is perfectly safe whether by day or by night, as the merchants who have used it report. . . ." This last statement Pegolotti qualified to the extent of conceding that on the worst stretch, the first, from Tana to Sarai on the Volga, a company of sixty men could pass in perfect security.

Enough Europeans had by then made the trip that a European (mainly Italian) colony flourished in Peking; the pope sent a legate who founded the Latin church of China and became archbishop of Cambaluc. The indefatigably aggressive Genoese established a warehouse at Zaitun (Amoy). A historic connection had been made; the Commercial Revolution of Europe had reached the wellsprings of Asia.

At this critical moment something went wrong, and the mighty door opened by Marco Polo swung shut once more. The Il-Khans of Persia, old enemies of the Muslims, after trying for half a century to persuade the Europeans to take up Crusading again, gave up on Christianity and did a religious-diplomatic about-face, embracing Islam. Thereafter Persia was a less congenial staging area for the merchants from the West.

When in 1368 the Chinese overturned the Mongol dynasty in favor of the native Mings, who instituted an antiforeign policy, it was merely the locking of an already closed door. This might in time have swung open again, but at the turn of the fifteenth century Tamerlane's armies galloped through central Asia, Russia, India, and Persia like hordes of mounted locusts, wiping out Tana, Sarai, Baghdad, Shiraz, and other commercial centers. His successors, unlike those of Genghis, did not erect a new empire on the conquered territory. Central Asia remained in chaotic fragments, and the Eastern trade was left in the hands of Arabs and Asians. The next effort the Europeans made to take it over was directed along other routes.

The *Description of the World* remained. A century and a half after its protagonist's death, Christopher Colombus of Genoa studied it and made notes in the margin of his copy. Martin Behaim's globe, based on Ptolemy, showed the space between Spain and China as 130° of longitude instead of 230°. This error, added to Marco Polo's statement, duly noted by Columbus, that Japan was 1,500 miles east of China ("That region is very inaccessible and out of the way.

Moreover, Messer Marco Polo never was there"), led him to place Japan about 3,900 miles west of the Canary Islands, approximately where America is located. Thus the Venetian traveler added posthumously to his feats an assistance in the discovery of America.

II

Cities and Bankers:
the Crespins of Arras

In the year 1299 the Flemish city of Bruges found itself saddled with a public debt of 140,000 pounds. Of this enormous sum no less than 110,000 pounds was owed to two individuals, Robert and Baude Crespin of Arras. The Crespins lent money to burghers and countesses, to knights, bishops, and kings, but in the last quarter of the thirteenth century increasingly to communes. Bruges was by no means the only town on their books; their name was known and feared throughout northwest Europe.

The Crespins were originally millers or bakers, perhaps both, a family of poor craftsmen attached to the large monastery of St. Vaast, the nucleus around which the city of Arras had formed in the early Middle Ages. The mills started them in commerce, and in the second half of the twelfth century a Jean Crespin appeared among the Arras merchants trading in Italy; Crespins were recorded in Dieppe, and in England, including, curiously, a Crespin named Aaron, lending some credence to the otherwise dubious speculation that the family may have originally been Jewish. In the early decades of the thirteenth century the Crespins of Arras grew rich, but had not yet attained the highest ranks of the patriciate. They were evidently in the cloth trade—one is recorded as having exported eighty sacks of wool from England—but were investing in other fields, including real estate and banking. Crespins, probably younger sons, also turned up frequently among the clergy and military.

In the middle of the thirteenth century the Crespin family shifted to banking. The father of Baude and Robert Crespin made numerous loans to private individuals, including such prominent figures as the countess of Flanders, the bishop of Liège, the count of St. Pol, and other members of the aristocracy. Occasionally he lent to communes, such as the city of Calais. But following their father's death in 1276 Baude and Robert Crespin, operating sometimes singly, sometimes together, introduced a radical new policy; in place of the countesses and bishops, the names of the cities of Flanders— Ghent, Bethune, and several smaller towns—appeared more and more exclusively on the Crespin books. Then suddenly, in 1281, the prominent cloth city of Ypres contracted loans from Baude Crespin totaling over 12,000 pounds. This transaction signaled not only a new departure in the Crespins' business activities, but a new development in the history of the Flemish communes. The debits of the cities in the Crespins' books grew astoundingly; Bruges borrowed twenty times between 1284 and 1287, and eight more times in 1287. By 1290 Ghent, Ypres, Damme, and Cassel had appealed to the Arras financial lords.

If moneylenders sometimes had collection problems, the Crespins did not; their long association with the counts and countesses of Flanders and Artois and the king of France gave them all the bailiffs and provosts they needed. Ypres, summoned by the bailiff of Lens, hastily sent a four-horse carriage loaded with silver to Baude Crespin. The king of France threatened seizure of "body and goods" of merchants of Ghent, Ypres, and Bruges who visited the Champagne Fairs while in debt to the Crespins. The inhabitants of St. Omer were reported to be so "terrified" of the Crespins that they did not dare venture outside their walls.

Given their resources, their power to collect, and their clients' rising demands for funds, the Crespins' vault to great wealth is not surprising. Neither is the borrowing power of the cities in this age of patrician affluence. What is surprising is the financial plight of the rich cities of Flanders and northwest Europe. Some cities, like Noyon, went through bankruptcy, and citizens had to forfeit all their property to the bondholders. The cities' financial calamities were not the result of expensive public services but of two other forces. The count of Flanders, Guy de Dampierre, was one of the most spendthrift members of an improvident class, the feudal princes. Count Guy had stopped borrowing from the Crespins for the simple reason that they refused to lend him any more money. To supply himself, therefore, he turned to his cities, levying feudal aids and contracting personal loans. The cities borrowed the required sums from the Crespins, often without telling them that the money was intended for the count; from 1292 to 1295, the Crespins loaned Ypres 45,000 pounds and Bruges 68,600 for this purpose. The patricians of the town councils found the count's importunities difficult to resist; in any case, they were not lending their own money but that of the taxpayers, and they themselves rarely paid taxes. The second element in the fiscal crisis was graft. City government, in its infancy, displayed enduring traits, including the concentration of political power in the hands of a small group and a penchant for corruption which, in thirteenth-century Flanders, achieved spectacular proportions. No exception was the government of the Crespins' own city of Arras; on the contrary, it supplies an especially illuminating example.

Arras was one of the principal cities of medieval Europe, the commercial and cultural capital of the economically advanced province of Artois (the deep, or Artesian, well was a medieval Artois invention), which belonged to the count of Flanders until he gave it to the king of France as a dowry for his daughter. Three of the outstanding poets of the Middle Ages, Adam de la Halle, Jean Bodel, and Baude Fastoul, were citizens of Arras. The Arras poets devoted many verses to the Arras merchants. Jean Bodel recalled, "The merchants did me many favors" (Les marchands m'ont fait beaucoup de bien!); Baude Fastoul echoed the sentiment with the recollection of a patron who supported him for five years; Adam de la Halle saluted one patron as "wise, courteous, patient, generous, as happy as he was brave, and laughing at table"; another as "courteous, gentle, and with the air of a king's son"; another as having the qualities of an emperor.

Their own patrons aside, however, Arrageois poets tirelessly denounced the avarice and fraud of the merchants. Adam de la Halle wrote in a famous verse:

> Arras, Arras, city of deceit,
> Of hatred and of degradation,
> In former times so glorious,
> The whole world says you are undone;
> If God does not restore your honor,
> I know not who will give you peace;
> Money is too much worshipped here.
> They are so stupid in this city
> That we're all in a muddle.
> A hundred thousand times, farewell!
> I'll hear the Gospel read elsewhere,
> For here men know but how to lie! *

According to the poets, the Arras patricians cheated on their taxes, listing only half their assets or less. One patrician distinguished himself by accounting for his fortune accurately, but in Douai pennies instead of those of Arras, which reduced it by three-fourths. Patricians whose malversations were exposed escaped by turning cleric and appealing to the ecclesiastical courts, staffed with their friends and relatives.

The Arras city council was selected by the widespread custom of co-optation, by which the outgoing councillors elected their successors. The councillors, while evading taxes for themselves and their friends, were scrupulous about collecting them from other people, to such a point that the basic property tax, the *taille*, produced the very large revenue of 35,000 pounds. What became of the tax money was the council's secret. True, the Arras council kept the municipality from falling into the catastrophic fiscal condition of many other towns—Arras appeared on the books of the Crespins

---

* See appendix 2 for original text.

only once in the 1290's—but the combination of outrageously high tax rates and deficiency of public services soon inspired popular protest. Not only the poor were cheated, but the better off craftsmen and tradesmen, and even the newer families among the wealthy. Complaints grew noisy; the arrogant councillors brushed them aside. The plebeian taxpayers managed to get two councillors, Philippe de la Vigne and Robert Nazart, to take up their cause. Their fellow councillors promptly voted to bar the troublemakers from the council; several declared that if Nazart named God himself as his successor they would refuse to admit him.

In 1285 the Pentecost celebration, a major public event in Arras, disintegrated into a riot around the casket containing the relics, which the commoners seized from the councillors and carried to the cathedral themselves. The mob grew. Somebody proposed marching on the Petite Place, lined with the tall houses of the best families and with luxury shops; the roar of "Death!" was heard. The bailiff's men arrived just in time to break up the demonstration and arrest several rioters, who were beheaded, hanged, or drawn.

Despite the harsh penalties, protests resumed. A popular leader named Jean Cabos made his voice heard; three councillors who were especially famous for not paying their taxes instigated a movement to silence him. Cabos was thrown into prison, first in Arras, then for safer keeping in a deep dungeon in St. Omer. His wife succeeded in getting him released through an appeal to the bailiff of the absent count of Artois at Amiens. When the count returned from abroad he agreed to an investigation, which turned up information damaging to the corrupt councillors. Andre Hauwel, one of the persecutors of Cabos, had been convicted of perjury and should have been barred from the council; another councillor had turned cleric to avoid taxes and had later returned to the burgher class; a third was illegitimate, violating a prohibition meant to keep commoners out of the council—"C'est mout grans outrages à soufrir en tel cité le bastard soit échevins" ("We suffer a great outrage in this city when a bastard becomes councillor"), stated the complaint.

A democratic reform was instituted in Arras in 1302, in the

form of a Commission of Twenty-Four, a sort of lower house of government given the mission of "knowing all the revenues, all the debts and all the expenses of the city," as well as that of scrutinizing individual tax returns. The Twenty-Four were chosen, eight from the guilds, eight from the cloth merchants, and eight, chosen by the other sixteen, who were neither guild nor cloth merchant nor councillor.

Far from tamely submitting to this intrusion on their prerogative, the council fought back vigorously, filling the next several years with a conflict that was half class war, half defense of privileged corruption. Their alliance with the king of France, who made good his hold on Arras during the Flemish conflict that prefaced the Hundred Years' War, helped the patricians in the end to maintain their grip on the city's government.

Through troubled times Baude and Robert Crespin carried on business as usual, lending equally to the city of Bruges, hotbed of social unrest, and to the count of Flanders. A modern scholar estimates the Crespin fortune at between 250,000 and 300,000 pounds; the Loucharts, next richest family of Arras, he puts at only 100,000 pounds, and calculates only five other families at over 50,000 pounds. In their adjoining houses in the Rue des Meaulx (two of the twenty-two they owned in town) the brothers and their wives and children lived the beautiful life. "Dinners, tourneys and illuminations" enlivened their days and evenings. As they acquired property in the countryside and purchased the favor of princes, the Crespins gained titles of nobility. The family seal was a shield with six hearts alternating with diamonds, with a *fasce brochant*, a horizontal band. The hearts have been identified with the "Arras hearts," a species of pastry, lending support to the theory that the earlier Crespins were bakers.

In a characteristic union of patrician dynasties, Robert Crespin had married Marie Louchart, daughter of the second wealthiest family in Arras. His children married into the Cosset and Wagon families, whose fortunes ranked just below those of the Crespins and Loucharts. A son of Baude Crespin married the daughter of a knight, Eustache de Bailleul, but Crespins did not need to marry into the nobility; they moved into it directly. Robert Crespin, financial prop of the count and countess of Flanders, became a knight banneret (entitled to a banner) and Sire de Harmaville, one of his country estates. Through financial services to the king of France, Baude acquired the distinguished title of royal valet, and was thenceforth addressed as "Messire." His son Sawale was knighted and became Sire de la Braielle.

The ennoblement of the Crespins of Arras had the effect of withdrawing them from their ferocious pursuit of business. Losing their identity as the Crespins of Arras, they became the "de Harmavilles," the "de Hestrus," the "de la Braielles," and gave up lending money. Their social advancement took them out of the economic mainstream, and as Crespins they disappeared, just as did the Zaccarias, the Embriaci and others.

At the very same time, in the first half of the fourteenth century, the corruption of the Arras city council was brought under control. The taille was reduced in 1340 to only 1,666 pounds, while a total revenue of less than 13,000 pounds produced a surplus in the budget.

Meantime the enormous sum collected by Baude and Robert Crespin had not gone entirely to establish aristocratic fiefs on earth. Some of it had gone to provide fiefs in heaven. Baude, who died in 1316, was buried under a sumptuous tombstone of marble, with copper fittings, in the abbey of St. Vaast. The old usurer had in fact become a Benedictine, and had made gifts to the abbey that assured him generous prayers.

His epitaph read:

> Here lies a man of goodly fame;
> Sire Baude Crespin was his name;
> Of Arras, vassal of the King.
>   [two lines no longer legible]
> Never will his like be found again.
> His bounty fostered many more souls
> Than a hundred other charitable rolls.
> Pray for his immortal spirit then,
> Laborers and working men.

In the time of the Incarnation, we hear,
The thousand three hundred and sixteenth year,
Did this honest citizen die,
On the eighteenth day of the month of July.
Then let us the God of hope implore
To give him joy forevermore.*

* See appendix 2 for original text.

I 2

The Calimala Guild:
the Alberti Company of Florence

In the twelfth century, a narrow street in Florence near the timber bridge over the Arno, future site of the Ponte Vecchio, became the center of a remarkable industry. The merchants of Calimala Street combined in the Calimala Guild (*Arte di Calimala*) whose coat of arms was an eagle clutching a bale of cloth. The finely finished and beautifully dyed cloth of the Arte di Calimala was famous throughout the Mediterranean and indeed throughout the world.

The craftsmen of Calimala Street did no spinning or weaving. The cloth came into their hands woven, but mere cloth; it left their shops as a luxury commodity and a work of art. Their raw material was the best Flemish cloth, transported undyed to the Champagne Fairs and sold to the Calimala agents. Italy itself produced wool cloth, but the sheep of the rocky Italian countryside did not compare with the long-fleeced English Cotswold sheep that supplied the weavers of Ghent, Ypres, and Bruges; thus Europe's best export was an international product, grown in England, manufactured in Flanders, bought and sold in France, and finished in Italy.

This splendid cloth made many fortunes. From a power in Florence the masters of the Arte di Calimala grew to a power in Europe, venturing into other commerce and especially into banking. For their enlarged operations they organized in "companies," a word they helped bring into Western language. The largest Calimala companies had branches all over Europe, and financed the wars of kings and communes.

Typical of these powerful family firms was that of the Alberti del Giudice (an ancestor had been a judge). The Alberti had arrived in Florence early in the thirteenth century from Catenaia, near Arezzo. Partisans of the papal (Guelf) faction, they went into exile from 1260–67, when the Ghibellines were in power. Although they were "magnates"—representatives of old, established wealth —they joined the popular party in 1293 in order to qualify for public office under the democratic "Ordinances of Justice."

In the earliest Alberti account book that survives, for the years 1302–29, the partners were Alberto, Neri, and Lapo, three sons of Jacopo degli Alberti, and two outsiders who within two years disappeared from the firm. In 1307, Alberto's son Jacopo joined the company; eight years later, Lapo's three sons followed. As the years went by, sons of the original partners took the place of their fathers, until only Alberto, the eldest of the three original brothers, remained. He headed the company from 1302 to 1328, when he was succeeded by one of Neri's sons.

At first the company's main business was the importation of raw Flemish cloth from the Champagne Fairs to be dyed in the company's Florentine dyeing establishment managed by Lapo, the youngest of the three brothers. The dye-stuffs, kermes, brasil, and orchil, were imported to produce shades of scarlet, crimson, and purple. The Calimala Guild exercised close supervision over the work, particularly with the scarlets, which had to be dyed in grain (kermes), without any addition of brasil, madder, or orchil. The guild inspected shops and warehouses and regulated the terms of sale, including duration of credit, discount, penalties for late payment, and lengths and breadths in which the cloths could be sold.

In the early years, the Alberti company's agents, like those of Symon di Gualterio, journeyed to the Champagne Fairs in caravans; in 1307 the account book records the return of three factors to

Dyers at work. Wool from English sheep was woven into cloth in Flanders, then transported to Florence, where the master dyers of the Calimala Guild turned it into a luxury commodity. They specialized in producing shades of scarlet, crimson, and purple. (Trustees of the British Museum)

Florence from France, bringing a shipment of 466 bolts of cloth. But already the company had permanent representatives abroad in Venice, Naples, Barletta, and Milan, as part of the transition to sedentary commerce. At various times during the period from 1302 to 1348, the Alberti had branches or factors in Avignon, Barletta, Bologna, Constantinople, Flanders, Genoa, London, Majorca, Milan, Naples, and Venice. From its early specialization in cloth from

Flanders and Champagne, the company gradually diversified its activities, dealing in raw wool, spices and dyes, and finally banking. In 1307, the Alberti employed fourteen factors, four of whom shuttled between Florence and Champagne, with three stationed in the kingdom of Naples, two in Bologna, one in Milan, and one in Venice. Two years later they employed twenty. These factors were salaried employees who worked under explicit directions from the company; they were not financially responsible for the firm and thus did not share in its profits or losses. Seldom did they become partners. The best paid were those at the Champagne Fairs, who received 100 to 150 pounds a year. Raises and bonuses rewarded special services. Factors worked under a contract which specified salary, duration of employment, duties, and obligations; they were forbidden to become partners in any other company, to work for others or for themselves, or to accept gifts except for the firm, and were enjoined to be honest and upright. Gambling was expressly forbidden. Salaries were paid in money, on an annual basis, usually on the first of July, at the time when balance sheets were drawn up. Often advances had to be made to tide over employees, who sometimes overdrew their salaries, a fact that did not escape the home-office bookkeeper. Agents were discouraged from putting down roots abroad. In spite of all precautions they sometimes got into trouble. A dishonest Alberti branch manager was jailed; two factors in Avignon embezzled, gambled away the stolen money, and were discharged. If defalcation was discovered after an employee had resigned, the company sued for damages; if he had died, they sued his heirs. Nevertheless, the problem of controlling agents and enforcing a concerted course of action at a distance, compounded by slowness of communication, plagued all the companies; the Alberti handled it more effectively than most, and managed to survive war, depression, and economic change.

On the same social level as factors were accountants and cashiers, led by a head accountant who was the next most important person to the *capo* (head), and the notaries, who drew up contracts and other legal papers. On the lowest rung of the ladder were the *garzoni*, the shopboys, office boys, and messengers, and the "disciples," who were learning a particular phase of the business—accounting, sales, cash handling. These minor employees commonly received part of their wages in kind, especially cloth, a hangover from the apprentice system.

Although the Alberti company lasted almost half a century in its original form, and various offshoots of it endured another century, the partnership was never concluded for more than two or three years, after which a new contract had to be drawn up continuing the arrangement. These contracts spelled out the shares due each partner in proportion to his capital and services. During the partnership no one was permitted, on pain of a heavy fine, to withdraw capital.

The Alberti partnership contract of 1308 specified that the partners were to invest all their available funds in the company's *corpo*, or capital, with a foreseen minimum return of eight percent, remaining profits to be apportioned at the rate of three-tenths to each of the three brothers, and one-tenth to Jacopo, son of the eldest brother. At each renewal, the allocation was slightly modified, the partners always receiving eight percent on their investment, plus a share of surplus profits at a predetermined rate. A partner who failed to supply his part of the capital was penalized and charged eight percent interest per year on the deficiency. A special provision allowed a partner or an outsider who wanted to put additional funds into the company to do so. This fund, called the *fuori del corpo* (outside the capital), also drew eight percent interest.

Apparently Neri di Alberto was something of a black sheep, and constantly drew out money. In 1310 he had to turn over to the firm land worth 10,000 pounds to rebuild his equity. To force him to keep a suitable investment in the business, a new contract in 1323 set up a capital of 25,000 pounds divided into twenty-five shares of 1,000 pounds apiece, eleven of which were allotted to Alberto di Jacopo and his sons Jacopo, Nerozzo, and Francesco; four to Neri; and ten to Caroccio and Duccio, sons of Lapo, the deceased third member of the original company. Profits and losses were to be divided in proportion to the shares, and every two years books were to be closed and a statement of profit and loss drawn up for that purpose. Wastrel Neri was unable to put up the required sum. Alberto and nephews Caroccio and Duccio temporarily supplied him with funds by buying his share of a farm the firm owned at Legnaia for 1,450 pounds, but before long Neri was drawing on the partnership again.

For the original Alberti firm, the average rate of return on invested capital was about 12.5 percent from January 1323 to August 1325 and 20 percent from that date to November 1329. One significant problem which the Alberti books reveal was the gradual accumulation of uncollectable accounts. There were bad debts, such as those of French knights in the service of Walter de Brienne, "Duke of Athens," the soldier of fortune who ruled Florence briefly in the 1340s. There were outright frauds, such as that attempted by Catalan merchants who wrecked a ship secured by a cambium contract drawn by Alberti correspondents in Constantinople, supposedly carrying a cargo of alum but actually sailing in ballast. There were honest business failures. That of the Bardi company in 1346 left Caroccio di Alberto and his heirs with an assignment on the English Exchequer which was worthless.

War played an important role in the vicissitudes of all medieval companies. The Alberti balance sheets showed five profitless years, from 1310 to 1315, when war cut the trade routes to France. The company also suffered from its own slowness to react to an important change in the industry; competitors were importing fleece from England, Spain, and North Africa and manufacturing their own wool cloth, at substantial savings. The Alberti invested in a wool shop of their own barely in time to ride the new current.

From January 1312 to 1316 the partners all were forced to forego the 8 percent return theoretically guaranteed in the contract of 1310. During these lean years, they had to pool their property, including land, and to raise cash even sold a parcel of pearls that belonged to Alberto and Lapo. When the property was reapportioned among the three brothers, the crisis had reduced their fortunes from 72,000 to 40,000 pounds. Outside investors earned no interest from 1312–14 because of "bad times and wars." Finally business picked up; the firm recovered its losses and began again to increase its capital.

Neri's son Agnolo was evidently a more sober head than his father, for when Alberto died in 1329, Agnolo became director of the company and remained in that position until his death in 1343. By that time the family fortune had increased so that Lapo's heirs alone had an estate worth about 37,000 pounds, about ten percent in real estate, the rest in the family business.

After Agnolo's death, the company broke up. Caroccio formed a short-lived partnership with Alberto's son Jacopo, but in 1345 they separated; thenceforward there were two Alberti companies, the Alberti Antichi, headed by Jacopo, and the Alberti Nuovi, headed by Caroccio. The more successful was the Alberti Antichi.

The most illustrious member of the Alberti family, the richest and most important man in Florence in his day, was Niccolo, son of the Jacopo who headed the Alberti Antichi in 1345. After serving his discipleship in the company's branches, Niccolo was promoted in 1359 to head of the office in Avignon, where the firm became for a time principal bankers to the pope. Ten years later, Niccolo succeeded to the codirectorship of the company, and soon became sole *capo*. He was elected a prior of Florence—a member of the commune's governing body—and served as a gonfaloniere of justice—the commune's chief executive. He also became a captain of the Guelf party, and was a member of every embassy sent by Florence to the pope.

In 1372, five years before Niccolo's death, the Alberti Antichi itself split, Niccolo heading one of the two offshoots, and by 1400 there were several Alberti companies operating in and out of Florence, with at least three represented in Bruges.

An enterprise such as the Alberti's, with its distant branches and complex transactions, demanded bookkeeping techniques of an advanced order. Five account books of the Alberti company have survived, dealing with the family's business investments and uncollectable debts. The accounts were entered in paragraph form, with debts and credits on facing pages or in separate columns. Each book, like each partnership contract, opened with the words, "In the name of God and of Profit." If the first entry was a payable item, it was labeled *"de avere"* (he must have), followed by the formula *"avegli dato"* (we have given him), to show how the debt was discharged; if the entry was an amount due to the company, it began *"de dare"* (he owes, or he must give), and the payments were indicated with *"anne dato"* (he has given). To simplify arithmetic, the Alberti bookkeeper often rounded off figures, a practice not universally followed; even in transactions involving hundreds of thousands of pounds, the Peruzzi company's bookkeepers used precise figures. At the end of every fiscal period, the Alberti deducted liabilities and initial investment from total assets, with provisions for accrued salaries, to arrive at net earnings. All accounts were "personal," relating to partners and clients; the "impersonal" account for items like office expenses had not yet been invented.

An Alberti inventory of 1348 gives a picture of the furnishings of the company's countinghouse: several desks, some with compartments for books; large tables for displaying and measuring cloth; shelves along the walls; a wardrobe with pigeonholes for sorting mail; a strongbox, a couch; a portable balance; and brass and copper inkwells. One of the partners kept the "secret books" locked up in a chest in his own home, rather than in the countinghouse.

The front of the company's headquarters served for transactions with customers. The range of merchandise sold was broad—metalware, jewels, skins, furs, silks, and spices as well as wool cloth. Even the greatest of companies, while dealing in wholesale merchandise and lending money to cities and princes, continued to sell at retail. At a time when the Bardi company was financing Edward III's wars in Flanders and France and exporting shiploads of wheat from Apulia, it still maintained its drapery establishment, with retail store.

In the rear of the shop the accountant worked, his figures protected from casual glances. Here the disciples learned bookkeeping and the use of the abacus. Near the bookkeeper's desk lay a volume of a special kind, a merchant manual, providing information about classes of merchandise, brokerage fees, markets, trade routes, currencies, and other useful matters. These texts became indispensable in the fourteenth century as trade ceased to be concentrated in the Champagne Fairs and was dispersed to Bruges, Paris, and London; the sedentary merchant needed a reliable source of information on the practices of the different commercial centers, their weights and measures, coins, taxes and tolls, regulations and customs.

The best known of the merchant manuals was the *Pratica della Mercatura*, compiled about 1340 by Francesco Balducci Pegolotti, who headed the branch office of the Bardi company in London, and served in Antwerp, Cyprus, and elsewhere. Pegolotti furnished a glossary in several languages of such terms as market, customs, freight charge, boat, shop, bale, interpreter, bolt of cloth, and watchman. He described in detail the weights and measures, the products to be bought and sold, and the charges to be paid in some forty different cities. He listed the lengths in which different kinds of cloth were sold in France, Flanders, and Brabant, the regulations in Florence on the sale of cloth, the weights of gold and silver coins of various origins, kinds of spices, of silk, of leather, of fur. He furnished tables for reckoning interest, for finding the date of Easter, for determining the day of the week on which the first of each month would fall. He explained how to weigh pearls and precious stones, and how to convert weights of spices into dry measure ("Francesco Balducci Pegolotti tested these in Cyprus," he wrote with some pride). He described the powdered sugar of Cyprus, its value, appearance, and packaging; Cyprus syrups, the bottles which contained them, and the cases which contained the bottles; he weighed all the parts of the packages in which Alexandrian ginger was packed and came to the conclusion that weighing methods in Cyprus concealed twenty-five percent of the weight of the packaging. He told how to buy and sell grain, how to choose a ship to carry one's merchandise, how to refine gold, how to alloy silver, how to judge the quality of merchandise. Hardly a subject escaped the pen of this experienced merchant, whose manual was widely quoted for decades.

Toward the end of the fourteenth century, the Alberti became involved in the bubbling kettle of Florentine politics. In 1378, Benedetto degli Alberti reluctantly accepted office in the democratic government instituted after the Ciompi revolt; when the reactionary oligarchy returned to power in 1382, its leader, Maso degli Albizzi, seized the first opportunity to exile Benedetto and several other members of the family. As time went on, Maso issued increasingly harsh decrees against the Alberti, finally putting a price on the heads of several members; one was executed for returning secretly to Florence. Some of the family's property was seized, but their branches abroad continued to operate. For forty years no male Alberti over the age of sixteen was allowed to live in Florence. This decree was repealed only in 1428, and the confiscated property was restored sixteen years later, after Cosimo de' Medici came to power.

The international merchants of the Florentine companies amassed fortunes and rapidly acquired all the symbols of wealth of their age: palaces, coats of arms (the Alberti's was a ring and chains on field of azure), villas, and splendid memorials when they were dead. The Alberti palace still stands in Florence at the corner of the Borgo Santa Croce and the Via dei Benci. Agnolo Gaddi executed the frescoes for the Alberti chapel in Santa Croce (the Bardi and Peruzzi both employed Giotto).

Outside Florence, the Alberti had a palatial villa, built by Jacopo's son Niccolo. Niccolo, head of the firm in its heyday, had a fortune amounting to some 240,000 florins. His "Villa of Paradise" was described by Boccaccio, himself a Bardi employee and son of a Bardi factor: "A very fair and rich palace, somewhat raised above the plain upon a little eminence. . . . Having walked about and admired the great halls and the curious and elegant rooms all appropriately furnished, they highly commended the place and pronounced its owner magnificent. . . . The garden which surrounded the palace was intersected with walks bordered with trellised vines in blossom. . . . These walks were all walled about with roses, red and white, and jasmin. . . . In the midst of the garden . . . was a carpet of very fine grass, so green that it seemed nearly black, enameled with a thousand kinds of flowers and enclosed by the greenest and lushest of orange and lemon trees. . . . In the center of the grass was a fountain of the whitest marble, carved with wonderful sculptures, and from it . . . there sprang, by a figure that stood on a column in its midst, a great jet of water high into the sky, falling back with a pleasant sound into the limpid pool; the water . . . ran under the lawn by a hidden way and resurfacing, encircled it in very attractive and curiously wrought courses. . . . The sight of this garden . . . so pleased the ladies and the three young men that they all of one accord swore that if Paradise could be created upon earth, they could not conceive in what form other than this garden. . . ."

Philanthropy consumed less of his wealth than this expensive caprice, but Niccolo gave generously to the Church of Santa Croce, to the foundation of a hospice for old women, to alms for the poor. When he died in August 1377, five hundred poor people were hired to follow his coffin, behind the patrician mourners in elegant red and black; the casket itself was draped in red, and the cortege included horses, torches, and the proud banners with the arms of the company. Royalty was often buried with less pomp than this master-merchant of the Calimala Guild.

IV

THE FOURTEENTH CENTURY

Capitalists in Crisis

The first three hundred years of the second millennium in Europe were a time of universal expansion: economic, technical, and cultural. Abruptly and brutally the fourteenth century brought contraction. The European surge ran afoul of calamity, war, famine, revolution, financial disaster, and the unique catastrophe of the age, the Black Death.

Class tension in Flanders at the end of the thirteenth century led to antilabor legislation. Weavers and fullers were forbidden to assemble, to bear arms, or even to carry their tools on the street. They were forbidden to strike on pain of banishment or death. Towns, under the rigid control of the old established wealthy class, made treaties with each other to extradite fugitive artisans accused of conspiracy. In the Flemish capital of Ghent, the patrician rule assumed a particularly autocratic form in the "Thirty-Nine," a municipal body which rotated offices for life; councillors might be senile, incompetent, and corrupt, but there was no getting rid of them. From the ranks of this narrow clique were excluded not only the workers but the newly rich.

In 1287 the reactionary Flemish patricians concluded an alliance with the French king, Philip IV, against an unlikely entente formed to curtail their power, between Count Guy de Dampierre of Flanders, Philip's vassal, and the craft guilds and lesser merchants. The lily banner of the Capetian kings was hung from the belfries of the towns, a symbol of oppression. The patricians called themselves the *Leliaerts* (men of the lilies). The count's party were the *Clauwaerts* (men of the claw—of the Flemish lion). In the first battles of this civil war, the Leliaerts were victorious; in 1300 Flanders was annexed to the crown of France, a French governor was sent to Bruges, and Philip IV paid a triumphal visit to his new province, for which the patricians presented the bill to the cities in the form of an extraordinary tax. The cloth workers immediately took up arms under an obscure weaver, Peter de Coninck, and massacred the French occupying army in Bruges in the "Matins of Bruges," a Flemish counterpart of the Sicilian Vespers. The weavers and fullers set up revolutionary governments in all the towns and organized an army of artisans which, under the command of the count's sons, startled the world by defeating the French knights at the battle of Courtrai (1302).

The French, however, made a military and political comeback, and the years after Courtrai saw alternating revolution and reaction in Flanders. In 1328 a new pro-French count, Louis de Nevers, reversed the alignment of Courtrai. Educated in Paris and married to a French princess, he sided with the patricians, appealing to his father-in-law, the newly crowned Valois king Philip VI, for help against the commons, again in rebellion. Philip sent troops to wipe out the Flemish insurrectionaries at Cassel. The revolutionary leaders were executed, their property confiscated, the privileges of the rebel towns abolished, the walls of Bruges and Ypres dismantled.

Such was the situation in Flanders in 1337, when skirmishes between French and English privateers marked the beginning of the Hundred Years' War, a dynastic struggle which continued intermittently until 1453, bringing widespread calamities not only to the two countries involved, but to Flanders and Italy. The source of the quarrel was the marriage that had been solemnized during the truce of 1298, at the time when Benedetto Zaccaria was blockading Flan-

Statue in Bruges of Peter de Coninck and Jan Breydel, instigators in 1302 of the "Matins of Bruges," the uprising of weavers, fullers, and other artisans in which the occupying French garrison was massacred.

ders, between Isabella of France, daughter of Philip IV, and the future Edward II. The product of this union, Edward III, was a grandson of Philip IV; the present king of France, Philip VI, was only a nephew. But Edward's descent was through his mother, Philip's through his father, and French lawyers maintained that ancient custom limited succession to the male line.

Flanders was now riven between the count's loyalty to France and the needs of the wool industry which bound its economic life inextricably to England. Large-scale Flemish cloth production and large-scale English sheep farming were, in the striking words of Eileen Power (*The Wool Trade in English Medieval History*), "exceptional in the intimacy of their connection with each other. The economic, and a good deal of the political history of Europe has been profoundly influenced by the fact that the earliest homes of the cloth manufacture were not identical with the most important centres of wool production. . . . To trace the three-cornered political relations between England, France, and Flanders is to recall an unforgettable lesson in mischief wrought by dynastic ambitions in sundering an economic unity." This dislocation, which took place in 1336 when Edward III placed an embargo on wool, touched off the revolutionary forces which were always smoldering in Flanders.

England's wars with France at the end of the thirteenth century, the preliminaries of the Hundred Years' War, had been financed by Italian bankers who came to grief through their loans to Edward I and II. The Italians who backed Edward III collapsed with a crash that had resounding repercussions in Italy, not only economic but political. Some firms, among them the Alberti, survived the crisis and managed to adapt to changing business conditions, such as the shift in Florence in the fourteenth century from cloth finishing to cloth making. In spite of depression and war, Italian business techniques continued to evolve.

Ten years after the start of the Hundred Years' War, an infinitely worse cataclysm struck Europe. Carried by flea-infested rats from central Asia, where the bacillus had always been endemic, to the Crimea and thence by returning Italian ships to Europe, the plague that was later known as the Black Death manifested itself in a terrifically lethal combination of three forms of the same disease: bubonic, characterized by swollen lymph glands; pneumonic, which attacked the lungs; and septicemic, infecting the bloodstream. It struck terror in Sicily early in October 1347, brought by Genoese ships from the Crimea, the crews of which had "sickness clinging to their very bones." From Messina, the disease spread to North Africa, to Corsica and Sardinia, the Balearics, Spain, and southern Italy, following the trade routes. Florence was among the first to be engulfed by the epidemic. Boccaccio wrote: "Many breathed their last in the open street, whilst others, though they died in their houses, made it known to the neighbors that they were dead by the stench of their rotting bodies; and of these and others who died everywhere the city was full. . . . The bodies were brought forth from the houses and laid before the doors, where, especially in the morning, passersby saw innumerable corpses; then biers were fetched, and some, for lack thereof, they laid upon a board. More than one bier carried two or three corpses; nay, many bore husband and wife, two or three brothers, father and son or the like. . . ." The most desperate measures proved futile. A Sienese named Agnolo di Tura wrote, "Father abandoned child, wife husband, one brother another; for this illness seemed to strike through the breath and sight. And so they died. And no one could be found to bury the dead for money or for friendship . . . And in many places in Siena great pits were dug and piled deep with huge heaps of dead . . . And I, Agnolo di Tura, buried my five children with my own hands, and so did many others likewise. And there were also many dead through the city who were so sparsely covered with earth that the dogs dragged them forth and devoured their bodies."

The sickness quickly reached France, spreading from Marseille northward. Among those who died at Avignon was Petrarch's Laura; "Oh, happy posterity who will not experience such abysmal woe and will look upon our testimony as a fable," Petrarch wrote. The pope took refuge in a castle on the Rhone and refused to see anyone. As the plague moved on to Germany and Flanders in 1348, Jews were massacred as scapegoats. The contagion passed to England and Scandinavia. Finally, when pestilence had wiped out nearly one-third the population of Europe, it subsided, to return six more times in the next sixty years, growing progressively less virulent up to its final outbreak in the fifteenth century.

The social and economic consequences of this apocalyptic disaster are a subject of dispute. But historians agree that as labor became scarce wages rose, along with prices for manufactured products, and that farm prices fell as land became plentiful and demand declined. Matteo Villani, relative of a distinguished Florentine historian, wrote, "Those few discreet folk who remained alive expected many things. . . . They believed that those whom God's grace had saved from death, having beheld the destruction of their neighbors, . . . would become better-conditioned, humble, virtuous and Catholic; that they would guard themselves from iniquity and sin and would be full of love and charity towards one another. But no sooner had the plague ceased than we saw the contrary; for since men were few and since, by inheritance, they abounded in earthly goods, they forgot the past as though it had never been, and gave themselves up to a more shameful and disordered life than they had led before. . . . Men thought that, by reason of the fewness of mankind, there should be abundance of all produce of the land; yet, on the contrary, by reason of men's ingratitude, everything came to unwonted scarcity and remained long thus; nay, in certain countries . . . there were grievous and unwonted famines. Again, men dreamed of wealth and abundance in garments . . . yet in fact, things turned out widely different, for most [manufactured] commodities were more costly by twice or more than before the plague. And the price of labor and the work of all trades and crafts rose in disorderly fashion beyond the double. Lawsuits and disputes and quarrels and riots rose elsewhere among citizens in every land."

The aftermath of the plague heightened tension between rich and poor; the second half of the fourteenth century was marked by social disorders everywhere. In France the peasants rose in 1358 in the insurrection known as the Jacquerie; in the 1370s and 1380s there were riots and uprisings in France, Flanders, Germany, England, and Italy. In Florence in 1378 the guild of the poorest wool workers, the washers and carders, called the Ciompi, rose under the leadership of a carder named Michele di Lando and forced the formation of a democratic coalition government with representation of the minor guilds. Counter-revolution in 1382 restored the reactionary oligarchy.

In the midst of disaster, there was some forward movement: the mid-fourteenth century saw the institutionalizing of a great North German business organization, the Hansa. This association, which endured for half a millennium and embraced an area 900 miles wide from the Zuider Zee to the Gulf of Finland, uniting more than 150 cities, arrived at its full constitutional development in 1356 with the first meeting of the Hanseatic Diet (*Hansetag*). In a different form, it had been in existence since the founding of the Baltic trading city of Lübeck in 1158. Leader of the Hansa for five hundred years, Lübeck lay twelve miles inland from the mouth of the River Trave at the narrowest point of the isthmus of Holstein, directly opposite Hamburg on the other side of the isthmus. An overland route between the two cities united the North Sea and the Baltic, avoiding the long and dangerous detour around Cape Skagen and the Danish Straits.

From Lübeck, North German merchants reached out to join in a centuries-old commerce between Sweden and Russia. The Swedish base was Wisby, on the Baltic island of Gotland, east of Sweden. The Russian base was Novgorod, ancient Viking capital of northern Russia, on the Volkhov River south of Lake Ladoga. In Novgorod the Germans at first shared quarters with Gotlanders, but soon built their own establishment, the Peterhof (St. Peter's Court), and finally took over the Gotlanders' settlement. They negotiated commercial treaties with the local Russian princes, gaining valuable privileges, similar to those enjoyed by the Italian merchants in the Levant. Their guarantees included the security of goods and persons, freedom from taxes, and the right to have their own law courts, scales, standards of weights and measures, and to assemble and elect their own officers, the sum conferring a kind of diplomatic immunity. The product of the organized pressure of the merchants, these privileges lay at the heart of the institution of the Hansa.

From Lübeck, German merchants also sailed to Scandinavia, establishing at Bergen, Norway, their second great foreign agency or Kontor, the *Tyskebrygge* or German Wharf. As early as the thirteenth century, they had moved into England and the Low Countries. In London, they had joined Cologne merchants who already had an establishment and who called their organization a *Hansa*, a word borrowed from Flemish merchants in London, originally meaning a tax imposed on foreign businessmen. Lübeck and Hamburg merchants obtained the right to form their own Hansa on the

George Gisze, a Hanseatic merchant of the London Steelyard, by Hans Holbein. The *Stalhof* was the agency where the Hanseatic merchants did business; "Steelyard," the English term, is a misnomer, deriving from *stal*, meaning counter or stall, rather than *stahl*, the German word for "steel." (Staatliche Museen, Berlin)

model of Cologne's and set up their third Kontor, the *Stalhof*. "Steelyard," the English translation, is one of history's misnomers, Stalhof being derived not from *Stahl*, steel, but from *stal*, counter or stall; the Stalhof was the Merchant Court. At about the same time, North Germans appeared in Bruges, helping to launch that city on a two-century career as the commercial capital of the West. The Bruges agency became by far the largest and most important of the four Hanseatic Kontors. Until the first meeting of the Hansetag in 1356, the agencies were autonomous; the first diet was convoked to establish the authority of member towns over the Kontor of Bruges, and in the subsequent twenty years, the other three Kontors were similarly subordinated.

The organization was a loose one, in no sense a "league," a term which the Hansa never applied to itself; "Hanseatic community" was its term, in one locution or another—*communis mercator* (community of merchants), *der gemene kopman* (the united merchant), *die gemene stete* (the united cities). Although it had no treasury, no army, no navy, no seal, no officers, and only one permanent institution, the Hanseatic Diet, the Hansa had instruments which proved extraordinarily effective in the period of its prosperity—negotiation, boycott, and blockade, or finally, if negotiation and economic sanction failed, war. Hanseatic war, conducted principally against the traditional adversary of the Hansa, Denmark, was customarily sea war, and consisted of privateer attacks on enemy ships.

The first Hanseatic war began in 1360 when the Danish king Waldemar IV Atterdag landed at Gotland and pillaged Wisby. Hanseatic counterattack in 1362 ended in a disastrous defeat, threatening the solidarity and existence of the Hansa. Five years later a great diet was convoked in Cologne, forming the Confederation of Cologne, to raise funds, levy contingents, and make plans for counterassault against Denmark. The coalition razed Copenhagen, raided the Danish and Norwegian coasts, and subdued Scania. Victory was complete, ending in 1370 in the Peace of Stralsund, which marked the emergence of a remarkable new mercantile power in northern Europe, capable of defending its commercial interests with the weapons of war.

13

Italian Companies Go Bankrupt: the Frescobaldi in England

Even before the expulsion of the English Jews, a new species of financier, the Italian merchant company, had arrived to take their place as a source of funds for the English monarchy. The Italians operated on a much larger scale than the Jews, and suffered far less; yet in the end their story formed a parallel to that of Isaac Jurnet and his unhappy coreligionists.

Medieval rulers had no reliable source of revenues for war; often they could not even raise funds for the normal needs of government, but had to pawn crown jewels or pledge their nobles or even themselves as hostages for loans. Yet the military advantages of permanent mercenary troops over the six-weeks-in-summer feudal levy were enormous. Aids—extraordinary war taxes—could not always be levied, and at best took time to collect. To bridge the gap, rulers borrowed. In the early days they borrowed from the Church, using land as security. In the twelfth century, lay lenders, both Christian and Jewish, began to take the place of bishops and monasteries. Instead of mortgaging estates, rulers borrowed on their tolls and taxes, which they allowed merchants to collect in return for cash advances.

The relationship between English kings and Italian merchants began in the 1180s, when Richard Lionheart and his English knights borrowed money in Italy on their way to the Holy Land, and later obtained loans from agents of the Italian companies in Syria and Palestine. Serving as bankers to the pope and collectors of papal revenues, the Italian companies had considerable sums deposited in their branches throughout Europe, to be paid out at the pope's order, but meantime at the disposal of the companies. When Henry III's younger son Edmund needed financial backing as contender for the crown of Sicily, the pope, who favored his venture, borrowed 54,-000 pounds for him from Tuscan merchants. Though Edmund's project came to nothing, the size of the loan alerted English royalty to the potential of the Italian companies. Henry's eldest son Edward, pledging himself to a Crusade, borrowed from them, and continued to do so after he returned to England and assumed the throne as Edward I.

By that time the Crusades had led the Italians to England, to collect the money owed by the Crusading borrowers. Prohibited from taking cash out of England, the Italians converted their credits into the great English commodity, wool fleece. These first Italians were Placentines, Bolognese, and Romans, but men of the premier mercantile and banking region, Tuscany, soon followed: Sienese, Lucchese, and finally Florentines.

They found a backward country, far behind continental Europe in manufacture and trade. Although welcomed as importers of foreign luxury articles and purchasers of wool, the newcomers were regarded with suspicion and closely circumscribed by rules designed to prevent them from breaking the native merchants' monopoly of internal commerce. They were forbidden to stay in the kingdom more than forty consecutive days, to buy houses, to sell except at wholesale, or to venture outside the walls of the cities. By suitably bribing the king, the Italians got some of the restrictions relaxed, acquiring sojourn permits for longer periods and the right to live wherever they liked, maintain their own shops, and sell at retail. Not only did they provide the king important revenues through taxes they paid on their own exports, they supplied credit for wars in Wales, Scotland, and France, as well as for the ordinary expenses of the king's household.

Henry III was hampered in his use of the Italians by a lack of good resources to pledge, but his successor Edward I obtained a unified system of customs with new duties on exported wool. One of the Italian companies, the Riccardi of Lucca, became the principal royal bankers by financing Edward's conquest of Wales. The Riccardi lent the king some £392,000 between 1272 and 1294, a good part of which they recovered from customs, which were placed entirely in their hands for nineteen years. Such was their position that in 1279 Orlandino di Podio, head of the English branch of the firm, was named one of the eight household officials allowed, when at court, to sleep in the king's wardrobe. When war broke out with France in 1294, the Riccardi found themselves caught between the two belligerents. Edward, needing money, seized their wool, while Philip IV of France arrested all Riccardi representatives in his lands as enemy agents, sequestered their goods, and levied a heavy fine on the company. Other pressures had already damaged the company's position; the pope had ordered the Riccardi to pay out 35,570 marks on deposit with them to Edward, who had promised to go on a Crusade. Other clients withdrew funds, precipitating a panic. Edward, a fair-weather patron, coolly took the customs away from the Riccardi and seized their assets, driving the firm into bankruptcy.

The fall of the Riccardi opened the door to successors bold or foolhardy enough to take their place. In 1299 the Frescobaldi company of Florence became the royal bankers. They might have profited by advice later incorporated in a poem by Giovanni de' Frescobaldi, one of the family's several literary men:

> To the Italian in England, a word or two;
> In dress be sober, and in bearing meek,
> Keep counsel, let them think your brain is weak;
> Cursed be the Englishman who injures you.
> Keep clear of trouble, enemies eschew.
> Loosen your pursestrings, let your money speak;

Pay as you go; politely debtors seek,
Explaining that you need the money due.

Those who show idle curiosity are fools.
When prices are at bottom, purchase then.
Deal not with courtiers; you'll regret it sore;
Observe the ordinance of him who rules,
Be loyal to your fellow countrymen,
Go to bed early, double-bolt your door.*

The Frescobaldi family, prominent in the aristocratic consular government of Florence in the twelfth century and the first popular government in the thirteenth, lived near the Arno in a street which still bears their name, where they had a palace and several smaller houses. A member of the family built a timber bridge nearby, the first Ponte Santa Trinità, later replaced with the famous stone structure of Bartolommeo Ammanati. Like the Alberti, the Frescobaldi were of the magnate class. In the second half of the thirteenth century, the family split into two feuding branches, the Whites and the Blacks, representing Florentine factions corresponding roughly to magnate and popular, or to Ghibelline and Guelf. In the 1270s, at the time of the Frescobaldi's first appearance in England, both factions were represented. In a few years, the schism healed, or the Black Frescobaldi retired from competition; by the end of the thirteenth century only the White Frescobaldi remained in England.

The earliest English operations of the Frescobaldi were modest participations in loans with other Italians. They first appeared as sole creditors in a document of 1293 in which they were conceded the right to "keep until the next collection" of the papal tithe 5,000 silver marks which the Church had deposited with them to be turned over eventually to the king. Five years later came their first operations of moment with Edward himself; in May 1298, they loaned £4,666 to the king, and the following August they ransomed a "faithful subject of Edward," Hugh d'Andeley, taken prisoner in Gascony, pledging £2,000 to the king of France in case the English

* See appendix 2 for original text.

violated their truce in that region. Shortly after, in October, they loaned £11,000 to the king's wardrobe, "for the expenses of maintaining the Royal Household," to be repaid by the treasury of Dublin. The following June they agreed to pay debts of the king's, adding up to some £2,642, to Spanish merchants. By the end of the century when the Riccardi company was ruined, the Frescobaldi were in a position to take over, and when the king seized the Riccardi's wool in Ireland in 1301, he turned it over to the Frescobaldi at their own valuation, to be deducted from their loans to the Exchequer.

The Frescobaldi company rapidly increased its scope of operations, lending not only to the king but to his friends, to members of the royal family, and to other nobles and clergy. For a journey to France, the Prince of Wales borrowed 2,000 marks "for palfreys and other expenses." The queen borrowed £1000. When Edward was crowned in 1307, representatives of the Frescobaldi, sent to Bordeaux to collect Edward's revenues from the duchy of Aquitaine, contributed one thousand barrels of wine for the festivities. In 1299, together with seven other Italian firms, they loaned 2,000 marks to the City of London so that the London burghers (who had always bitterly resisted giving rights for foreigners) could buy back their own municipal liberties which had been abolished by the king in 1285.

But the Frescobaldi's chief client remained the king himself. By 1302 he was on their books for £32,886; in the next eight years his prodigal borrowings raised the total to £150,000.

In return, the Frescobaldi company received a succession of privileges and concessions, some of them of dubious value. They were given a lease on the silver mines of Devon, though when they visited the site they found the equipment so primitive and the mines so poorly maintained that they abandoned the concession. The right to collect royal revenues in the counties of Ponthieu and Montreuil, south of Calais, and in Ireland, proved more worthwhile, though these resources took time to develop, and the expenses of collection ate into the profits. They were placed in control of the "exchanges" of a number of principal towns, under the central control of

London—Newcastle-on-Tyne, Exeter, Dublin, Bristol; they were named Keepers of the Exchange of London and Canterbury, in charge not only of money changing but of the mint, with seigniorage revenue. In 1305 Edward I appointed the company collector of the royal revenues of Aquitaine, and three years later Edward II appointed to the office of Constable of Bordeaux, highest financial office of the Duchy, the director of the London branch, Amerigo, son of Berto de' Frescobaldi, the company's head. Amerigo remained in London to run the Exchange and direct the branch office, appointing an associate, Ugolino Ugolini, known to his English connections as Hugelin Hugelyn, to act as his deputy in Bordeaux.

Finally the Frescobaldi company was awarded control of the customs of the kingdom, held at the moment by shipowners and wine merchants of Bayonne who had loaned the king funds for the defense of Aquitaine against Philip IV. The king ordered the collectors of all ports to turn over receipts to the Frescobaldi. The customs seal of Ireland was delivered to them. Thus a company of Italian moneymen found themselves virtually in control of the revenues of the kingdom of England.

At the pinnacle of power, the members of the Frescobaldi company in England lived like lords. Old Berto de' Frescobaldi remained in Florence, but most of his numerous sons flocked to England to share in the profit and glory of being the king's "beloved merchants." Not only the director but partners and factors enjoyed a privileged citizenship which gave them full rights and no obligations. They were excused from serving in the public offices, unremunerated or poorly paid, to which burghers were customarily drafted; they were freed from tallages, aids, and other feudal dues, and from any tributes imposed by the cities. Berto himself was given the honorific office of private councillor to the Crown. The directors of the London branch received life grants of land. In 1308 Amerigo was awarded four manors in Lincolnshire and two in Dorset; two years later, he received two more manors in Lincoln belonging to a vassal of the king who had died leaving a minor heir. The director of the company and his brothers could name their own candidates to certain church offices. They and their friends were forgiven infractions of laws, including murder and the even more serious crime of contravention of laws about coinage. When they were accused of "carrying over the sea" English gold money and gold and silver objects and jewels and selling them at a profit, they were pardoned "in consideration of their services to the King." In 1308 one Gracius di Freso, who had killed Roger Bonaventura, asked Amerigo de' Frescobaldi for protection. The company not only gave sanctuary to the guilty man and his belongings, but Amerigo successfully petitioned the king that he be pardoned and allowed to "return in the King's peace."

The king also made the merchants gifts of money, usually representing payments of concealed interest. These grants were described as restitution of "damages suffered by delays in repayment of loans to the King," or "in consideration of great service to the Crown." The company was paid £13,000 in three installments for "delay in repayment" of loans by Edward I. This scarcely balanced the account; in 1307, shortly before the king's death, probably beginning to be alarmed, the firm presented a long list of alleged damages: over £10,000 lost because depositors withdrew funds in 1296–97 in alarm over a loan to subsidize the Burgundians against the king of France; some £3,000 for the expenses of three or four factors kept in England to sue the king for payment; over £10,000 borrowed from colleagues for the Court; substantial losses on occasion of other loans in England, France, Flanders, Lombardy, Rome; £11,000 lost in collecting money owed them by the king in Ireland "which is a country, as you well know, where only by great effort and with great danger were we able to collect anything"; finally, sums lost during the lease of the silver mines of Devon. The king nominated a commission to investigate the claims, an inquiry which continued under Edward II, resulting in a compromise newly assigning the customs on wool, hides, and wool-fells (sheepskins) to discharge the debt.

With the king still on their books for huge sums, the Frescobaldi were not entirely happy; yet their favored position drew virulent suspicion. The Italians, with their money, privileges, and intimacy with the king, had long been objects of jealousy not only for native merchants but for the English nobility. At the height of their prestige, the Frescobaldi found themselves overtaken by the same furious resentment that had destroyed English Jewry. The barons, defending their feudal rights against monarchical encroachment, drew up a list of ordinances containing a distinct anti-Italian thrust. One provision stated that customs could not be assigned to foreigners; another, even more threatening, that foreign merchants should be arrested and their goods seized "until they have rendered reasonable account of what they have received of the revenues of the Kingdom, in the aforesaid time, before the treasurer and the barons. . . ." Edward II found it politic to sign, but delayed enforcement. Already in November of 1310 he had given Amerigo and Bettino de' Frescobaldi permission to move with their goods into the Tower of London, for safety against mob action. Pressure was put on the company's nonroyal debtors, many of whom were in Newgate prison. But English xenophobia was reaching explosive proportions, and in February 1311 the king granted safe conducts to several members of the Frescobaldi family upon the occasion of the death of old Berto in Florence (though Berto had never set foot in England he was described as "clerk of the King"), nominally to collect their inheritance, actually to give them an opportunity to flee the gathering storm.

In June popular pressure forced a royal order to the collectors of the ports to send their receipts directly to the king, even those already earmarked for the Frescobaldi; a month later officials of England and Aquitaine were commanded to seize the company's goods and arrest its representatives before they fled the country. Execution of the order was postponed by the king who said he had a "full and formal promise from them that they would remain."

That was Edward II's last stand in favor of his Italians. As in the case of the Jews, the overpowering of the royal protection by popular fury was followed by a royal change of front. In October his delaying order was annulled in Aquitaine, and in March 1312 the royal sheriffs of London arrived at the Tower and at the Frescobaldi's establishments with an order of arrest.

But unlike the Jews, the Italians had a home to return to, and had profited from ample warning. The sheriff found only Pietro de' Frescobaldi, "yeoman of the King." All the rest had vanished, without passports but with the complicity of authority. Pietro was interrogated by the angry barons of the Exchequer as to where certain goods were hidden, particularly "silver and gold vessels worth £500 deposited in the Tower of London for safekeeping, for use of the King," which had unaccountably disappeared. While Pietro was being questioned, the silver and gold vessels and all the other *care cose* (precious things) were on their way to Italy, hidden in bales of wool provided in Bruges, whither the treasure had been transported by a well-paid Channel skipper.

The Lords Ordainers, a committee of the barons, issued a solemn decree "that Emerigo Frescombald and his followers were to come and render accounts in the manner previously ordained, notwithstanding the account they said they had rendered between September 22 and October 6, 1312, and meanwhile their bodies and goods were to be arrested and the lands of Emericus in the realm seized," adding, "If Emericus does not appear within the time, he is to be banished." Reminded that Amerigo was still director of the Exchange, the Lords Ordainers discharged him and asked the king to nominate another man to the post. The manors which had been assigned to Amerigo were expropriated one by one: in 1311 the properties in Dorset, in 1312 those in Lincoln.

The fugitives had left England in relays, by way of Bruges, where their factor Guido Donati furnished them with funds and helped them arrange for transportation of the bales of wool "among which were concealed our precious things." Giovanni, Filippo, and Dino de' Frescobaldi arrived in Bruges with three of the company's factors in February 1311. They were soon followed by the brothers Amerigo and Guglielmo, for whom England had become particularly dangerous. Pepo di Bettino arrived late in 1311, then his father Bettino, Amerigo's brother, at the head of a large party. They proceeded to Vienne, south of Lyon, where the pope had convened a council, and where the papal court was therefore being held. The company counted on finding support, or at least protection, from the pope and the high prelates who formed an important part of their clientele. The bales of wool arrived and were repacked, shipped to Avignon and on to Marseille, and by galley to Italy and finally Florence. The entire company was reunited in Vienne in April 1312, except for Pietro, of whose fate in England nothing is known. When the council ended, they returned to Avignon where the pope now resided, Pepo di Bettino, who was convalescing from a serious illness, traveling by boat on the Rhone.

Arriving in Avignon, the company rented a suitable house for their headquarters and bent their energies to rescuing Ugolino Ugolini, Amerigo's deputy in Bordeaux, and other employees who were under arrest in the English province. Twice they sent delegations into Aquitaine with gifts of money and horses, but when the second expedition skirmished with the law at La Réole and had to flee, its members returned to Avignon and reported that nothing more could be done for Ugolino.

Guglielmo and Bonaccorso de' Frescobaldi left for Italy. Meanwhile the Lords Ordainers had learned that the Frescobaldi were in Avignon, and dispatched two ambassadors to demand that the pope arrest them and seize their goods. But this act had already been accomplished under other auspices. An English bishop whose property had been confiscated by the Frescobaldi to turn over to the king arrived in Avignon and, discovering his former oppressors, brought suit in the papal court against them. The members of the company were placed under house arrest.

Rather than fight the case, they found it expedient to bribe their jailers (eight florins for two sergeants), meanwhile smuggling out money and possessions to an associate, Cornacchino Cornacchini. At the same time, they hired five lawyers, including the father of Francesco Petrarch. Privately the lawyers recommended bribes. On November 14 a gilded silver cup costing twenty-one florins was presented to "Beltrano, companion of the vice-treasurer." In December Cornacchino Cornacchini was arrested too. The Frescobaldi lost no time; on the day of the arrest, fifty florins was paid to the head guard, six florins seven sous to the sergeants, and Cornacchini was out of jail.

The Frescobaldi now repeated their London maneuver of departure in installments, until only Pepo di Bettino and the factor Lapo della Bruna remained. In March 1313 the King asked Pope Clement V to extradite Pepo and Lapo della Bruna. By this time his "beloved merchants" had become smugglers, robbers, and criminals, but Edward promised not to have them executed or maimed if they returned. Lapo della Bruna was actually brought to England, but in the course of time broke out of prison; the fact that his jailer Geoffrey Nichol was absolved of complicity in the escape probably only indicates the success of the bribery. In Avignon, Pepo also succeeded in slipping away.

Rather surprisingly, the Frescobaldi did not give up the idea of returning to England. The anti-Italian Ordinances had been enforced only against the Frescobaldi; other Italian merchants had been left unmolested. In 1316 the company even obtained safe conducts "to render their accounts to the King for the time in which they were receivers of his revenues in the kingdom of England, in Aquitaine, Ireland and elsewhere." Probably Edward wanted them back. But the opposition was on the alert; two separate inquiries were made into the company's affairs, in 1316 and 1318, examining account books, letters, and notarial acts.

Most of the money and belongings which the Frescobaldi had smuggled out of England eventually reached Italy. The rest was entrusted to colleagues who promised to repay it by means of letters of exchange to their companies with headquarters in Florence. One by one these business associates restored the Frescobaldi's property—Cornacchino Cornacchini, the Scali, the Bardi, the Peruzzi, and many smaller clients.

The Frescobaldi finally abandoned hope of returning to England. They were luckier than they realized. In England their places were taken in the next generation by the Bardi and Peruzzi companies, who took over all the privileges which the Frescobaldi had enjoyed—safe conducts, exemptions, money gifts, and, notwithstanding the famous Ordinances, the assignment of revenues. Their position with the king was even more favorable than that of the Frescobaldi, and they were even more cordially hated by the London population, which rioted against them in 1326 and burned their shops. For Edward III's wars with Scotland and for the first battles of the Hundred Years' War, the Bardi and Peruzzi opened their coffers to the king, to pay for arms, mercenaries, supplies. When their resources were exhausted they met the same fate as the Frescobaldi; they were investigated and jailed, and as soon as it was clear they were of no further value, they were dropped. Back home in Florence the news of the disaster came as a thunderclap; the first reaction was to blame the London branch managers. The Bardi manager, dying in his London palace, dictated a pathetic testament to a notary from Pistoia and charged him with carrying it to the partners in Florence: ". . . Those who vilify us speak evil, claiming that we have cheated and injured them, but everything that we have done was for them and at their request, and they knew what we were doing all the time. . . ."

The calamities of the Italian bankers in England were matched by losses at home, where the Florentine commune's wars in Lombardy and Lucca forced the government to exact heavy loans from private firms. The great companies reacted by attempting to seize the government, but they were decisively defeated in a series of violent street clashes in September 1343. The signal for the popular party to begin the battle against the magnates was given by members of an obscure family, the Medici; and the last of the magnate party to lay down arms were the Bardi. During the struggle, some twenty-two houses belonging to the Bardi were sacked and burned. The vandalism of the mob was followed by the reprisals of the commune. Some of the magnate families "who appear less guilty than the others" were admitted to the popular party, so that they could take part in the government. The Bardi and Frescobaldi were excluded.

The foiled coup d'etat was followed by a series of resounding bankruptcies. The first to fail were the Peruzzi, in 1344, followed by the Acciaiuoli and finally the Bardi. In each case, bankruptcy was declared and delegates from the creditors were chosen to examine the company's accounts. Settlement was recommended at a fixed percent, twenty or thirty, some creditors making their own arrangements. The proceedings were protracted. All the companies owned valuable real estate; land and houses were sold precipitously under depressed market conditions, and the members of the bankruptcy commissions seized the opportunity to feather their own nests.

From the Frescobaldi to the Bardi and Peruzzi, the Florentine bankers had been ruined by two historic upheavals: the crisis of the English monarchy, and the crisis of the commune of Florence. Like the English Jews in the thirteenth century, the great capitalists of the fourteenth were still subject to typical medieval turns of fortune, including popular sentiment and royal rapacity.

14

Moneyman in a Revolution:
Jacob van Artevelde of Ghent

On Sunday, December 28, 1337, a vast conclave of men and women thronged a field in front of the Cistercian abbey of Byloke, on the outskirts of Ghent. They had gathered to listen to the eloquence not of a preacher but of a businessman, discoursing not on the perils of damnation but on the hazards of the cloth trade.

The man who addressed the people of Ghent was about fifty years old, known and respected for his authority and strong will, sometimes expressed by a violent temper. Jacob van Artevelde was the son of a *Clauwaert*, a Flemish patriot of the Franco-Flemish war of a generation earlier, and a member of a family of cloth merchants which had served in the municipal government and which had on occasion lent money to the commune. A representative of a newly rich class that was more and more disputing power with the old patriciate in Ghent and other Flemish towns, he had, after the death of his first wife, married a wealthy woman, Kateline de Coster; they lived in a house inherited from his father in the most exclusive quarter of town and owned three other houses in Ghent and land in the country. On the face of it, he was scarcely a revolutionary; in 1326 when the town levied a punitive tax on the weavers of Ghent after a riot, Jacob van Artevelde was the collector. His wealth and prestige were essential to his role in the present crisis. Yet the stirring appeal he now made to his fellow citizens was the tocsin for one of the largest and perhaps the most dramatic of the revolutionary movements of the Middle Ages.

The crisis to which Jacob van Artevelde addressed himself that December Sunday had its origins in the maneuverings of Edward III of England and Philip VI of France to gain Flemish support for their claims to the French crown. Philip's advantage was the gratitude and feudal loyalty of Louis de Nevers, the Count of Flanders; in the Flemish revolt of the 1320s, Philip's help had won Louis the victory of Cassel. But Edward had an even better diplomatic weapon. In the summer of 1336 he suddenly enforced an embargo of English wool to Flanders. To show he meant business, Edward moved the "staple," the continental town where for tax purposes all English wool was shipped, from Bruges, in Flanders, to Antwerp. The manufacturers and weavers of Bruges, Ypres, and Ghent at once faced ruin and starvation. The three cities exchanged frantic counsel, and with Ghent taking the lead, appointed the commander of the Ghent militia, Sohier de Courtrai, to head a mission to Edward to negotiate an agreement. During a conference of representatives of the three cities at Bruges, Count Louis had this emissary seized. Edward III riposted by sending a convoy carrying 10,000 sacks of wool to Dordrecht, in Holland, tantalizingly close to the desperate Flemings. A delegation from Ghent visited Count Louis, urging him to consider the wool industry's dire situation, but Louis stood fast.

Thus on the December Sunday in 1337 Jacob van Artevelde made his entrance on the stage of history at a moment when the smoldering conflict of the capitalists and proletarians of the Flemish cloth industry was temporarily quenched by common interest.

In this situation van Artevelde made a forthright, convincing speech, declaring that there was no way out of the crisis for Flemish businessmen and workers except through alliance with England. He suggested that negotiating with Edward might make Philip VI more conciliatory. But the main thrust of his argument was the revolutionary concept that the united communes of Flanders could effectively stand together in defiance of their feudal lord.

Van Artevelde's speech persuaded Ghent. A few days later a junta was established, composed of five captains, representing the districts of the city, with one of the five, van Artevelde, at their head. Alongside the wealthy burgher captains served the deans of the craft guilds, principally the weavers and fullers. Deputations were sent to parley with the duke of Brabant, the count of Hainaut, and the count of Guelders, all of whom were Low Country allies of Edward, and in mid-February 1338, an agreement was reached. Edward's brother-in-law, the count of Guelders, acted in the king's name. In March the wool from Dordrecht began to arrive in Ghent, ending an eighteen-month famine in raw material for the wool industry. All Flanders rallied behind Ghent and acclaimed Jacob van Artevelde.

As so often, for a moment it seemed as if a revolution could triumph without bloodshed. But neither Count Louis nor his feudal lord could afford to let the revolution go unchallenged. Philip formally ordered the court to have the walls of Ghent demolished, and demanded that the Church place the city under interdict. More immediately he told Louis to execute Sohier de Courtrai, the commander of the Ghent militia whose arrest had started the trouble.

Sohier was taken from a sickbed in the count's castle at Rupelmonde and beheaded. Most of Flanders was appalled, but the rural Flemish aristocracy and some members of the old patriciate, angered and alarmed by the pretensions of van Artevelde's burghers and proletarians, applauded the act. On Easter Eve, the rustic nobility and its reactionary allies presented themselves before the walls of Ghent. Van Artevelde had his people open the dikes and flood the ground, driving them off. When they came back a few days later the Ghent sailors and carpenters demolished a bridge over the Lys to block the attack. Finally the rustics retreated, and Jacob van Artevelde sallied out at the head of the communal militia. After two days' fighting, the feudal army surrendered; van Artevelde moved on to Bruges and wiped out pockets of resistance there.

Suddenly Jacob van Artevelde was the unchallenged master of Flanders, which in June swore allegiance to the new regime. A delegation from the triumphant revolutionary government journeyed to Paris, where Philip VI, seeking at all costs to prevent an open alliance between Flanders and Edward III, agreed to Flemish neutrality and commercial relations with England.

From London, Edward III also recognized the county's neutrality. He gave Flemish merchants the right to do business freely in England, specifically to buy wool there, and promised that his troops would respect Flemish territory if Philip's would do the same. In a rather tenuous legalistic compromise, he also granted the count freedom to assist Philip with his own vassals, but not with the burghers of the cities.

The revolutionary character of the situation in Flanders in this hour has been underlined by the Belgian historian Henri Pirenne, who pointed out the analogy between Count Louis' situation and that of Louis XVI during the French revolution: "He pretended to have entire confidence in [the new regime]. . . . In the great procession of Tournai, where the citizens of Ghent sent a large deputation every year, he appeared in their ranks and wore their colors, just as the King of France wore, in 1792, the Phrygian bonnet."

All parties—Edward, Philip, Louis, and Jacob van Artevelde—now tried to reconcile opposing factions into some pattern that would accord with their own interests. Philip VI made concessions designed to restore the Flemings' loyalties to their count, of whose loyalty to his own person Philip was sure. Characterizing the manufacturers and workers of Flanders as "simple and ignorant" people toward whom he had always shown "liberality" and on whom he had bestowed "graces and benefits greater than any of my predecessors," he declared that he renounced any damages, since he had no desire to "enrich himself at their expense," and wanted nothing more than their "good deportment" and friendship.

From Antwerp, Edward III made overtures in the reverse direction. He proposed a marriage between his daughter Isabella and Louis de Nevers' son Louis de Mâle, and offered to restore the ancient frontiers of Flanders—Arras, Lille, Douai, Tournai, and Bethune. The count, clinging to his feudal loyalty, announced that the countess was ill and departed for Paris.

Left in unchallenged command of Flanders, Jacob van Arte-velde showed statesmanship. An illegitimate but nevertheless noble sister of Louis de Nevers had married a wealthy knighted burgher named Simon van Halen, known as Mirabello, scion of a Florentine banking family long settled in Flanders. Van Artevelde established Mirabello as regent for the vanished count, thus maintaining an appearance of constitutionality.

In December 1339, Flanders, in the name of the absent count, but in the hand of Jacob van Artevelde, concluded a treaty of alliance with Edward III's ally, the duke of Brabant, tantamount to a declaration of war on Philip VI. The next month King Edward and Queen Philippa made a ceremonial visit to Ghent. In the Friday Marketplace he was hailed by the councillors of Ghent, Ypres, and Bruges as legitimate heir to the throne of France. In return he swore to maintain the rights and independence of the towns, and promised additional rewards, including a wool staple at Bruges and a large subsidy for the cities' military effort. To demonstrate his faith in his Flemish allies, he left the pregnant queen behind in Ghent, a circumstance that caused the royal son presently born at the Abbey of St. Bavo to go down in history as John of Gaunt.

In the summer of 1340 a Flemish-Brabanter-English army besieged French Tournai, while the fleets battled in the Channel. The English and Flemings won a smashing naval victory off Sluys, sinking almost the entire French fleet; but Tournai held out, while the allies fell to quarreling. Jacob van Artevelde, commanding the Flemish contingent in person, contributed to the trouble. A soldier of the Brabant army, suspected of communicating with the enemy, denied the charge; choleric van Artevelde had him subjected to water torture until he admitted that he had been sent by the duke of Brabant to parley with the French. When the Brabanter escaped to his own camp, his story seriously exacerbated inter-allied relations. Soon after, in the tent of Edward III himself, under the very eyes of king and duke, hot-tempered Jacob killed a Brabant knight who had dared to insult him.

When the fragile alliance was shaken by a proletarian revolt in Brabant, the Brabant patricians put domestic tranquillity before foreign conquest and hastened home to suppress the rebellion. Together with Hainaut, Brabant made peace with Philip VI. Edward gave up and went home.

The victory of Sluys had lifted Jacob van Artevelde's prestige to the pinnacle; the check at Tournai and Edward's departure had the effect of canceling Sluys. The political tide ebbed with the military. Flemish dissensions which had been papered over rather than healed by the revolution appeared again. Not only did Brabant and Hainaut draw away from Flanders, but jealous Bruges and Ypres drew away from Ghent. The divisions went deeper. The three great cloth cities were hated by their own respective countrysides for brutally enforcing their metropolitan monopoly of cloth manufacture. All three had sent armed expeditions into the neighborhood to break the looms of weavers and smash the vats and frames of fullers; Ghent had destroyed the cloth industry of little Termonde, Bruges that of Eekloo, Ypres that of Poperinghe. Even more deep-seated was the unresolved conflict inside the cloth cities which pitted the weavers against the fullers and other lesser crafts.

In the winter of 1342–43, it was the turn of Philip VI to apply pressure to Flanders by blockading the frontier to keep French wheat from reaching the cities. Famine followed. Edward III's promised subsidies did not materialize. Count Louis once more appeared in Flanders, and in January 1343 a counterrevolutionary insurrection broke out in Ghent; headed by a wealthy burgher named Jan van Steenbeke, the rebels demanded that van Artevelde surrender his post and turn the government of the city back to the old town council. Van Steenbeke's partisans gathered in the Friday Marketplace and marched on the town hall. The councillors succeeded in averting bloodshed by inducing the two leaders to accept confinement respectively in the city's two strongholds, van Steenbeke in the Castle of the Counts of Flanders, van Artevelde in the older Castle of Gerard the Devil, a brooding pile in the middle of town, overlooking the Scheldt. From his castle-prison, van Artevelde sent messengers to summon his partisans from Bruges and

Castle of Gerard the Devil, Ghent, where Jacob van Artevelde, who led the Flemish artisans in their struggle for independence, was briefly imprisoned during the counterrevolution of 1343.

Ypres; contingents from Bruges arrived shortly and camped before the gates of the city. When a few days later troops arrived from Ypres, the councillors gave way, banished van Steenbeke's party, confiscated their property, and reinstated van Artevelde.

During this strenuous period, Kateline de Coster van Artevelde, Jacob's second wife, with a hardihood and independence often displayed by medieval women, undertook three trips to England in an attempt to collect from the king the subsidies long promised to the Flemish cities, who paid the expenses of the trips. Only the first of her voyages was crowned with success; she returned to Flanders with a large sum of money. On the second journey, accompanied by her brother Jan de Coster, a priest of Ghent, she arrived in England to find that the king was in Britanny leading his troops against Philip. An English chronicler records an attempt to assassinate the brother and sister while they were in London, but does not reveal the motive. Kateline and her brother recrossed the Channel and sought King Edward in Brittany, but the mission came to nothing.

For a precarious year, van Artevelde maintained himself in power. In the spring of 1345, Edward once more made plans for an offensive on the Continent. Before Edward completed his preparations, a violent clash broke out in Ghent between the rival guilds of weavers and fullers. On May 2, the two parties, in armed array behind their leaders, confronted each other in the Friday Marketplace. Van Artevelde threw the influence of the government to the support of the powerful weavers' guild; fighting broke out, and the weavers cut their adversaries to pieces. Hundreds died, many while trying to swim the Lys to safety, in what went down in Flemish history as "Bloody Monday."

Whatever van Artevelde's motives in supporting the weavers, who he may have felt constituted the core of his own popular support, Bloody Monday was no real victory for him. Instead, it raised a new power in the form of the now unchallenged weavers' guild of Ghent and its leader, Gerard Denijs.

When van Artevelde set off in July for Sluys to confer with Edward III, he left behind him an uneasy city, alive with enemies

jealous of his personal power, with whispered suspicions of his intentions, and with shifting loyalties. What went on aboard Edward's
ship with the Flemish delegates, van Artevelde, and the councillors
of Ypres and Bruges, no one will ever know. The rumor, rife in
Ghent and repeated by all the chroniclers, was that Edward III
urged the Flemings to abandon Louis de Nevers and his line and to
accept in their place Edward's own son, the Prince of Wales, to
whom he would give the title duke of Flanders. The rumor went
further; it accused Jacob van Artevelde alone of the delegates from
the Flemish cities of accepting the proposal. The story is out of
keeping with van Artevelde's past policy toward the count and supported by not a single clause of the agreement finally drawn up between Edward and the Flemish cities, but it testifies to the captain's
growing unpopularity. During the conference, messengers arrived
warning van Artevelde that the very weavers whom he had supported on Bloody Monday were conspiring against him. Hastening
home, he arrived on Sunday, July 17, to find an ugly crowd gathered around his house, many of them weavers. Stones began to fly,
and the mob attacked the house. Van Artevelde tried to escape by a
side entrance, but was overtaken and killed.

For a short time after Jacob van Artevelde's death, his policy
was continued; the alliance with Edward was renewed and brought
to fruit in the successful siege of Calais, which Edward made the
staple town for English wool. Count Louis de Nevers, meanwhile,
was among the slain at the battle of Crécy. The weavers of Ghent
hoped his heir, sixteen-year-old Louis de Mâle, would remain in
Flanders as a docile figurehead. The boy instead escaped to France,
leaving Flanders in a state of interregnum.

On January 13, 1349, the fullers and lesser crafts of Ghent
turned the tables on the weavers and massacred them in the streets
in what the conquerors dubbed "Good Tuesday," in revenge for
Bloody Monday. The weavers were summarily excluded from political power, and the rich burghers, the fullers, and the lesser crafts invited Louis de Mâle to return with full rights. The English alliance
was at an end; many weavers left the country and settled in Eng-

land, where Edward III helped them establish themselves and in doing so encouraged a native English cloth industry which presently competed with that of Flanders.

After her husband's assassination, Kateline van Artevelde fled to England with Jacob's brother William. Her brother Jan de Coster and her sons Jan and Jacob remained in Ghent until the counterrevolution, when they too crossed the Channel. The property of many refugees was confiscated; the van Arteveldes got off with heavy fines. The exiles remained in England until 1359, when Louis de Mâle, secure in his power, permitted them to return.

Twenty-three years later, in 1382, Jacob van Artevelde's son Philip led a revolt against Louis de Mâle and died losing the battle of Rozebeke. "Thus ended the van Arteveldes," wrote Froissart a few years later, "who in their time were great masters in Flanders: the poor people raised them up in the beginning, and wicked people killed them in the end."

A more modern view of the van Arteveldes' fate is that they were crushed between the irreconcilable forces of class conflict in industrial-feudal Flanders. Jacob demonstrated genuine political sagacity and leadership, and his failure to establish a new government on a solid basis may be compared to similar failures by Cromwell and Napoleon. The old regime had too much strength, and the basis of the new one was undermined by too many internal divisions.

The weavers and fullers of Flanders were revolutionary proletarians only in a limited sense; their dream, as Pirenne pointed out, was the essentially conservative one of a petty capitalist world in which each craftsman had his own small shop and produced his own goods, which he would sell in the local market, dispensing with the wholesalers, the importer-exporters, the bankers, and the great merchants. Yet these latter, who exploited and tyrannized, were creating an economic revolution of far deeper moment than that of Jacob van Artevelde.

15

Francesco di Marco Datini of Prato, the Man Who Survived

In 1870 an old house in Prato, a few miles northwest of Florence, was subjected to alterations. Knocking out a partition, the workmen discovered a long-disused stairwell in which were piled a vast number of sacks stuffed with letters and books, evidently discarded there. Thus was discovered perhaps the most important single collection of commercial documents of the Middle Ages, and one of the most fascinating of all historical archives.

Jumbled together in the sacks were all the letters, documents, and account books of Francesco di Marco Datini, meticulously filed in the fourteenth century by the head of an import-export firm and his branch managers; besides these, there were Datini's household accounts and private letters. This priceless treasury, which owed its preservation to the very fact that it had been forgotten, comprised 150,000 letters, more than 500 account books and ledgers, 300-odd deeds of partnership, some 400 insurance policies underwritten both by and for the Datini firm, and several thousand miscellaneous papers providing specimens of every commercial instrument of the Middle Ages—bills of lading, bills of exchange, letters of credit, checks.

Italian scholars set to work mining this discovery, classifying the business letters under the principal Datini branches and sorting the documents, business records, and personal papers; scholars of many countries are still at work today on the top floor of the Datini palace, in archives consisting principally of room after room of shelves filled with the Datini letters and documents. The collection is absolutely unique, providing the only comprehensive record of the career of a fourteenth-century businessman, private and public.

The picture that emerges from the Datini archive is that of a man who survived childhood tragedy to make his fortune in a tough world by the classic ingredients of driving determination, intelligence, patience, and the circumstance of being in the right place at the right time. This enormously successful man controlled a network of companies with branches in Genoa, Pisa, Majorca, Avignon, Barcelona, and Valencia, as well as his native Prato and neighboring Florence; he was a banker, cloth manufacturer, retail merchant, and importer-exporter, dealing in wool, wool cloth, skins, silk, armor, wheat, art works, and many other kinds of merchandise. Yet his origins were humble, and at the outset fortune seemed to do anything but smile on him. Beginning his business career soon after the collapse of the great Florentine companies, Francesco Datini learned a lesson from them. He kept aloof from politics, refusing office and avoiding factional struggles. He loaned money to the government only when he was forced to, and then with bad grace; by choice his borrowers were sound merchants like himself, not irresponsible city councils or arrogantly defaulting kings. Finally, instead of forming a single large company with branches all over Europe, in the style of the Alberti, the Frescobaldi, the Bardi, and the Peruzzi, he set up a series of autonomous partnerships, in which he himself was the only common element, a separate partnership for each branch office, in Pisa in 1382, in Genoa in 1392, in Barcelona in 1393, and in 1394 in Valencia, Majorca, Ibiza, and Catalonia. This arrangement of independent agencies was a pattern later adopted by the Medici bank.

Born in Prato about 1335, Francesco Datini was the son of an innkeeper who had saved enough money to buy a bit of land where he raised cattle to sell in the marketplace. Francesco's first job was as an apprentice butcher, helping his father cut up meat.

He was thirteen when in 1348 Tuscany was devastated by the Black Death. Francesco's father perished, followed by his mother, his sister, and one of his two brothers. Francesco and his brother Stefano were the sole survivors. Of four executors their father had appointed in his will, only one was still alive, a relative named Piero di Giunta del Rosso. Articles of clothing and household goods belonging to the family were sold, and the two boys sent to live with a foster mother, a friend of the family for whom Francesco came to feel a son's affection.

A year later, Piero di Giunta accompanied Francesco to Florence, taking the boy from one shop to another until he found him a place as an apprentice. Many Florentines were taking advantage of business opportunities at the papal court, still in its "Babylonian Captivity" in Avignon. In 1350 Francesco, only fifteen years old, sold a small piece of land, part of his inheritance, for 150 florins, and set off for Provence. Except for one brief visit, he did not return to his native land for more than thirty years.

Francesco arrived in Avignon at the apogee of its glory: a small town packed with functionaries of the court, full of the luxury shops of Italian merchants. Taking lodgings with a Florentine, he soon found work. His guardian in Florence received no requests for money, only from time to time for shirts and lengths of cloth, charged off to his inheritance. Eight years after his arrival, hardworking Francesco was prosperous enough to send for his brother Stefano, and directed Piero di Giunta to buy him land and a house in the Via del Porcellatico in Prato. In April, 1359, now a young businessman of twenty-four, he at last returned to Prato to go over accounts with his guardian, buy another piece of land, and persuade Piero to entrust him with 100 florins belonging to Stefano to invest in Avignon. In July he was back in the papal city, going into partnership with another Tuscan. They opened a shop in the main square, Francesco living in an apartment on the second floor. The firm dealt, among other things, in armor. When Bertrand du Guesclin's army threatened Avignon in 1360, enterprising Francesco seized the opportunity to sell arms both to du Guesclin and to the Provençal defenders, supplying coats of mail, helmets, breastplates, cuirasses, and gauntlets brought on mule back, packed in bales of straw wrapped in canvas, across the Alps from Milan.

His profits helped him expand his business, taking in another partner. According to Francesco's own account, the capital of 400 florins apiece put into the partnership grew in the next eight years to more than 10,000. He set up a money changer's table and opened a tavern and a draper's shop. The flourishing main store carried not only armor but jewelry, hides, harnesses and saddles, cloth, and such religious articles as vestments, altar cloths, saints' pictures.

The pictures were painted to order and priced by size. In July 1373, Francesco ordered from Florence, "A painting of Our Lady, with gold background . . . by the best master who is painting in Florence, with several figures. In the middle, Our Lord on the cross, or Our Lady, whichever you find. The important thing is that it be beautiful, with fine big figures, the fairest and best that you can find for 5½ to 6½ florins, but not more. . . . A picture of Our Lady of the same kind, on gold background, but a little less grand, for the price of 4½ florins, but no more. . . . I want them for people who demand the best, and I'm in no hurry. . . ." Later one of his partners wrote to Florence, "You say that you can find no pictures at our price, because it is too low, then we say, if you cannot, let it go. Pictures are in no great demand here; they are occasional items which one must buy when the painter is in want. . . . If, however, one day you find a good picture and the artist needs money, then buy it." Art buyers came from a wide range of classes, from a tailor who bought a medium-sized picture of the Virgin for two florins, to the papal official, a brother of the cardinal of Naples, who bought a large triptych for six florins and the Lucchese banker Philip Rapondo, a member of a family who financed the king of France and the duke of Berry, who bought "a square picture with gold background" for ten florins. Only once was the name of a painter mentioned, Jacopo di Cione, a brother of Andrea Orcagna. Artists, according to Francesco, thought far too well of themselves and those with reputations overcharged their clients. "Are they all brothers or

Madonna del Ceppo, by Fra Filippo Lippi. In the right foreground, Francesco Datini, with four other citizens of Prato. (Commune of Prato)

cousins of Giotto?" he inquired sarcastically. Yet this traffic in paintings had obvious significance in the development of Italian art.

Not until 1376, when he was forty years old, did Francesco marry. He chose a sixteen-year-old Italian girl living in Avignon, Margherita di Domenico Bandini, whose family belonged to the petty nobility of Florence; her Guelf father had been executed by a victorious Ghibelline faction. At this moment, a quarrel between Florence and Pope Gregory XI led to the expulsion of the Florentine colony in Avignon and confiscation of the property of the merchants. Francesco, profiting from his Prato citizenship, remained. Two years later the pope returned to Rome, taking half the wealth of Avignon with him, and in 1379 Francesco began to make preparations to go home, leaving two partners in charge of the business. In December 1382, sending his household goods by sea from Arles to Pisa, Francesco set off across the Alps for Prato with wife and servants. The little party took the road to Sisteron, followed the Durance River to the Mont-Genèvre Pass, then to Turin and Milan. The first part of the journey, over the Alpine passes in the dead of winter, took two weeks; another ten days were spent traveling via Parma and Bologna, the whole trip, with a week's respite in Milan, taking thirty-three days.

Francesco returned to Prato a wealthy middle-aged man. His formerly autonomous native city was now a Florentine dependency, its wool cloth trade, long the city's pride, producing *panno pratese* (cloth of Prato), slowly being absorbed; many cloth merchants had already moved to the nearby capital.

Settling down in Prato, Francesco built a fine new house on the land he had commissioned Piero di Giunta to buy, on the Via del Porcellatico. Tall, square, adorned with a loggia and frescoes, it was the finest residence in Prato. Like Benedetto Zaccaria's mansion on the banks of the Bisagno, it accommodated royalty: Louis II of Anjou, pretender to the throne of Sicily, was twice Francesco's guest. On the second occasion the prince and the commoner made a characteristic deal; Louis added the lily of France to Francesco's coat of arms, in return for a loan of 1,000 florins.

Many an ambassador, lord, and prince of the Church, not to

mention aristocrat of the counting house, was entertained in the mansion on the Via del Porcellatico, whose basic function, nevertheless, was as a business headquarters. Francesco's warehouse and central office were established on the grounds. The warehouse soon held wool from Spain and Provence, alum, soap, dyestuffs, linen, leather. Other goods arrived for the house itself—paint, gold leaf, furniture, velvets, and brocades. To handle the imports, Datini opened a branch in Pisa. A year after his return to Prato, he enrolled in the Wool Guild and entered the cloth business with his guardian Piero di Giunta and a distant cousin; the next year he formed a dyeing company with Piero's son Niccolo, who was a master-dyer, engaging to supply cloth which Niccolo finished, using chiefly indigo and woad, which Francesco obtained from his other branches. Through Francesco, the Pratese were now able to import fine "garbo" wool from Spain and Africa, Minorcan wool, and best of all, English wool.

Unlike the great Florentine firms of the early 1300s, Francesco showed a healthy diffidence toward London and never established a branch in England, but depended upon Tuscan firms already in the English capital to do his buying for him. These companies sent their representatives to the Cotswolds, to farms, abbeys, great estates, or to the summer fairs to buy up the clip. The wool was carried on Venetian or Genoese ships sailing from London and Southampton.

Wool from the western Mediterranean, garbo and Minorcan, was collected in Catalonia and in Palma di Majorca, and brought to Italy by ships putting in at Nice, Marseille and Aigues Mortes, then heading for Genoa; thence it was forwarded by sea to Pisa, or carried overland to Prato and Florence. The finished cloth went back to Spain and North Africa by similar routes, except during the frequent periods when political troubles closed Pisa to Florentine trade, or when mercenaries in the pay of the Visconti of Milan were plundering the Tuscan countryside. Then cloth from Florence was packed across the mountains to Bologna and Ferrara, shipped downriver to Venice, and by sea to the West. Pisa was the port normally used by Francesco, with minor Tuscan ports and Genoa frequent alternatives and Venice a last resort. Sometimes goods were sent across the Alpine passes via Mont-Cenis for northern France, or Mont-Genèvre for Avignon and the lower Rhone.

The profit-making process was slow; on one occasion it took more than three years to realize an investment in wool, between the purchase of the clip and the sale of cloth. From the proceeds had to be deducted considerable overhead: the cost of raw materials, packing, expense of agents, transportation, customs, insurance, taxes and tolls, commissions, and labor. The profits of the Prato cloth company ran just under nine percent per year.

Four years after his return to Prato, Francesco transferred his headquarters to Florence, where the new conservative oligarchy that had taken over after the suppression of the proletarian Ciompi revolt seemed to promise comfortable stability to a businessman. He opened a warehouse in the Via Porta Rossa and formed a new partnership with Stoldo di Lorenzo, a Florentine who had worked for him in Avignon and Pisa, and a third partner, Falduccio di Lombardo. The company dealt in Minorcan, Spanish, and Provençal wool; wool cloth from Florence, Prato, and Perpignan; silk and velvet from Lucca and Spain, as well as hides, wax, spices, wine, grain. In 1388 Francesco joined the silk merchants' guild and opened a shop in Por S. Maria where he sold wool cloth, silk, velvet, table linen, veils, and notions—needles, thread, scissors, knives, hammers, soap. Like all the great Italian merchants, he carried on a variety of undertakings. In 1404 he joined the Calimala Guild; for a time he farmed the meat and wine tolls of Prato; he underwrote insurance; in 1398 he opened a bank in Florence and the next year joined the money changers' guild, the Arte del Cambio.

Like Benedetto Zaccaria, in one important Mediterranean commodity Datini failed to deal. He did not engage in the slave trade which flourished in Europe as a result of the labor shortage created by the Black Death. In theory only non-Christians were enslaved; most slaves consequently came from Spain and Africa, the Balkans, Constantinople, Cyprus, Crete and, most productive source of all, the Black Sea region. Most were women and young girls, sold by their parents or kidnaped, taken to the slave markets of Tana on the

Sea of Azov and Caffa in the Crimea and thence to Venice and Genoa. Those from the western Mediterranean were sold in the Balearics. Their usual fate was to become servants in well-to-do households. The Datini ménage employed several such domestic slaves, their status that of well-treated servants. Francesco's slave cook did not even hesitate to express her annoyance when he brought unexpected guests to dinner.

Like the great Calimala companies, each of the Datini agencies, under the direction of Francesco's partners, had a staff of salaried employees, factors, notaries, accountants, couriers, and office boys. Francesco, the capo, regarded himself as the father of a large family, maintaining a patriarchal relationship with his employees, including those abroad. He held the reins tightly, rebuking the branch managers when they made foolish investments or incurred losses, and keeping a close watch over their private lives. In the business area, he was successful in controlling their actions; their morals eluded his authority. Simone d'Andrea, the manager in Barcelona, kept a Moorish slave girl who ran the shop and gave him venereal disease. Cristofano di Bartolo in Majorca kept a succession of slave women and brought up their children in the company headquarters. (Francesco's own position in this matter was weak; he himself had a daughter by a young domestic slave and brought her up in his otherwise childless Prato house.)

Perhaps the greatest value of the Datini archive is the light it casts on the progress of European business methods. Francesco's complicated enterprises required expert management and advanced techniques of bookkeeping. The Datini accounts show a gradual evolution in that art. The early books, from the Avignon period, use a system similar to that employed earlier by the great Florentine companies, with each of the "great books" divided into two sections, one for debits, the other for credits. Taking a balance was difficult. Francesco's early account books, however, did make use of an advanced technique: the "impersonal" account, representing such factors as office or administrative expenses.

In the company's later books the debit and credit of each

account were presented on facing pages, a system known as "Venetian style." Finally, from 1386 on, Datini's companies began to use double-entry bookkeeping, which had evolved in Tuscany or in Genoa (scholars are not certain) earlier in the century. In this system, every receipt and every expenditure was allocated to a particular function—to office expenses, brokerage, profit, loss—making it possible for a businessman to strike a balance and determine his financial situation at a moment's notice. "Here will be entered, God forbid, losses incurred on merchandise: 2 loads of wax, which Francesco di Boncorso bought for us at Genoa as shown on page 342. 2 florins, 7 s., 6 d."; "Profits on merchandise will be entered here, God grant us health and profits, Amen. For profits on leather and sugar sold, as on merchandise A, the account is on page 174. 12 florins, 12 s." By 1400 all the Datini companies were using this system. In the course of the following century, the method spread through Italy and reached Flanders, though elsewhere in Europe it remained unknown. Two developments finally established it universally: the invention of printing, which gave wide currency to manuals of instruction (among them the first treatise on accounting, the *Summa* of Luca Paciolo), and the discoveries which deflected commerce from the Mediterranean to the Atlantic and led the businessmen of northern Europe to take over Italian methods along with Italian trade.

Francesco Datini's statue in the main square of Prato shows him holding a sheaf of bills of exchange. This instrument, widely used by the Datini firm—more than five thousand examples survive in the archives, in many languages—had come into use in the period when Italian merchants stopped going to the Champagne Fairs and conducted business by letter through permanent agents in other cities. It took the place of the earlier cambium contracts used by Romano Mairano and by Symon di Gualterio; it was at once a way of supplying money to someone in another country and in another currency, and a form of loan in which the interest was disguised in the rate of exchange. The new version replaced the clumsy, verbose notarial document of the cambium with a simple direction to a correspondent abroad to pay a certain sum to a certain person after a lapse of time (called "usance") which depended on how far away the foreign city was. Collection was always specified in a different currency and a different place. The parties to the bill were usually two pairs of correspondents in two cities. Unlike modern bills of exchange, these were not discountable—they could not be sold at a reduction before maturity—and they were always paid to the payee named in the bill; but it was possible to use them to speculate on the rate of exchange.

In addition to issuing and accepting bills of exchange, for which they exacted a commission, banking services provided by the Datini company included letters of credit, loans to merchants, and many services to businessmen. Among the documents in the archive are some primitive examples of checks, although this instrument did not come into general use until the sixteenth century. The established custom had been to withdraw or transfer money by verbal order, entered into the bank's journal before the eyes of the party or parties involved, and sometimes to open a temporary account in the payee's name for the transfer. Bankers and money changers often had accounts with each other in a kind of anticipation of the modern clearing house, making it possible to hand over credit from one person to another even when they had accounts in different banks. At first, written orders were used only when a client could not be present. Some of the checks used by the Datini companies fit this category, but some seem to have been drawn in favor of a party in town by a client in town.

These advances in commercial technique were made in the face of political upheavals and other troubles. In 1390 harassment by the Visconti of Milan disrupted Florentine trade, and in 1391, when an anti-Florentine faction took over Pisa, Manno di Albizzo degli Agli, the manager of Francesco's branch, had to hide out in the shop of a friend. Pisa made peace again and trade was resumed, but Francesco decided to close the branch. To replace it, he opened an agency in Genoa through which the bulk of his merchandise thenceforward passed; from the Genoese branch he then extended his operations to Spain and Majorca.

Piracy and looting aside, the troubles with Milan distressed

Statue of Francesco Datini in the Piazza Communale in Prato. In his left hand is a sheaf of bills of exchange, widely used by his firm as a form of speculation and to transfer money from one country to another.

Francesco in another way: the Florentine commune levied forced loans to pay for its military expenses. Protesting that he paid taxes in Prato and Avignon, Datini refused. He was summoned before the Signoria, where he appeared dressed in a taffeta-lined robe with scarlet hood, black silk hose, and scarlet cloak, with two defenders, his close friend the notary Ser Lapo Mazzei, and the gonfaloniere of justice Guido del Palagio. The case was finally dropped and Francesco excused from the tax. But it was not the last time he was subject to such exactions. In 1401 he complained that he had paid 6,000 florins in six years, and now in his old age was liable to find himself penniless.

Toward the end of the fourteenth century the Black Death suddenly reappeared in Italy. After the first onslaught of 1348, it had lain dormant for thirteen years, then resurfaced four times between 1361 and 1375. Its recurrence in 1399 inspired a penitential movement in Tuscany. Companies of men, robed and hooded in white, marched barefoot through the countryside singing hymns, praying at shrines, and scourging themselves while they begged God for mercy. At first the bands were made up of poor people, but gradually their ranks were swelled by prosperous merchants. Francesco Datini joined a pilgrimage of 30,000 men, heading his own little group of twelve well-to-do citizens: his brother-in-law, his Florentine partners, and eight factors. Dressed in white linen robes, they set out on August 18, 1399, taking communion at Santa Maria Novella and then marching through the city in ranks of three, each carrying a lighted candle, striking themselves with rods as they went. They trudged along the Arno, stopping at Pieve a Ripoli to say a mass for the bishop of Fiesole, who led the pilgrimage, then lunched on bread, cheese, and fruit—having vowed not to eat meat for the nine days of the pilgrimage, or remove their white garments, or sleep in a bed. In spite of these exigencies, Francesco's party was not without creature comforts, for he had brought along two horses and a mule loaded with saddle-packs full of sweetmeats, cheese, wafers, cakes, and with a sack of warm clothing, in case of inclement weather. The pilgrims spent three days skirting the banks of the Arno to San Donato, San Giovanni, Montevarchi, and finally

Arezzo, where they heard mass in a meadow and spent the night in the Franciscan monastery, returning to Florence via Castelfranco and Pontassieve. Back home, they kept on their white robes through the bishop's mass in the square, then dispersed to their houses.

In spite of this penitential outing, the plague continued to converge on Florence. A pilgrimage was organized in Prato, and the shops were closed for nine days while the procession wound around the neighboring countryside. Francesco joined this one too. Finally, under the influence of the sermons of Fra Giovanni Dominici, he relieved his conscience by having Ser Lapo Mazzei draw up a will leaving half his fortune to Florence's foundling hospital and the rest to a foundation, the *Casa del Ceppo dei poveri di Francesco di Marco*, which would administer it for the poor people of Prato. He later amended his will to leave everything to the Ceppo—his house in Prato, all his other dwellings and farms, his interest in all the companies.

Once the will was made, Francesco left for Bologna, with his wife, illegitimate daughter, servants, and two factors. He was none too soon; the plague was already raging in Florence and Prato. Ser Lapo Mazzei wrote him on July 6 that 201 people had died the day before, "without hospitals, priests, friars or monasteries, or gravediggers . . . and today we have about 250 sick. See how God smites us! But my family is still well." In August he reported that the plague had passed from the areas of the poor to those of the rich. "Most of the shops here remain closed; the judges have deserted their benches; the Priors' Palace is empty; no one can be found in court; there is no one to mourn the dead." A few days later Francesco replied that his partner in the bank, Bartolommeo Cambioni, who had gone to Bologna soon after Francesco, had come down with the plague and died. Death followed death—Niccolo di Piero and Francesco Bellandi, Datini's partners in Prato; his notary, Ser Schiatta di Michele; his Pisan partners, Falduccio di Lombardo and Manno d'Albizzo, and the head of the Genoa branch, Andrea di Bonanno. The heaviest blow fell on Ser Lapo: his sons Amerigo and Martino died on the same day, "the oldest and the middle one, in my arms, within a few hours. God knows what hopes I had for the eldest, already a companion to me, and, with me, a father to the others; and who was doing so well in Ardingo's bank. . . . and God knows how for many years he never failed, night and morning, to say his prayers on his knees in his room, even when it was so hot or cold that I felt sorry for him. . . . And at the same time [Ser Lapo's daughter] Antonia was in bed, sick to death, and the middle boy with her, and he died there. How my heart broke, when the little ones cried, and their mother not well herself or strong, hearing the words of the elder boy. And now all three of them dead!"

Francesco languished in Bologna. He was uneasy when Ser Lapo wrote him that the priors were levying new loans, especially on those who were absent. Furthermore, a particularly testy and tactless comment of his had reached Florentine ears—to the effect that he would stay on in Bologna for a time because he was sure that God would again punish "the most evil folk in the world, the people of Florence, Prato, Pistoia and Pisa." Afraid of his reception at home, Francesco momentarily considered transferring his business to Venice, but Ser Lapo urged him not to. Finally, after fourteen months' voluntary exile, he returned to Florence.

Francesco Datini lived nine more years, mostly in Prato. In July 1410, at the age of seventy-five, he took to his bed with kidney trouble, and died two weeks later. He was buried at the foot of the High Altar of San Francesco, a church he had endowed and embellished with paintings and altar furnishings. The Latin inscription over his tomb reads: "Here lies the body of the prudent and honorable man, Francesco di Marco Datini of Prato, citizen and prosperous merchant of Florence, who died on the 16th day of August, A.D. 1410. May his soul rest in peace." The council of Prato ruled that Francesco's eulogy should be delivered in the cathedral every year on the anniversary of his death; to this day a mass is said for him there. His statue stands in the Piazza del Comune, and over the door of his house can be read the words: "The Ceppo of Francesco di Marco, Merchant of Christ's Poor." But Francesco Datini's greatest and indeed incomparable monument is the archive in the house in Prato, an irreplaceable treasure for economic historians, and a memorial to a businessman who weathered the storms of the fourteenth century and helped keep the Commercial Revolution moving forward.

16

Merchants of the German Hansa: Hildebrand and Sivert Veckinchusen

Around the middle of the fourteenth century, a merchant family of Westphalia, in northwest Germany, moved east to the frontier region of Livonia (modern Latvia and Estonia). Eventually the Veckinchusens included nine children. Among them there were two boys, Sivert and Hildebrand, whose business careers, preserved in letters and other documents, supply an invaluable insight into the life of North German merchants. Family connections of the Veckinchusens were spread throughout the Hanseatic towns, east and west, from Flanders to Estonia. The two brothers began their careers in Reval (now Tailinn, Estonia). Uncles, cousins, and nephews lived in Dorpat (Tartu) and Riga, as well as in the Hanseatic capital of Lübeck, and in the Hansa's western outposts of Bruges, Ghent, and Cologne.

The family belonged to the wealthy class which controlled the Hanseatic towns, and whose position was based on property, urban and rural, as well as on business investments. Some members of this class had noble antecedents, but the majority traced their origins to commerce, to shipowning, or to industry: silver or copper mining, salt extraction and refining, brewing. Almost everywhere in the

Hanseatic area the patricians were organized in closed associations: at Cologne the Rich Men's Club (*Richerzeche*), at Dortmund and Riga a "great guild" that came to be called the *Junckergesellschaft*, at Danzig the Brotherhood of St. George, at Lübeck the Society of the Circle. Intermarriage was part of their way of life; at Lübeck in 1380 most of the members of the town council were related at least as closely as cousins. Strength and exclusivity were characteristic of the Hanseatic patriciate; rarely was it forced to bow to the rule of a popular government, and never, as in Flanders and Italy, for long periods of time. And never was it easy for outsiders to enter the circle of the elite.

By the late 1380s Sivert and Hildebrand were operating in Bruges. Here Hanseatic merchants rented lodgings or houses from Flemish landlords who served as interpreters and brokers, and who were legally responsible both toward and for their guests—an arrangement which caused endess friction. In the other three Hanseatic agencies, the merchants lived in walled enclaves, but in Bruges the Hanseatic Kontor owned no buildings. Members lived dispersed in the city, and meetings were held in the refectory of the Carmelite monastery.

Hildebrand and Sivert probably participated in debates over the question of whether to conduct one of the Hansa's periodic boycotts against Flanders. Ten years before, in 1378, in retaliation for various grievances, the Kontor had decided to leave the city secretly and set itself up in Dordrecht. But the plan leaked out. All the Hanseatic merchants were arrested, their goods were seized, and the Kontor had to submit and remain in Bruges. The revolutionary movement led by Philip van Artevelde intervened before the Hanseatic Diet could take action. Commerce was disrupted between the German cities and Flanders for several years. This was followed by counterrevolution in 1382 and the take-over of the County of Flanders by Philip the Bold, duke of Burgundy. When the Hanseatics returned to Bruges, they presented Philip with a list of demands: not only money indemnities for the seizure of the merchants' persons and goods, but a chapel to be erected by the city of Bruges where perpetual masses would be said in memory

Hanseatic Commerce in Europe

of Hanseatic merchants who had been killed in the disorders. The demands were not met, and in 1388 a diet at Lübeck decreed that the blockade should take place. The Kontor quit Bruges and moved to Dordrecht, where two years later Hildebrand Veckinchusen is recorded as buying two bolts of cloth and twelve barrels of wine which he shipped to Estonia.

The quarrel with Flanders ended in 1392, after four years of negotiations, the Hansa settling for official apologies and pilgrimages to Rome, Compostella, and the Holy Land by Flemish officials. The Kontor returned to Bruges, and in 1394 Hildebrand was elected one of the six aldermen of the agency, two of whom were chosen every year to represent each of three geographic areas, Lübeck-Saxony, Westphalia-Prussia, and Gotland-Livonia (Estonia). That same year he was entrusted with another office, as a member of a committee delegated to inspect the Kontor's scales. Together with the mayor of Bruges, two jurors, two toll-collectors, a gauge master, and a weigher, he was invested with the task of testing the agency's twenty-four silver weights, which were kept in the Minorite cloister. In 1395, Sivert's name appeared in Bruges' records, selling his share in three houses which he owned with three other merchants, near the St. Giles Bridge.

In 1398 Hildebrand was reelected alderman, and left Bruges to get married. A third brother, Caesar, a member of the town council of Reval, acted as matchmaker. The bride was fifteen-year-old Margarete Witte of Riga, pretty, well brought up, and accompanied by a dowry of furniture, jewels, and 200 pounds in cash. In addition, her father, Engelbrecht Witte, contracted to pay 100 marks to the groom at Witte's own discretion, an ambiguous provision that clouded relations between father-in-law and son-in-law until Witte's death, although they continued to do business together. The sum was never paid. Hildebrand claimed it, Witte refused; when Margarete's mother died, Hildebrand made a claim on her estate for the 100 marks which, according to his calculations, had grown considerably on compound interest.

The couple were married in Riga, but Hildebrand did not stay there long, apparently because of trouble with his in-laws; the following March, he was in Novgorod, where he appeared with thirteen bolts of Ypres cloth to sell for furs.

Hildebrand probably arrived at that remote northern outpost on the Volkhov River in the autumn of 1398, having traveled overland from Riga via Pskov, with the contingent of merchants, who had come to Novgorod to spend the winter. Another band of traders appeared after the spring thaw and left at the end of summer. The two parties—sometimes there were as many as two hundred in a group—were not ordinarily allowed to overlap their stays, and the Kontor was vacant for a period in the spring and in the fall. The merchants had a choice of two routes: overland from Riga, or (the ancient Viking Gotlander route) by sea to the mouth of the Neva, where they loaded their merchandise onto light river craft to

Wisby, the Hanseatic stronghold on the Baltic island of Gotland, east of Sweden, from which the North German merchants first sailed to Novgorod, the ancient Viking capital of northern Russia, on the Volkhov River. (Trustees of the British Museum)

be guided by Russian pilots up the pirate-infested stream to Lake Ladoga, thence down the perilous rapids-filled Volkhov, with frequent portages, to Novgorod.

Novgorod was one of the most exotic as well as one of the northernmost commercial centers in Europe, a trading republic in the midst of a vast country of forest and marsh covered with snow for half the year. It served as a sort of northern Champagne Fair for German merchants from the Baltic who brought western European manufactured goods to exchange with trading partners who included Russian fur trappers from Carelia and Smolensk, and traveling middlemen carrying products from the Far East by way of the Black Sea and Kiev. In this alien place the Germans lived a garrison life in a walled enclosure, the Peterhof, facing the marketplace, on the right bank of the Volkhov River, and accessible by a single gate. Inside were the Church of St. Peter, barracks, a meeting hall, warehouses, a bathhouse, a malt factory, the priest's house, and the prison. All business was conducted within the enclosure. During the day Russians were admitted to buy and sell, but at night the gate was locked and watch dogs roamed the yard. The archives and coffers of the community were nightly deposited in the church, along with the most valuable merchandise (there were strict injunctions not to pile goods on the altar). The German merchants retired to their barracks, the clerks and apprentices to theirs, to spend the long Russian evenings in talk and drink, in moderation, for in the strict discipline of the Peterhof, excess was severely punished by fines and imprisonment.

Furs reached the agency in an almost infinite variety. The most valuable was sable, then marten (widely enough distributed to serve as a monetary unit), then castor and ermine, lynx, otter, and finally, squirrel and rabbit. Skins were designated by origin, or by color, or by quality. Each two bolts of Hildebrand's Ypres cloth bought a thousand fine skins. These were carefully packed in a huge barrel and shipped to a business associate, Johannes Stoltevot, in Reval. Stoltevot sent them on to Sivert, who, after himself serving a term as alderman in Bruges in 1399, had settled in Lübeck.

How long Hildebrand remained in Novgorod is not known; a year later he had traveled the thousand miles back to Bruges. His brother Sivert, in Lübeck, sent a shipment of cloth to Dorpat to a brother-in-law, who sold it and bought 15,000 skins with the proceeds. These he dispatched westward to Bruges, to Hildebrand, who had brought his wife from Riga and taken up permanent residence in Flanders; Hildebrand had become a citizen of Lübeck, appearing subsequently in Bruges as a representative of the Hanseatic capital.

These transactions, bringing cloth from Flanders to Novgorod and furs from Novgorod via Reval to Lübeck, then cloth to Dorpat and furs back to Bruges, comprehended one important axis of Hanseatic trade, linking the North Sea and Baltic routes in a continuous flow of traffic. Like the Mediterranean in the south, the two northern seas provided a highway for the exchange of goods between East and West. The advanced West supplied chiefly manufactured goods, the underdeveloped East raw materials. Two other areas of North German commerce, England and Scandinavia, were never visited by the Veckinchusens in person, though they had correspondents there. The brothers also extended their orbit south, to South Germany and to Venice.

Neither the Veckinchusens nor the other Hanseatic merchants operated on the scale of the Italian companies, but nevertheless, they carried on long-distance trade, with an extensive use of credit. In earlier days, German merchants had customarily traveled with their goods, usually in company with other businessmen from the same city, but by the Veckinchusens' time they had become increasingly sedentary, though not to the extent of their Italian counterparts. Sometimes they did business alone, with hired agents traveling for them, but often they formed sleeping partnerships similar to the Italians' commenda.

Hildebrand found his family connections indispensable: Sivert in Lübeck and later in Cologne; another brother, a brother-in-law, and a father-in-law in Riga; a second brother-in-law in Dorpat: nephews available to travel to Venice and to Estonia. These relations could buy, pack, and ship goods to Bruges and could attend to the sale of the merchandise he sent them. In addition, Hildebrand had a number of salaried employees, couriers, carters, sailors, and apprentices. The couriers sometimes carried merchandise as well as letters. Apprentices traveled, too. They were usually hired for a specific period, their wages paid in cash or clothing or both; sometimes they had to post a bond as security, particularly if large sums passed through their hands.

From Bruges, Hildebrand traded in all directions: east, to Holland, Hamburg, and Lübeck, Riga, Dorpat, Luneburg, Reval, Wismar, and Stettin; west, to the cities of Flanders; south, to Nuremberg, Strasbourg, Frankfurt-am-Main, Constance, Aachen, and Cologne. His commercial contracts encompassed Italy, especially Venice; France (Bordeaux, Bayonne, La Rochelle, and Rouen); and England (London and Boston). The merchandise in which he dealt was as varied as the markets in which he sold. Flanders furnished cloth; Russia, Estonia, and Prussia supplied furs, wax, wood, and grain; from South Germany came wine; Sweden provided copper, iron, and lead. Salt came from the Bay of Biscay; silk, spices, sugar, alum, and incense from Italy; dried cod from Norway; salt herring from Scania, the peninsula at the southern tip of Sweden; linen from Westphalia; beer from Hamburg. Precious amber, used principally for making rosaries, he bought from the Teutonic Knights in Koenigsberg, who had a monopoly on this fossil resin, which was found along the peninsula of Samland, near that city. Sometimes products arrived by land, but more often by water, carried for the most part in a ship that was characteristic of the Hansa, a large shallow "cog" about 100 feet long and 23 wide, powered by a single sail, and capable of carrying more than 100 *last*—about 220 tons.

Hildebrand's commerce was not only in merchandise but in credit operations; he dealt in letters of exchange, accepting sums in Flemish currency from merchants who were traveling to Lübeck, Danzig, Cologne, and London, and giving them letters to business associates in those cities who furnished them with local currency. In Lübeck, Frankfurt-am-Main, and Cologne, Sivert carried on a similar activity, and occasionally lent money. When a Hansetag was scheduled for Lübeck in 1407 and the representative from Riga, Tideman van Nyenlo, needed an advance on his expense money, Sivert lent him 200 marks in Riga currency, to be paid in Dorpat.

The Veckinchusens thus made extensive use of credit, which had been an important factor in Hanseatic commerce since the thirteenth century, when the Germans were exposed to Italian business methods at the Champagne Fairs, and in Bruges, London, and Cologne. But though credit had proved indispensable to the development of the Hansa, and though Hanseatic merchants perforce used it, at heart they distrusted it. They moralized that credit caused instability of prices and encouraged recklessness and dishonesty. Hanseatics were never bankers, and their occasional attempts to open banks invariably failed. Conservatism was partly responsible for the Hansa's narrow hostility to a practice without which trade could not flourish and expand, a shortsighted attitude which eventually became a severe handicap to Hanseatic merchants. Resistance to foreign competition was another element; the Hansa wanted its members to shun credit arrangements and partnerships with foreigners, and thus to avoid sharing the precious Hanseatic privileges on which North German prosperity was founded. Again and again, particularly in the fifteenth and sixteenth centuries, towns, agencies, and diets legislated against credit transactions with foreigners.

In Hildebrand Veckinchusen's time this antipathy had not yet reached its height. When, after several years of prosperity, Hildebrand became involved in financial difficulties, his plight seemed to vindicate the Hansa's phobia about credit. Overreaching ambition, rash borrowing, and unwise investment were certainly partly to blame. But in addition, the second decade of the fifteenth century began a period of recession for the Hanseatic world. The causes included class turmoil in the Hanseatic cities, a ban on trade with Venice decreed by Holy Roman Emperor Sigismund in 1417, and war between the Hansa and Castile, beginning in 1419 and lasting for more than two decades. In the economic sphere, a saturated market for luxury goods, a shortage of money, and tight credit were probably aftereffects of the depression of the fourteenth century.

Hildebrand had rented a house in Bruges in 1402, with a shop, living quarters, and storerooms. Here he and his wife lived and raised seven children. Conservative Sivert, worried about his brother's extravagances in the heady atmosphere of the sophisticated western metropolis, repeatedly admonished him to be prudent. "I've warned you again and again that your stakes are too high," he wrote. He urged Hildebrand to rejoin him in Lübeck. The Livonian relatives, on their part, importuned Hildebrand to buy a house in Riga. But the luxury and elegance of Bruges and its alluring business opportunities kept him in that city. In 1417 reverses caused him to send Margarete and the children to Lübeck where he owned a house and where living was cheaper; but he himself stayed on.

Sivert, who had managed to attain a position of respectable wealth in Lübeck, was presently in trouble of a different kind. Lübeck had experienced tremors of social upheaval in 1380 and again in 1384, in the so-called Bone-Cutters' Revolutions, led by the butchers, and both quickly put down. In 1408 an eruption took place that threatened the Hansa itself. It was the same sort of class war that had shaken the cities of Italy and Flanders—an attempt

The Customs House at Bruges, where the Veckinchusen brothers began operating in the 1380s. Here cargoes were weighed and merchants paid duty before going on to unload in the Grand' Place.

by the guilds and the artisans to wrest from the entrenched patricians a share in the government.

In Lübeck, as had so often happened elsewhere, trouble started with a financial crisis. In 1405 the town council needed additional funds; the guilds insisted, in return for their compliance in new taxes, that a commission of sixty members be set up to consult with the council on financial questions. The council gave in; the commission was formed and became the weapon of the malcontents. It drew up a long list of grievances against the council, such as its excessive expenditures, its attacks on the rights of the guilds, and its taxes favoring the rich. The commission demanded radical constitutional reforms, giving the guilds a part in electing the councillors. After a bitter struggle the council yielded (1408). Fifteen diehards among the twenty-three members of the Old Council forthwith left the city. The commission proceeded to elect a New Council of twenty-four members, in which the guilds were represented equally with the patricians.

Sivert Veckinchusen was elected to the New Council; but his sympathies were with the exiles. He had, in fact, recently been admitted to the exclusive Society of the Circle, the power center of Lübeck. In April 1409 he slipped out of town and rode to Cologne; just before Christmas his wife joined him there. He remained in self-imposed exile, while the New and Old Councils battled for recognition by the Hansa and the Holy Roman emperor, under whose sovereignty Lübeck stood, as an Imperial City. With Lübeck in chaos, the Hansa was without a "head." "The community doesn't know where to address itself," the Kontor at Bruges complained. Similar revolutions had taken place in Wismar, Rostock, and Hamburg, and those towns supported the New Council; but the majority of the Hanseatic towns favored the Old.

In 1410, Lübeck was placed under imperial ban, and its privileges—autonomy, tax exemptions, revenues—as a "city of the Empire" were withdrawn. When Sigismund became emperor the following year, the New Council offered him 6,000 florins to lift the ban. Sigismund demanded 24,000. Apparently the New Council could not raise the money; at any rate the first installment, due in 1415, was never paid. Sigismund then canceled the arrangement and ordered Lübeck to submit to the Old Council; on top of that blow, the king of Denmark declared against the New Council and arrested all Lübeck merchants in Scania. The New Council gave in.

Sivert had spent a homesick and difficult period in Cologne, cut off from business connections as well as friends. His house and merchandise were in Lübeck—they had not been confiscated, like the property of most of the Old Council members—plus outstanding accounts and interest which he could not collect. The silkworkers owed him 1,200 marks; he wrote Hildebrand that he would gladly settle for a third of the sum. He wanted to buy a house in Cologne, but could not afford it. He lacked capital, and as a foreigner found it hard to get credit; it was easier to borrow 6,000 marks in Lübeck, he wrote bitterly, than 600 gulden in Cologne. The pressure of his need of money kept him constantly on the road. In 1411 he spent less than sixteen weeks at home. In July 1412 he was in Augsburg in such need of ready cash that he had to send a messenger to Bruges for funds; in 1413 he wrote from Luneburg that his traveling expenses were higher than his profits; in 1414 when he made a trip to Speyer from Cologne, he had to borrow 100 gulden from an Italian moneylender. He could not even clothe his wife suitably; most of her wardrobe was in Lübeck, and he could not afford to buy her a new one. He spoke enviously about a friend whose wife was kept "in the latest fashion." Meanwhile he followed events in Lübeck with anxious attention and kept Hildebrand informed. Finally, abandoning hope of recovering his position in Lübeck, in 1411 he applied for Cologne citizenship.

From Cologne, he carried on commerce with South Germany, Frankfurt-am-Main, Augsburg, and Italy, especially with Venice. In 1407 Hildebrand and Sivert had formed the "Venice Society," with a capital of 5,000 marks divided among five investors. Peter Karbow and the brothers' nephew Cornelius Veckinchusen were dispatched to the Italian city, whence they sent sugar, spices, cotton, and silk to the north, receiving in return English cloth, amber rosaries, and—most important of all—furs. At first the enterprise prospered. The capital investment rose to 11,000 marks in 1409; in 1411, Karbow wrote that he had sent off merchandise worth 70,000 ducats and had received merchandise worth 53,000 ducats. But after that things began to go wrong. The brothers were unable to control Karbow's activities; he bought unwisely, drew too many letters of exchange, and committed other blunders. Sivert, at first enthusiastic about the venture, began to cool toward it; he tried to persuade Hildebrand to drop it. "I wish I had never gotten involved in Venice," he wrote Hildebrand, and advised him to go back to the Flemish-Prussian-Livonian trade, "the good old places," where one could earn a steady income.

There were other mishaps. Some were the everyday accidents that befell merchants. A shipment of figs intended for Hamburg spoiled on the way and had to be sold at a loss. Wool cloth which Hildebrand transported to Livonia was moth-eaten. A shipment of rice from Bruges to Danzig was damaged by water. The goods did not always suit the customers: silk sent to Lübeck was not fine enough; oil and figs shipped to Danzig did not measure up to the prospective buyer's standards; a shipment of coral to Berg-op-Zoom was returned because the client no longer had use for it. Piracy and brigandage were constant problems. Heinrich Slyper, a Veckinchusen agent, was captured on his way to Venice and despoiled of 1,700 gulden by a robber baron.

Beyond all these minor disasters lay the fact that the market was depressed. Furs, the Veckinchusens' stock-in-trade, which usually brought a good profit, were not selling well. "Dear brother," Sivert wrote from Cologne in 1418, "your six lots of fish and the shipment of furs have arrived, but I am afraid I will not be able to dispose of them easily. No one wants to give 28 gulden for mackerel or 35 for turbot, and the furs are not worth 80 gulden cash; besides no one wants to pay cash for anything here. And according to your letter you paid too much for the fish. Today I sold on credit two thousand fine furs, payable at the next Lenten fair of Frankfurt, for 87 gulden a thousand. . . . I would have gladly given my furs for 80 gulden cash, not being able to raise any ready money. I don't know how to get back to Lübeck, with my debts. . . . I have never been so pressed for money in my life, and I don't know how to escape. May God help us out of this fix. . . ." Everywhere the market was glutted with the merchandise that the brothers were trying to sell: in 1416 figs and spices remained unsold in Novgorod, in Danzig in 1418 and 1419 alum, cloth, raisins, and almonds could not be moved; in Venice, amber rosaries went begging; at Frankfurt-am-Main and Cologne in 1418, fish and wax were sold at a loss. When goods did find a buyer, the terms of credit were often very extended—sometimes over a period of two or three years.

Undiscouraged, in 1420 Hildebrand took a flier in salt; learning that the annual shipment from the Bay of Bourgneuf, near La Rochelle, was canceled, he set out to corner the salt market in Livonia. His agent Philip Sporenmaker rode out of Bruges on January 14 to Cologne, Dortmund, and on to Danzig, thence to Koenigsberg, Dorpat, and Riga, stopping along the way with business associates for fresh horses, a change of clothes, and pocket money. In Dorpat he bought 100 lasts (220 tons) of salt for 800 marks, and another 50 lasts to be delivered to Reval. From Dorpat, the Veckinchusens' brother-in-law, Hildebrand van den Bokel, wrote that in Reval and Narva there was not a last of salt still for sale. Other merchants were soon alerted to the situation, and four days' ride behind Sporenmaker galloped another courier with similar instructions. He succeeded in buying 60 lasts in Riga before Hildebrand's agent could carry out his instructions. In the end, Hildebrand's Three Musketeers' scenario did not produce the hoped-for killing.

Hildebrand suffered yet another financial blow. He had been named in 1417 as one of six Hanseatic delegates sent to pay homage to Emperor Sigismund, in the name of the Kontor at Bruges. The honor proved costly; the emperor seized the occasion to borrow 3,000 crowns from the delegates. Back in Bruges, the Kontor promised to assume the loan, but years passed and Hildebrand still did not receive his share of the money; he was not repaid until 1421.

Ten members of the Old Council had returned to Lübeck in 1416, co-opting five of their colleagues who had remained in the city; these fifteen then named twelve more members, two from the Circle Society, five merchants, and, as a conciliatory gesture, five members of the New Council. Thus bloodlessly ended a revolution which had been carried on with characteristic Hanseatic restraint —no violence on either side. Meanwhile Sivert's wife died in Cologne in October 1418. Sivert wound up his affairs—he had already relinquished his Cologne citizenship—and returned to Lübeck the next year. For a time he entertained the idea of retiring to a monastery, but instead accepted his friends' advice and remarried, taking a young girl name Mette van Lune, who brought him a dowry of 1,600 marks. With that capital, he was soon back in business, forming a company to manufacture amber rosaries and investing in saltworks at Oldsloe.

In Bruges his brother Hildebrand's situation looked superficially sound, as evidenced by his election to another term as alderman. But where Sivert had succeeded in retrieving himself through marriage and fortunate investment, Hildebrand's business steadily deteriorated. When relatives and friends refused to advance him money, Hildebrand turned to the Italian moneylenders of Bruges, borrowing most heavily from a Genoese company, the Spinolas, known in Bruges as the Spinghels. Hildebrand rapidly became more and more dependent on the moneylenders, and his prospects of digging his way out of debt grew dimmer. He constantly importuned Sivert for loans. Sivert replied that money was short in Lübeck and he had none to spare. Besides, he was ill; he suffered from eye trouble, a rash, swollen glands—his letters were full of symptoms.

By 1422 Hildebrand's situation was so desperate that he began to contemplate flight. His idea was to go to Antwerp for the Whitsuntide Fair in May, as he did every year, and instead of returning

Salt warehouses in Lübeck. The Veckinchusen brothers imported salt from the Bay of Biscay. In 1420, Hildebrand, learning that the annual shipment from France had been canceled, tried unsuccessfully to corner the salt market in Livonia.

to Bruges, to head for Cologne. He forwarded some of his clothes to a friend in Cologne and had household articles purchased for him there.

Hildebrand left for Antwerp as planned, but he was outmaneuvered by his landlord-broker, Jacob Schotteler, who, aware of Hildebrand's financial troubles, guessed his intention. Schotteler, who was legally responsible for the debts of a defaulting client-lodger, wrote to Hildebrand in Antwerp urging him to return to Bruges and negotiate with his creditors, promising to mediate. One of Hildebrand's cousins who had talked with Schotteler warned Hildebrand not to yield to the pressure—the man was not to be trusted; instead, Hildebrand should invite his creditors to come to Antwerp. Schotteler pleaded and threatened, begged Hildebrand not to abandon him, insisted that he had always been a good landlord. Finally, in a contract witnessed by several of Hildebrand's friends, including the clerk of the Kontor at Bruges, Schotteler guaranteed his personal security. Hildebrand would meet his creditors, and Schotteler would help him wind up his business; if the whole affair could not be concluded satisfactorily, Schotteler would help him leave the country.

Hildebrand returned to Bruges, but matters did not go as Schotteler had promised. The discussions with creditors took place; however, no settlement could be reached. Hildebrand's letters to his wife grew less and less optimistic; they were full of anxious instructions: she should take good care of the children and see to their discipline and education; she must keep on good terms with their friends. In Lübeck, Margarete prayed everything would turn out all right; meanwhile she wept, and asked her husband to send her medication for eyes inflamed by too many tears.

By the end of the year, Hildebrand was in debtors' prison. As prisons went, the Stein, the debtors' prison of Bruges, an imposing two-story stone structure facing the Town Hall, was mild. He and his fellow debtors lived in bedroom-cells with curtains instead of doors so that prisoners could be subjected to surveillance. A prisoner had to rent his room; otherwise he lived in the common room, sleeping either on a pallet or a rented bed. He paid for his board—bread, beer, soup. The discipline was strict (somewhat like that of the Peter-hof); dice and "other odious games" were forbidden, except playing for drink at table. On holidays, the prisoners were occasionally given special leave.

For four years Hildebrand sought release, through petitions to the authorities and pleas to his relatives and his friends. Sivert and the Livonian relations excused themselves. Hildebrand's bitterness increased; he was sure that Sivert could help him if he wanted to. "I beg of you, do not write me so angrily about your brother and your friends," Margarete wrote; as for herself, she had found her broth-er-in-law's help invaluable.

At last, in 1426, Hildebrand was released, perhaps through Si-vert's intervention, perhaps because his creditors had relented or agreed to a settlement. He returned to Lübeck and died shortly after. His wife was still trying as late as 1433 to get the 100 marks of her marriage settlement from her brother, who replied that he had no money and besides the matter had been settled long before. Si-vert died in Lübeck early in the 1430s.

A grandniece of Hildebrand and Sivert married Hinrich Cas-torp, who became burgomeister of Lübeck in 1472. Hinrich shared a number of enterprises with his brother Hans, whose name a twen-tieth-century Lübecker, Thomas Mann, borrowed for the hero of his novel *The Magic Mountain*. Hinrich Castorp was, like many other Hanseatic statesmen, a notable diplomat. He headed the em-bassy which negotiated the Peace of Utrecht (1474), ending the An-glo-Hanseatic War of 1470–74 with a triumph that strengthened Hanseatic commerce and reestablished the flagging prestige of the Hansa, while hampering English expansion into the Baltic area.

After Hinrich Castorp's time, the Hansa went rapidly downhill. Competition had raised a threatening head even in the Veckinchu-sens' time, from the English, invading Prussia and Poland with their cloth; from the South Germans, who opened a new trade route on the southern border of the Hanseatic zone, preparing the way for the Fuggers; and especially from the Dutch, who man-ufactured their own cloth, rivaled Hamburg in beer production, and established their own herring industry, operating on the high seas with new large nets and specialized boats. The naval power of the Hansa could not compete with that of the increasingly powerful European monarchies. One by one the four great Kontors declined and disappeared. First, Novgorod fell to Ívan the Great in 1478; the Kontor at Bergen declined and disappeared; Queen Elizabeth closed the Steelyard of London and banished the Germans from the kingdom. But worst of all was the decline of the Kontor at Bruges, coincident with the decline of Bruges itself, torn by political upheavals which drove foreign merchants to seek refuge in Antwerp.

In the middle of the sixteenth century, an attempt was made to stave off the inevitable. An alliance of Hanseatic towns created a special officer, a "syndic," with the mission of reviving the community. To the office was appointed the head of a distinguished old patrician family of Cologne, Heinrich Sudermann, who set himself to reorganize the Kontor of Bruges, now relocated in Antwerp. He contracted to build a great center, the largest Hanseatic civil structure, where merchants could live communally and do business, as they had always done at the other Kontors. But the edifice was hardly finished when the disturbances caused by the outbreak of religious war bankrupted the Kontor and ended Sudermann's dream.

The decisive force behind the founding of many towns of the north and east and the expansion and prosperity of many others, the Hansa had provided northern Europe for centuries with products to sustain life and develop industry. Its military capability, though striking, has long been overemphasized. Less noted is the fact that the Hansa taught a remarkable lesson in peacekeeping. It pioneered arbitration and negotiation as a means of settling quarrels both among its members and with the outside world. On one occasion of crisis, Hinrich Castorp gave advice remembered long after and hardly out of date today:

"Let us assemble to deliberate; for although it is easy to pitch the tents of war, it is costly to conduct it with honor."

V

THE NEW
FINANCIERS

After the troubled fourteenth century, the European sky slowly cleared. The fifteenth century saw a regathering of economic energy, surpassing anything that had gone before. It was as if a team of strong horses, after blundering into the mire, losing its footing, and tangling its harness, had at last been set right, and with an open road ahead, was breaking into a gallop.

In the eleventh century it was possible for a robust peddler-saint to rise in the world, and for a soldierly venturer to win fortune by joining the First Crusade and looking out for himself. Two hundred years later a merchant could sit in his countinghouse in Genoa or Florence and invest his capital abroad, or remain in his shop in Douai and exploit weavers scattered through the town. Now businessmen's horizons expanded with a rapidity that brought personal success stories so spectacular that they put all previous moneymen's careers in the shade.

The middle of the fifteenth century has been generally accepted as the end point of the Middle Ages. The accidental confluence of the fall of Constantinople and the end of the Hundred Years' War, both in 1453, gave this date a particular attraction for old-fashioned political historians; scholars with a broader orientation have noted the proximity of the invention of printing and the first voyages of exploration. All four events are basically technological-economic; Constantinople and the English strongholds fell to the new artillery firepower made possible by gunpowder, metallurgy, and cash, while the Commercial Revolution created both the technical basis for ocean navigation and the motivation for seeking an ocean route to the East.

In the four events may also be seen the interaction between East and West which lay at the bottom of many of the elemental stirrings of the Middle Ages. Gunpowder was first known in China; whether it was introduced to Europeans by the Arabs or discovered independently is still in controversy. The lateen sail and compass likewise have Eastern origins, though the history of the transmission is obscure. The silk and spice trades of course had an ancient Eastern-Arabic history. Printing had been done in China from wood blocks for a thousand years. What held China back from the concept of movable type was the multiplicity of Chinese characters which, however, did not prevent movable type being introduced in Korea a generation before Gutenberg. How much of the Chinese and Korean inventions was known in Europe is one more tantalizing question; oddly, Marco Polo says nothing of printing though he mentions the printed Chinese paper money. When and where both gunpowder and movable-type printing first appeared in Europe has never been satisfactorily determined; both inventions seem suddenly to appear full-fledged with only baffling early references to suggest a history of experimentation. The important point is that the invention of both firearms and printing was probably inevitable in the high Middle Ages, given Europe's developing technology and the powerful demand, on the one hand for knowledge, on the other for weapons, supported by a swiftly increasing capacity to buy both books and guns.

Both inventions played roles in the giant explosion of European imperialism. Columbus annotated a printed edition of Marco Polo which helped him optimistically to misconstrue the size of the earth, and Vasco da Gama used gunpowder weapons in pushing his way into the Eastern waters where no European had ventured. Six years after da Gama's voyage, in 1504, no spices arrived at the Levantine ports for the Italian merchants to buy; the entire harvest had been preempted by the Portuguese in the Indies. Perhaps 1504 should be taken as the date of the end of the Middle Ages.

Despite this, and despite the fabulous adventures of Cortes and Pizarro in America, the overseas expansion was only one of several elements in the sweep of European advance at this dawn of modern times. Equally or perhaps more significant were the development of mining and metallurgy, the continuing growth of cloth manufacture (now become a major industry in Germany and England as well as Flanders, France, and Italy), the proliferation of commerce inside the continent and along its shores in foodstuffs (fish, wine, cereal grain) as well as consumer goods, the growth of cities (Milan and Venice had populations of over 100,000, and a dozen other cities were at least close), and the multiplication of schools and universities (Paris and Bologna of the twelfth century had been joined by Oxford, Cambridge, Glasgow, St. Andrews, Laon, Louvain, Cologne, Montpellier, Avignon, Grenoble, Pisa, Florence, Siena, Padua, and many more). Among the masses, literacy had vastly increased to meet the Commercial Revolution's need for clerks, storekeepers, supercargoes, notaries, lawyers, and other vocations, and among the elite, intellectual achievement was competing for status with military adventure and moneymaking. A new view of life, focusing on man himself, was beginning to compete with the old God-centered universe of the Church scholars.

Writers and poets had flourished throughout the Middle Ages; the fifteenth century merely added a few illustrious names—Villon, Malory, Alain Chartier, Commines, Machiavelli, and many lesser lights. But painting and sculpture blossomed with extraordinary vigor. Francesco Datini's fourteenth-century jibe, "Are they all brothers or cousins of Giotto?" seemed to receive an affirmative answer in the fifteenth and early sixteenth centuries, as Michelangelo, Leonardo, Andrea del Sarto, Botticelli, Donato, Cellini and scores of equal or only slightly lesser talents flooded Italy with a torrent of masterpieces such as the world had not seen since the Age of Pericles, if then. The no-longer-backward northern countries produced Dürer, Memling, the Holbeins, the van Eycks. Whatever other explanations lie behind the phenomenon of Renaissance art, the rise of medieval commerce and industry are surely decisive contributing factors. Besides their direct patronage, the businessmen of Florence, Augsburg, Bruges, and the other cities contributed significantly to the enrichment of that greatest of art patrons, the Church, whose revenues from the tithes of the masses leaped as the masses grew in number and improved in condition.

The Church's extravagances in art and architecture contributed to the Protestant Reformation, an event which some historians have tied to the rise of capitalism. The view seems foreshortened; capitalism had already risen. Whatever the economic roots of Luther and Calvin, the great tidal upsurge of the medieval businessmen—selfish, grasping, materialistic, daring, innovative, constructive—had gone beyond the point of no return.

17

Jacques Coeur,
the King's Moneyman

One spring morning in 1432 a tall, strong-featured, fur-capped burgher of about forty bade his wife good-bye and rode through the south gate in the town wall of Bourges. Jacques Coeur was setting out to implement a breathtaking project he had conceived entirely himself, that of taking from the Genoese and Venetians the rapidly growing trade in luxury imports to France.

Coeur was at the moment no rival to the financial magnates of Italy. He was a reasonably successful businessman who had inherited the fur shop his father had transferred from the village of St. Pourcin to wealthy Bourges, capital of the province of Berry, whose duke Jean de Berry was renowned for his free spending (one of his little luxuries, the illuminated "Très Riches Heures," gained him immortality among art connoisseurs). The duke and his court were lavish in their display of ermine, silver fox, and marten; even their horses wore fur as tournament trim. The elder Coeur established his fur shop near the ducal palace, in a street today called the Avenue Ducrot. There Jacques grew up; by 1418 the family had sufficient status for him to marry Macée de Léodepart, daughter of the provost of Bourges and valet de chambre to Duke Jean. Macée's grand-

Statues of Jacques and Macée Coeur in the palace that he built in Bourges. Macée's father had been provost of Bourges and valet de chambre to the duke of Berry, the province of which Bourges was the capital. (Archives Photographiques)

father, like the Rozos of Milan, had been master of the mint, and in 1427 Jacques joined the staff as an assistant to the new master, a certain Ravant le Danois. The mint by this time was no longer ducal, but royal, for the Dauphin Charles, driven out of Paris by the pro-Burgundian party, had retreated to Berry. The English army sought to use Paris as a base for a final offensive against the Dauphin in the Loire Valley, but instead encountered a check at Orleans (1429) which proved the turning point in the long second round of the Hundred Years' War.

Jacques Coeur was soon in trouble in the Bourges mint; his superior, le Danois, was accused of making underweight coins. Both men were fined and dismissed, but they succeeded in disproving the charges; their fines were remitted, and le Danois was given charge of all the mints in the realm. Jacques Coeur, however, did not return to his former employment. During the two years (1429–31) that Joan of Arc was playing out her epic, Coeur, behind the humdrum façade of his fur shop, was maturing his ambitious scheme. His fur business, which depended partly on imports from as far off as Russia, gave him an insight into the anatomy of long-distance commerce and a glimmer of the potential of the luxury market. Coeur was not the only man in France thinking of a direct trade link with the East. At this very moment an emissary of Philip the Good, duke of Burgundy and lord of the Flemish cloth towns, was reconnoitering a possible land-sea route from Dijon to the Levant. But Philip was a wealthy sovereign; Jacques Coeur was a plain man, armed only with modest capital and vast effrontery. The enterprise on which he set out that spring morning of 1432 must go down as a prime example of creative commercial genius.

His first destination was Narbonne, the busy port of Languedoc, where he boarded the "Narbonne galley," a large sail-and-oar vessel named *Notre-Dame-et-Saint-Paul*. The *Notre Dame* stopped in Montpellier long enough to complete its loading of merchants and cargoes, and set out for Egypt and Syria. The voyage was without incident; arriving in the East, Coeur cast what proved to be the eye of a Napoleon on that fabled battlefield of commerce. He took note of the kinds of merchandise available in the bazaars of Damascus, Beirut, and Tripoli, saw the Baghdad caravans arrive and their cargoes pass smoothly from Arab to Italian hands, and picked out the weak spot in the enemy's line. In their long and fierce competition in Syria and Constantinople, the Genoese and Venetians had neglected another potential entrepôt for the Eastern trade: Cairo, capital of a powerful sultan who maintained a ten-station carrier-pigeon service between Damascus and Cairo. Chinese junks and Arab dhows brought fine porcelain and other exotic products; sugar and cotton were available in the Cairo markets, along with rubies, ivory, and beryl. Cairo was also the source of "sultan's balm," water from the miraculous spring where the Holy Family rested on the Flight to Egypt, popular in Europe for medicinal purposes and as holy water. The silk of Mosul also reached Cairo, as did musk from

Tibet; incense; aloe wood; amber; indigo; alum, and cochineal, a carmine dye extracted from an Oriental beetle.

Italian merchants did business in Cairo, but they were less numerous because they lacked the privileges they had won in Syria. Coeur made the important observation that the Orient was long on gold, short on silver. If silver could be exported from Europe, gold could be purchased and resold at home for a 100 percent profit.

The voyage out had been without incident. Not so the trip home; off Corsica the *Notre-Dame* ran into a gale and was thrown on the rocks. The crew and passengers managed to get ashore but were unable to salvage their cargo, the Corsicans claiming eminent domain over all wrecked ships; while permitting the merchants to escape and even courteously pointing the way to the nearest port, they preempted all salvage rights, threatening to kill anyone who interfered.

No matter; Jacques Coeur had accomplished his mission. Back in France he set to work at once, exhibiting organizational genius backed by inexhaustible energy. The company he set up first had its headquarters in Montpellier, in Languedoc, using the port of Aigues Mortes, employing factors in France and abroad. To balance his imports from Egypt, Coeur launched a wool-manufacturing enterprise in Berry and Languedoc, selling his cloth to the Venetian market.

The flowering of Coeur's enterprise was favored by a major political event, the ten-year truce of 1435 which saw the tacit withdrawal of the duke of Burgundy from the Hundred Years' War. This gave Charles VII the opportunity to put affairs in his realm in order, principally by suppressing the bands of "scorchers," mercenaries for either side who had turned bandit. Jacques Coeur, close to the royal government by geographic propinquity and personal contact, planted his factors as fast as the royal power made towns secure. He made his success agreeable to the king; in 1436, when the new dauphin, Louis, married Marguerite of Scotland at Tours, he lent the money for the costly nuptials. His factors soon numbered in the hundreds; success bred success. He persuaded the wool merchants of Montpellier to build dyeing establishments, utilizing the madder of Provence; Montpellier at once became a leading center for finished cloth. To furnish a reliable water supply, Coeur developed a spring, enclosing it in an attractive structure which won such popularity among Montpellier's ladies of the evening that it was nicknamed "la Font Putanel," "Whore's Fountain." In addition to his own handsome house he built a splendid Merchants' Hall, a combination of hotel and market from whose roof he could see his galleys in the bay. A Burgundian knight, Jacques de Lalain, dining with the great burgher, was impressed equally by his richness of attire—scarlet hose, velvet waistcoat, gold chain—and by the "originality of his views." After dinner the munificent host offered his guest his choice of an array of jewels and gold ornaments to complete his journey, a sort of traveler's check by which he could obtain cash from Coeur agents anywhere in France.

One of his most important exports was silver, the high price of which he had noted in the Levant. To obtain it, he bought up crown rights to several old mines in Beaujolais and Lyonnais in the Rhone Valley. The mines, some of which dated to Roman times, had long been abandoned as uneconomical, which leads to the suspicion that Coeur may have used them less as a source of silver than as a mask for his real source, the silver currency whose export was almost superstitiously forbidden. He could buy silver coin in Geneva or Bruges, or even in France, melt it into ingots and pass it off as a product of his Lyon mines. Genuine or spurious, the mine operations were profitable enough to enable him to buy several houses in Lyon, where just as in Montpellier he at once became a leading figure. At his residence in the Rue Mercière he entertained the Lyon notables at a table covered with Syrian damask. He soon made valuable business connections. Often he was a silent partner in enterprises which he had set going but whose direction he left to others, illustrating a favorite saying of his, "*Dire, faire, taire*"—"Speak, act, be silent."

Another Coeur enterprise was born of the fifteenth-century information explosion. Manuscript production had grown rapidly in the century before the plague; now, like other economic indicators, it was setting new records. In several places in Europe experiments were going forward on techniques for reproducing writing by me-

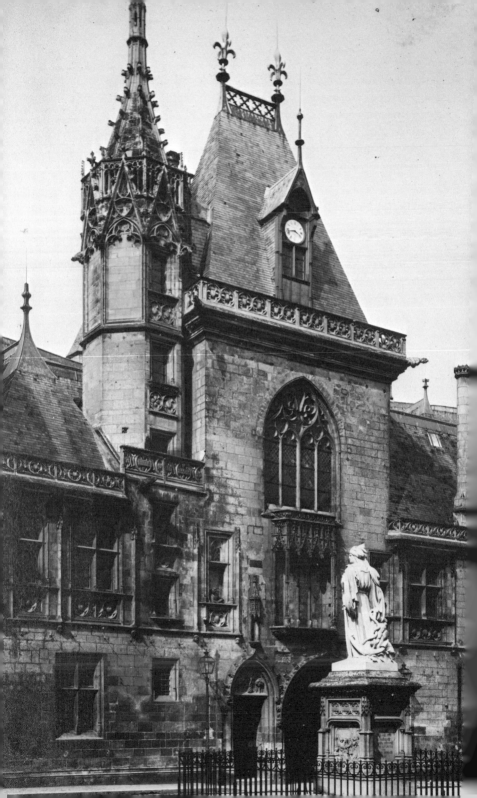

chanical means; even before their success, Europe exhibited an insatiable appetite for paper, the new cheap substitute for parchment. The medieval adoption of the linen shirt provided a source of discarded rags, basic raw material for paper manufacture. To take advantage of the conjunction of the two developments, Jacques Coeur built a paper mill.

Constantly on horseback, frequently aboard ship, personally overseeing his suddenly erected but far-flung commercial empire, he yet spent much time at home in Bourges, where Charles VII, no longer a dauphin but a king, maintained an alternate capital even after the liberation of Paris (April 1436). In 1439, Coeur was named *argentier du roy*. The title did not signify finance minister, but merely royal treasurer; Coeur had no control over the government's fiscal policy but only the privilege of supplying the king's needs. It brought him further honors; in 1441 he was ennobled, taking for his arms three cockleshells, the emblem of St. Jacques, and three hearts, with the device *"A vaillans coeurs, riens impossible,"* "For brave hearts, nothing is impossible." He was named royal commissioner to the Languedoc Estates, and in 1442 member of the king's Great Council. His brother Nicolas was nominated by the pope, on the king's recommendation, bishop of Luçon. For his merchant friends of Montpellier he won valuable royal dispensations.

In 1443 Coeur undertook an enterprise that proved to be his lasting monument for posterity: the impressive and highly original house in Bourges that came to be known as the Hotel Jacques Coeur, or Palace of Jacques Coeur. The property, known as "la Chaussée," backed up against the ancient, disused Gallo-Roman rampart in a fan-shaped plan, its outer rim on the walls. The name of the architect is lost; we know only that the work was carried out under the direction of a Coeur factor, Pierre Jobert. But what is evident is that the design was the master's own. Comparable to the great sixteenth-century chateaux in size and richness of detail, it was unique in conception, a new style in architecture. Where the Duke de Berry's palace consisted of five enormous rooms, fifty by one hundred fifty feet, all opening directly into each other, the palace

The Hotel Jacques Coeur, built by the wealthy burgher in Bourges in the 1440s, is comparable in size and intricacy of detail to the great chateaux of the sixteenth-century nobility. (Archives Photographiques)

of the wealthy burgher had a totally different architectural sense: fourteen principal rooms, the largest about thirty by forty-five feet, plus numerous antechambers, dressing rooms, and cabinets, each given an air of individuality and seclusion by ingenious arrangements of stairs and entries. Composed of four wings joined by stairway towers around a central court, the exterior of the hotel presented a double aspect—fortress and town house, like the little stone house of Isaac Jurnet in Norwich raised by several orders of magnitude. On the western side, resting on the old rampart, it was forbidding; on the elaborately decorated eastern side, inviting. Depicted in relief were many curiosities—portraits of the master and his wife Macée; the hearts and shells of his arms; mystic signs and symbols, exotic trees and plants, representing the Orient on which the fortune of the house was based; the family motto, "For brave hearts, nothing is impossible," with the central word *coeurs*, represented by two hearts, and "Speak, act, be silent," the other household motto, engraved on the central tower.

Everywhere comfort vied with luxury. An immense fireplace heated the dining room, a steam-heating system under the floor warmed the bathroom. The latrine was situated high up in the old rampart, the waste-water carried off into the soil outside. Each room had a name—the Chamber of Months, the Chamber of Winter, the Bishops' Chamber—and was appropriately decorated with sculpture and carvings. The Chamber of the Galleys contained a relief of a ship, with sailors rescuing a man who had fallen overboard; on the tower door leading to the kitchens a group was represented around a boiling pot. Adjoining the chapel were two small private sitting rooms for master and mistress, each with a window and a fireplace, the ceilings adorned with angels carrying the arms of relatives and friends.

The towers on the rampart, overlooking the plain, housed offices and miscellaneous small rooms. One, the Treasury, was guarded by a heavy iron door with a secret lock, and contained a piece of decoration which caused considerable gossip and speculation at a later date: a scene from the romance *Tristan*, in which Tristan and

Yseult meet in a garden, while jealous King Mark looks on from a hiding-place in a tree, and Tristan sees the king's reflection in a pool. A fiction circulated that the figures represented Jacques Coeur in a rendezvous with Agnes Sorel, the royal mistress—an absurd tale whose momentary credence is explained by later events.

In the 1440s, while the house was under construction, its owner oversaw the work only intermittently, distracted not only by the demands of his business but by diplomatic activity in the service of the king and the French business community. He undertook to free French and Provençal merchants from the tyranny of the Catalan pirates by a mission to Alphonse the Magnanimous; by judiciously mixing finance with diplomacy and lending money both to Alphonse and his brother, he won the king's cooperation. He arranged for the right to build warships for Charles VII in Alphonse's port of Collioure, in return for tax exemptions for Aragonese merchants in French waters.

In 1445 he intervened to save the Knights of Rhodes, whose island fortress was under siege by the fleet of the sultan of Egypt. Rhodes was an important base in his own eastern commercial empire; journeying to Rome, Coeur convinced the pope that the sultan should be conciliated in order to concentrate Christian energies against the more dangerous Ottoman Turks. With the pope's support he sent a ship to carry plenipotentiaries from Rhodes to Alexandria, where peace was negotiated.

The same year he moved his Mediterranean main office from Montpellier to Marseille. The artificial harbor of Aigues Mortes was silting up, while Marseille had a splendid natural harbor. To use it Coeur had to adopt a dual citizenship, because Marseille belonged to the independent realm of "good king René" of Provence, patron of the arts and brother-in-law of Charles VII. As usual, Coeur at once galvanized the local business community; his two powerful galleys, *Notre-Dame-St.-Denis* and *Madeleine*, carried Marseille merchants and cargoes of coral to the Levant, whither they had hardly dared venture before because of the pirates.

In 1447 he sent his most trusted captain, Jean de Village, to deliver a suit of armor, with the pope's permission, to the sultan of Egypt; in return the mission won valuable privileges for the French merchants.

An even more spectacular diplomatic coup involved the papacy itself. The long struggle among Rome, the secular princes, and the Church councils had led to an unseemly series of rival popes, or "anti-popes." The most recent was "Felix V," formerly duke of Savoy, who had abdicated his ducal throne in favor of his son Louis to take up religious meditation. He preferred to do his meditating in a castle rather than a monastery, and interrupted it with frequent feasting, or, according to hostile accounts, the feasting was occasionally interrupted by meditation. During one of his meditations Felix heard a call from on high and, without quitting his castle, announced his new papal title. Charles VII first seized this opportunity to extend his control over the French church, then supported the new Roman pope, Nicholas V; needing an embassy with plenty of fanfare, he called on his treasurer. Coeur paid for and stage-managed a mission which filled eleven ships. This impressive delegation first went to Rome, where it gained papal approval of Charles's actions in respect to the French church, and thence overland to Lausanne where the Church council was sitting. A bribe to Louis of Savoy, the anti-pope's son, smoothed the path to peace. The anti-pope agreed to put aside his tiara.

The amazing moneyman of Bourges had already made his personal alliance with the new pope by getting his twenty-two-year-old son Jean named archbishop of Bourges in return for financing the restoration of the Bourges cathedral. In 1448 the youthful archbishop made his solemn entry, and his father took the occasion to produce a memorable welcome lasting several days, with eating, drinking, and entertainment for everyone.

In the spring of 1449 the English broke the last of the truces that had made the stop-and-start Hundred Years' War last well over a hundred years. It was the last English mistake of the war. Instead of the antique French feudal levy, out for a summer's adventure in disorganized bands, that had clanked and bumped into disaster at Crécy and Agincourt, they found themselves up against a paid professional army, organized into disciplined echelons, and armed with high-powered crossbows and cannon. The transformation had more than one cause, but an indispensable basis for it was the cash loan of Jacques Coeur to Charles VII of the enormous sum of 200,000 écus —nearly a ton of gold.

Townspeople whose walls the cannon breached got a pleasant surprise when the troops broke in; now that they were paid regularly, the troops looted less. Rouen trusted the king's army enough to open its gates, forcing the English garrison to take refuge in the fortress. After a negotiated surrender, Charles made a ceremonious entry, accompanied by his generals, St. Pol and Dunois, by his brother-in-law King René of Provence, by the archbishop of Rouen, and finally by his argentier Jacques Coeur, who was *"monté, houssé et vêstus comme ledit comte Dunois"* (mounted, equipped, and dressed like the said Count Dunois). Coeur's armor was not for mere show; he had actively participated in the battles and assaults, and continued to do so as Dunois completed the conquest of Normandy that winter. In the spring a large new English army disembarked at Cherbourg. The outnumbered but well-paid and well-armed French won a decisive victory at Formignies, killing 3,500 of the enemy and capturing an equal number, who, the chronicler recorded, were "sold at auction, like slaves" (probably as speculations on their ransoms). Dunois took Bayeux in May and Caen in July (1450). Cherbourg remained in English hands. Jacques Coeur personally carried out negotiations with the English captain, Thomas Gower, who proved a shrewd bargainer—he held out for return of his captured son, the ransom of several English prisoners, and payment of the garrison's expenses. A project to capture Calais was canceled out of deference to the duke of Burgundy. The duke (Philip the Good) was inclining to the French side, but might be frightened back into English arms by a French presence in Calais, threatening Flanders. Apart from Calais, the English still held Gascony.

That December Jacques Coeur advanced "Charles the Victorious" another 60,000 pounds. Coeur seemed to be at the height of his fortune. Then, six months later, on July 31, 1451, he was suddenly arrested and taken, under a guard of the king's crossbowmen, to the castle of Lusignan. There he was placed under the surveillance of his bitterest court enemy, Antoine de Chabannes.

What had happened to bring about a reversal of fortune that resounded not only through France but through Europe? Like all such outwardly dramatic events, it was less sudden than appeared. For a decade Jacques Coeur had been the wealthiest man in the kingdom. Such immense and rapidly-acquired riches could not fail to arouse suspicion and envy. Fraud and alchemy were imputed to him; the mystic symbols with which he had decorated his house in Bourges and his Loge des Marchands at Montpellier were whispered about by the superstitious. The truth, that his import-export business had been launched at exactly the right time to meet a large and rapidly growing demand, and that he had pushed it with utmost skill and vigor, was not at all appreciated. Getting into the field ahead of all rivals, he had built up so large an operation— three hundred factors in France and abroad—as to discourage competition.

A tough-minded competitor like Jacques Coeur could not be unaware of enemies. His chief reliance was on his friendship, bought and paid for, with the king. But he sought to buy other influence by lending money freely to the Court—eighty pounds to Madame Aragonde, one of the queen's ladies, to buy a dress; four hundred pounds to the queen herself; eight hundred gold crowns to Jean de Breuil, admiral of France, for construction of warships; 2,980 crowns to Count Mathieu de Foix; thirty-seven gold crowns to Yves de Scepeaux, the dauphin's chancellor, and varying sums to the war hero, Dunois, to the president of the Parlement, to the Master of Requests, to bishops, bailiffs, councillors, and seneschals. Such openhandedness may itself have been self-defeating. Among the numerous properties he acquired, some of which were surrendered by their noble owners out of want brought on by misfortune or prodigality, was St.-Fargeau, fifty miles north of Bourges. The castle and dependencies were sold in 1442 by the marquis de Montferrat to the duke de la Tremouille for 21,000 gold crowns; La Tremouille did not meet his obligation, Montferrat repossessed, and in 1450 sold the property to Jacques Coeur. The millionaire did what the aristocrats had not been able to do; he renovated the tenth-century castle, adding a new tower (which bears his name to this day). But a contest developed between the new proprietor and the intermediate; instead of gracefully making a present of the property to La Tremouille, or giving it to him on easy terms, Coeur opened a legal battle to secure his rights. That added the powerful La Tremouille to an already formidable list of enemies among the Court intimates—persons he had injured directly, like La Tremouille, indirectly through his influence with the king, or merely psychologically, by his rapid rise. From Taillebourg, where Charles VII was preparing to attack the English in Guienne, Coeur had already got word to his wife and business associates in Bourges of the danger that threatened, taking the precaution to send the real message orally while entrusting the messenger with letters giving assurances that his "situation was very good, that he was on as good terms with the King as ever, whatever rumors might be abroad." The three Noir brothers of Avignon, trusted subordinates, hastily collected the most valuable merchandise and carried it to Avignon, papal territory. Similar precautions were taken elsewhere. When news of the chief's arrest arrived in Marseille, Jean de Village, whose sovereign was Charles' brother-in-law, "good King René," saved the galley *Notre-Dame-St.-Jacques* by a fictitious sale, and the *Madeleine* by an equally fictitious capture by pirates.

But if the arrest came as no surprise to Coeur, the charge under which he was seized did. The accusation was that he had poisoned the king's mistress, the beautiful Agnes Sorel.

Agnes, who had become Charles's favorite in the 1430s, had presented the king with four children, the last just before her death in his castle of Anneville, near Jumièges, during the Normandy campaign. She had journeyed thither from Bourges, despite advanced pregnancy, in order to deliver to the king a mysterious message, purporting to be an intercepted communication from the Dauphin Louis to Jacques Coeur, disclosing a conspiracy by young Louis and Coeur against the king and the Court. The king trusted Coeur enough to show him the letter; the moneyman at once pro-

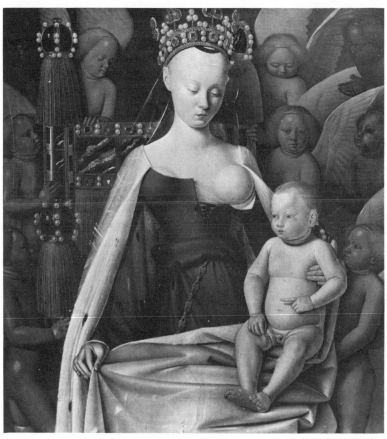

Agnes Sorel, mistress of King Charles VII, depicted as the Holy Virgin, by Fouquet. (Archives Photographiques)

nounced it a forgery. The king accepted the explanation but nevertheless had the letter read in Council, where it was received by Coeur's enemies with real or affected suspicion. The Dauphin Louis was known to be hungry for power; the letter spoke of assassination and enlisting the support of the English. When Agnes died, following the birth of her child, apparently of childbed fever, several of Coeur's court rivals seized the opportunity to form a cabal. The chief conspirators were Antoine de Chabannes, an ex-captain of "scorchers" who had married an heiress, won an amnesty from the king, and become a royal councillor, and Otto Castellani, royal treasurer for Toulouse, who coveted Coeur's position. Chabannes and Castellani enlisted Antoinette de Maignelais, a young cousin of Agnes whom the old favorite had introduced to her royal lover as a successor. As witness they brought forward Jeanne de Mortagne, a lady of the court who had attended Agnes in her last illness.

Coeur awaited trial by the Parlement of Paris without apprehension, certain he could clear himself before that impartial body. But at the urging of the cabal, Charles appointed a special tribunal, weighted with Coeur's enemies. Yet the evidence was too feeble to stand up even in a star-chamber proceeding. On her deathbed Agnes had named Coeur as one of her three executors; one of the other two was Robert Poitevin, the royal physician, who pointed out the impossibility of Agnes' fatal illness being due to poison when the child to which she had just given birth survived. Jeanne de Mortagne, the prosecution's chief witness, fell into a series of contradictions and ended by confessing perjury.

But Coeur's enemies refused to give up. They concocted a set of fresh charges: that the prisoner had accepted bribes as a royal official, that he had impressed citizens to serve in his galleys, that he had exported silver to the Saracens, that he had once ordered the return of a Christian slave to the Saracens, that he had given a suit of armor to the sultan of Egypt.

In themselves these allegations hardly interested the king, but the cabal successfully insinuated that in them lay the prospect of killing the goose and seizing all the golden eggs at once. It was the same temptation that had seduced the English kings with respect to the Jews and the Italians. The man who had abandoned Joan of Arc to her fate was not likely to count past services in the case of Jacques Coeur. Transferred from castle to castle and threatened with torture, Coeur was induced after twenty-two months' imprisonment to make a confession of guilt. Judgment was handed down on May 29, 1453; the prisoner was pardoned from capital punishment, thanks in part to the intercession of the pope, but sentenced to a "restitution" of 100,000 écus, a fine of 300,000, confiscation of all his goods, and imprisonment until the fine and restitution were paid. In vain the moneyman protested that there was no way he could pay the fine if all his property were confiscated and he himself kept in prison.

A solemn joke was added by way of insult. Coeur had to make public penance in the church at Poitiers with a ten-pound candle in his hand. The very same day (June 5, 1453), the perjured witness, Jeanne de Mortagne, also did her penance!

A little over a month later the French army, equipped and paid by Jacques Coeur, virtually ended the Hundred Years' War with the victory of Castillon. Pro-English Bordeaux held out till October.

By that time the affair of Jacques Coeur was in the hands of the procurer-general, Jean Dauvet, whom Charles appointed to confiscate the property. Dauvet proved an indefatigable collector; he traveled all over France—Tours, Orleans, Paris, Rouen, Bourges, Montpellier, Aix-en-Provence, Marseille—everywhere that the firm of Jacques Coeur had branch offices. He was pursued by endless calls from the king for money. In Tours he destroyed jeweled saltcellars in order to turn them more quickly into cash. At Rouen he arranged the liquidation of the ransom of two English lords, three-quarters of which belonged to Coeur, the other quarter to Dunois. At Bourges he held an auction of the prisoner's household goods, but—a remarkable testimony to Coeur's prestige in his native city—nobody came, even when the auction was repeated. Dauvet closely interrogated Coeur's majordomo about missing furniture, tapestries, rugs, pictures, and drove a Coeur debtor to take refuge in the church of the Dominicans at Bourges. Finding that one of Coeur's judges (and bitter enemies), Otto Castellani, owed the prisoner money, the incorruptible Dauvet forced him to pay up, and at once. In Marseille he attempted to seize the prisoner's house, but the town officials argued hotly that the house belonged to them, that Coeur owed the town taxes, and besides it was not *"une belle maison"* as his contract to become a Marseille citizen had specified; Dauvet, on seeing the house, was amazed at their impertinence, but wrote the king that he had found it more expedient to settle for three hundred écus than to risk losing everything to the stubborn Marseillais, subjects of King René, not Charles.

In Marseille Dauvet made contact with Jean de Village, Coeur's trusted lieutenant and able seaman, who freely assumed responsibility for two of the accusations against his master—he had urged Coeur to return the Christian slave More to the sultan, he said, and had personally presented the sultan with the suit of armor. On receiving Dauvet's report, Charles solemnly ordered the arrest of Jean de Village, which, of course, could not be effected.

Not till February of 1457 did Dauvet, estimating that "most of the execution" was accomplished, turn in his accounts. By that time Charles had long since distributed Coeur's estates among the Court, whose beneficiaries included Antoinette de Maignelais, cousin of Agnes Sorel and now the new royal mistress, who became Dame de Villequier.

Meantime the prisoner had succeeded somehow in escaping from the castle in Poitiers where he was confined. A letter from the king to Dauvet dated October 29, 1454, enjoined him to have "all the ports and passages" alerted. Whatever the means—bribed guards, outside accomplices—Coeur made his way to Montmorillon, thirty miles (fifty kilometers) away, where he took refuge in the Franciscan monastery; thence he reached a Dominican monastery at Limoges; from there he managed to cross the Massif Central and reach Beaucaire on the Rhone 370 miles (600 kilometers) distant, where he again found a haven in a Franciscan monastery. Across the river from Beaucaire was Tarascon, in Provence, outside France.

The king demanded surrender of the prisoner; the monks stoutly refused. The king's men patrolled the monastery day and night, anticipating a handsome reward for the prisoner's capture. They did not scruple to set foot on monastic grounds; one evening Coeur was suddenly assaulted, but the monks had provided him with a lead-weighted truncheon, and he beat his assailant off.

He wrote Jean de Village: "For all the love you have for me . . . help me escape, or in five days they'll get me . . ." He blamed the assassin's attack not on the king but on Castellani, and mentioned a threat of poisoning.

Jean de Village rode straight from Marseille to Tarascon. With the help of the Franciscan chapter in Tarascon, he communicated with the prisoner across the river, and learned that Coeur was more closely hemmed in than ever by Castellani's ruffians. Returning to Marseille, de Village recruited twenty reliable men—*compagnons de guerre*—and returned quietly to Tarascon.

At midnight Jean de Village crossed the river with his commando party; a prearranged guide on the Beaucaire side led them through a breach in the ancient city wall to the monastery. It was the hour of matins. Coeur was in the chapel with the monks; Castellani's ruffians roamed outside. Village's men fell on them with a rush; in the melee the monks assisted Coeur to escape. The entire band and their liberated prisoner regained the breach in the wall, raced to the river bank, jumped in the boat and bent to their oars, a single arrow from their pursuers splashing in their wake.

Provence was under good King René, but good King René was Charles VII's brother-in-law, and Coeur did not feel it prudent to test his independence too far. He did not tarry. Horses were ready; he galloped across the plain of Crau to a point where Jean de Village had a boat ready to sail to Marseille; from Marseille he rode to Nice; there an armed ship waited to carry him to Pisa. In a matter of days he was in Rome, where his good friend Pope Nicholas V welcomed him with open arms.

He was free. But his career as moneyman was ended, and he made no attempt to return to it. Shortly after his arrival in Rome, Pope Nicholas died, in the midst of preparations for a "Crusade," an expedition against the Ottoman Turks, whom Coeur had pointed out years earlier as the most dangerous element in Islam, and who had captured Constantinople in 1453, the year of the victory of Castillon. The new pope, Calixtus III, pushed Nicholas' project, which had the backing of Italian merchants. Within two years of Constantinople's fall, the Italian establishments were open again in Syria, but the Italians felt a military expedition would provide a salutary distraction for the Turks.

To command his sixteen-galley fleet, the pope wanted a man of resolution and experience; at hand he found Jacques Coeur, companion-in-arms of Dunois, experienced mariner, reliable friend of the papacy and above all man of resolution. He offered Coeur the command; Coeur accepted it, and as captain-general of an expedition that immediately attracted volunteers—Catalan pirates, who had lately been operating in the eastern Mediterranean—raided the Turkish islands of the Aegean. After a number of successful combats and a good bit of pillage, he fell ill either of wounds or disease, on the island of Chios, which a century and a half earlier had belonged to Benedetto Zaccaria. Realizing that he was on his deathbed, Coeur wrote Charles VII, declaring his innocence of the charges against him, calling for God's forgiveness of his enemies, and, getting to the point, asking the king to treat his children decently. He expired on November 25, 1456, and was buried in the choir of the Church of the Franciscans.

On the news of his death, his children petitioned Charles for restoration of the great house in Bourges. Charles gave them the house, a gesture he could certainly afford, but one which indicated how little he shared the vindictive hatred of Castellani and the rest of the Court cabal. He had pardoned Jean de Village, despite the rescue, and now made him captain-general of the French fleet!

Charles died in 1461. At once tables were turned; the dauphin, now Louis XI, made Jacques Coeur's son Geoffroy royal cupbearer, and sent Antoine de Chabannes to the Bastille. For a moment there was talk of reopening the trial, but that idea died quickly; in the case of Joan of Arc a fresh trial had merely dealt with affairs of the spirit, but in the case of Jacques Coeur there was money involved, and however much Louis sympathized with the Coeurs, he had no intention of restoring any cash or valuables.

Geoffroy Coeur, Sire de la Chaussée, de Beaumont, de Gironville, and various other places, married the daughter of the baron de Montglat. Behind this noble title was another bourgeois—one of the Bureau brothers whose cannons (paid for by Jacques Coeur) had won the Hundred Years' War. Other Coeur children made similar marriages; though the direct line died out, the descendants of the greatest of French moneymen, like the descendants of the Embriaci, the Zaccarias, and the Crespins, were all titled nobility.

18

Cosimo de' Medici,
Father of His Country

The funeral procession that wound through the streets of Florence to the Church of San Lorenzo on a February day in 1429 cost, by the reckoning of an admiring chronicler, three thousand gold florins. Behind the handsome open casket rode the dead man's two grown-up sons, followed by twenty-eight other male members of the family; then ambassadors, headed by the representatives of the Holy Roman Empire, the Venetian Republic, and the Holy See.

The man to whom this dignified homage was paid was Giovanni di Bicci de' Medici. He was a knight, with the right to wear golden spurs, and had served a brief term as gonfaloniere of justice of Florence. But he was no prince, and hardly an aristocrat; he had refused the title of count of Monteverde offered by the pope. "He was pious and gentle and assisted the poor without being asked," says Machiavelli. "He never sought after honors . . . [and] never set foot in the palace of the Signoria unless he was summoned there. Upright by nature, he refused to enrich himself at the public expense. At his death he was rich in property, but richer in the respect and love of the people."

Giovanni di Bicci had begun his career by following his father and older brother into a junior partnership in a banking house belonging to a distant cousin, Messer Vieri di Cambio de' Medici. Becoming a branch manager in Rome, whither a flood of tithes and other payments poured from all corners of Europe, Giovanni di Bicci established a reputation for skill and probity that permitted him in 1393 to found his own firm, with its home office in Florence but its principal branch in Rome. As junior partner he took Benedetto de' Bardi, son of a once-powerful financial dynasty now in decline. Though his family's capital was gone, Benedetto preserved its business acumen intact. A third partner who proved incompetent was soon eased out and in time ended his life in debtors' prison. The Vieri branch of the Medici family also ran out of talent in another generation, and disappeared into obscurity.

Giovanni and Benedetto pursued a business policy compounded of prudence, alertness, and thrift. They neither overpaid their employees nor lent money to doubtful clients. Profits of 10 percent did not discourage them, though they preferred 30 percent. They opened a branch in Venice; the manager, contrary to express orders, lent money to Germans, who were still considered bad risks by conservative Italians; when the Germans did in fact default the manager tried to juggle his books to cover up, but Giovanni soon learned the truth and fired him. In 1402 Giovanni diversified operations by opening a wool shop in Florence; six years later he added a second. After a number of years of operation it was discovered that the second made good profits and the first did not, doubtless because of bad management, and Giovanni closed the first shop.

Through the period 1397–1420 all operations of the Medici firm earned a total of 151,820 florins. A little over half this sum, 79,195 florins, came from the Rome branch, which acted as deposit bank for the Apostolic Chamber, and in addition handled the financial affairs of a number of wealthy prelates. The Rome branch's earnings ran to 30 percent per year and were so reliable that presently the branch's capital was withdrawn as not needed; papal deposits supplied adequate funds.

The figures covering the period are recorded in the closing of accounts which followed the death of Benedetto de' Bardi in 1420.

COSIMO PATER PATRIAE

Cosimo de' Medici, as adept at politics as at business, was hailed within his lifetime by the citizens of Florence as the "Father of His Country." This statue is in the portico of the Uffizi Gallery. (Alinari)

Benedetto's share of the profits had been one quarter, the rest going to Giovanni di Bicci. In the reorganization of the firm, Giovanni chose Benedetto's brother Ilarione, manager of the highly successful Roman office, which was now turned over to still another Bardi, while a new branch manager in Florence was also taken in as a partner; this was Folco d'Adoardo Portinari, a descendant of the family of Dante's Beatrice. The capital was set at 24,000 florins, of which Giovanni contributed 16,000.

The most important feature of the new partnership was the retirement from titular control of Giovanni di Bicci de' Medici. The new contract bore the names of Giovanni's sons, Cosimo and Lorenzo. Old Giovanni did not immediately relinquish the functions of management, but he gave the two young men, especially thirty-one-year-old Cosimo, increasing responsibility.

Tall, commanding, with an antique Roman profile, Cosimo de' Medici was every inch the patrician. Quick to grasp ideas, he was prudent in expressing his opinion, modeling his conduct on that of his father. He made it a special rule not to talk politics. While thus avoiding quarrels with his fellow patricians, he made sure of his popularity with the masses by openhanded charity, by discreet support of their causes, and, again imitating his father, by his geniality; he allowed himself to be seen chatting with workmen and peasants, whose company he professed to enjoy.

There was another aspect to Cosimo's personality. While old Giovanni was not uneducated, he was no intellectual, owning exactly three books, and those purely of a religious character. Cosimo had spent his adolescent years at the feet of Roberto de' Rossi, a Florentine Socrates who gave lessons and lectures in Latin and Greek, followed by walks with his students in imitation of the peripatetic Athenian philosophers. Drinking in rich draughts of philosophy on the walks and occasionally at the scholar's otherwise frugal dinner table, Cosimo acquired a lifelong love of wisdom and a lifelong taste for literature and the arts. Where Giovanni was an honest money-grubber, Cosimo was a gentleman in the world of finance. Yet humanism notwithstanding, he had both the taste and the talent for business.

His name had first appeared in the firm's books as titular head of the first wool shop (Lorenzo appeared as head of the second), but this was a mere ritual; his baptism came at seventeen when he entered the banking house and began his study of the recondite secrets of exchange. Working in the home office and abroad he gained the confidence of his father and the respect of his subordinates. From the same Bardi family from which Giovanni had taken two partners, Cosimo took a wife, Madonna Contessina de' Bardi. A conscientious and devoted bourgeoise, Contessina personified the old-fashioned virtues. She presented Cosimo with two sons, Piero (1415) and Giovanni (1421). A few years later, in 1427, Cosimo fathered a third son, Carlo, by a Circassian slave girl. Submissive Contessina made no objection to Carlo's eventual legitimization and entry into holy orders.

In 1422 Cosimo was named one of the six Florentine "sea consuls" stationed in conquered Pisa, a public office appropriate to his rank. His stay in Pisa was distinguished by the sailing of the first Florentine armed galley from Porto Pisano for Alexandria. On his return home he gradually took over control of the firm, so successfully that on Giovanni's death in 1429 the adjustments made in the reorganization were even more minor than those at the time of Benedetto de' Bardi's death in 1420. By chance Bartolommeo de' Bardi, the Rome manager, had also just died; Cosimo appointed a successor there, and added a new assistant manager in Florence. All branches, including a new one at Geneva, showed good profits.

Cosimo de' Medici seemed headed for a successful career of unobtrusive moneymaking, very similar to that of his father, only on a larger scale. But within a few months of his assumption of control of the firm, political events foreshadowed an unexpected, dangerous, and highly important new role for him. The businessman who had declined to discuss politics was now forced to accept a political role. He astonished everyone by adroitly combining statesmanship with business, ultimately carrying the Medici family to the forefront of the European stage.

After the proletarian Ciompi revolt of 1378, the Florentine oligarchy had regained power under the leadership of a strong man named Maso degli Albizzi, who waged a successful war against Pisa (and who persecuted and exiled the Alberti family). His son and successor Rinaldo waged unsuccessful wars, first against Milan, then against Lucca. Opposition to the oligarchy, never reconciled but only silenced, seized on the military failures to rally moderates. Left leaderless by suppression, this opposition looked for new leaders, and turned to Cosimo de' Medici, who now found himself forced out of his businessman's neutrality. In 1432 Milanese troops invaded Tuscany and defeated the Florentine army, and Siena and Genoa entered the war on Lucca's side. The demand for peace grew overwhelming. Cosimo and Palla Strozzi, another wealthy moderate, were chosen to head a Florentine delegation to a peace conference in Ferrara. News of the successful outcome of their negotiations was brought to Florence by two horsemen bearing the treaty and an olive branch.

Rinaldo, aware of the smoldering antagonism among the popular party and especially among the proletariat, saw the peacemaking Cosimo as the potential head of revolt; he resolved to crush it.

Cosimo himself held off, still hoping to avoid an open political commitment that might mean violence. As a precaution, he and his brother Lorenzo put several thousand ducats into safekeeping with two religious orders, transferred 15,000 florins to the Medici branch in Venice, and sold their Florentine government bonds to the Rome branch. Then Cosimo retreated to his country estate at Cafaggiolo, in the Mugello, north of Florence. There he received a summons to appear before the inner council of the Signoria.

Cosimo had precise details on Rinaldo's maneuverings; nevertheless he decided to answer the summons. He rode into the Piazza della Signoria, ascended the stairs to the great council chamber, and was at once arrested. He was conveyed to an apartment called the Barberia, a part of the upper floor of the palace used as a state prison. Two days later (September 9, 1433) he heard a confused roar from the square below and looked out to see it jammed with a ferocious crowd, demanding his blood.

Rinaldo was holding a *balia*, a special town council. This theoretically democratic safeguard in the Florentine constitution was a

wonderfully handy tool for any regime in power; by stationing ruffians armed with swords and daggers in the narrow streets and alerting his followers, Rinaldo filled the square with howling adherents. Under the pressure of the mob, the Signoria voted to condemn Cosimo, but only to banishment; until the sentence was executed, he remained in prison. He himself attributed his escape from death to the fact that his brother Lorenzo in the Mugello and his cousin Averardo in Pisa, also summoned to face the balia, heard of Cosimo's plight and refused to come. "If they had taken all three of us," Cosimo wrote in his memoir of the affair, "they would have made short work of us."

At that, his life was still in danger. Rinaldo, balked at his coup, kept the moderates at bay with a covert threat against Cosimo, who ascribed another reason for keeping him in the Barberia: "They thought that if, while in prison, I could not attend to my affairs, I would go bankrupt. But in this they failed, for our credit suffered nowhere."

Cosimo's friends and adherents continued to pull strings; Venice sent a special embassy to intercede for him. On October 3, after nearly a month in prison, he was brought once more before Signoria and told that his banishment was about to commence. The problem of safe exit from Florence immediately arose. Rinaldo, having agreed under pressure to banishment, could be counted on to recruit assassins to waylay Cosimo. Consequently the departure, though legal, was carried out clandestinely. Cosimo bribed two minor officials five hundred florins each; "Guadagni and Baldovinetti released me from the Palazzo on October 3 during the night, and conveyed me away through the Porta San Gallo. They were feeble fellows, for they could have had 10,000 and more for my escape."

Rinaldo, frustrated, warned his political allies that they would pay for their folly in leaving Cosimo alive, "for great offenders ought either to remain untouched or be destroyed." Machiavelli quotes Cosimo to the same effect: "One should either not lift a finger against the mighty or, if one does, do it thoroughly."

A friendly patrol escorted Cosimo over the Pistoiese mountains to the Florentine frontier. With a single companion, the architect

The Palazzo della Signoria (now Palazzo Vecchio), the fortified city hall of Florence, where Cosimo de' Medici was imprisoned in 1433. (Ente Provinciale per il Turismo, Florence)

Michelozzo, he rode north to Ferrara, and thence to Padua. Back in Florence, Rinaldo handed out rewards—the captaincy of Pisa, management of the salt depots, governorship of the citadel of Leghorn, meat provisioner to Florence. It was less a matter of spoils for the victors than patronage for the machine, as Rinaldo desperately worked to strengthen his still insecure grip on power.

Rinaldo's forebodings were well-founded. While Cosimo was being received with princely honors in Padua, at home in Florence his banishment served to make him exactly what Rinaldo had feared he would become, the hero of the dissident elements. A new military adventure, which Rinaldo sensibly opposed, was pushed through by the imperialist faction, always hoping for a successful war that would lighten taxes, but ended in another reverse. Pacific Cosimo became more popular than ever.

He decided to act. Driven to play politics, he played shrewdly. The papacy, with which the Medici had had close relations for forty years, was in difficulties. The wars had created three powerful mercenary leaders in central Italy: Niccolo Piccinino, Andrea Fortebraccio (also known as Braccio da Montone), and ablest of all, Francesco Sforza. Finding themselves unemployed, the three joined to rob the Holy See of some of its lands. The Romans blamed their government just as had the Florentines in similar circumstances, and Pope Eugene IV fled to Florence. From Venice, Cosimo made contact with the pope through his friends, and an agreement was reached. Choosing the most redoubtable of the three mercenaries, Francesco Sforza, Cosimo bribed the soldier of fortune to make peace with the pope and war with his fellow condottieri. In return the pope threw his influence into the scales on the side of Cosimo and against Rinaldo.

In September 1434, a new council was elected with a majority openly in favor of Cosimo's return. Rinaldo and his friends raised the specter of proletarian revolt, but the moderates refused to panic. Palla Strozzi, their leader, decided the issue by refusing to go along with a new attempt at a coup d'etat aimed at strengthening Rinaldo's power. Rinaldo again collected an armed band, but after some street fighting with Medici partisans, his bravos melted off in search of loot. The showdown was an anticlimax: a long, impassioned interview between Rinaldo and the pope at the monastery of Santa Maria Novella. Rinaldo argued and pleaded, but Cosimo had acted and produced; ambitious, underfinanced Rinaldo found himself deserted by his troops and rebuffed by the pope.

The Signoria voted the return of the Medici, the banishment of Rinaldo's family, and the appointment of Francesco Sforza as condottiere of Florence. On October 5, 1434, exactly one year after his departure, Cosimo reentered Florence, as quietly as he had left it, after dark, by one of the smaller gates, dismounting at the Palazzo della Signoria where, just as a year earlier, he slept with a guard at his door.

Next morning he paid a visit to the pope and returned to his own house. His friends had taken all necessary measures; the coup was virtually bloodless.

For the moment Cosimo accepted the insignia of gonfaloniere of justice but his power already was so great that the office was superfluous. "It has seldom occurred," wrote Machiavelli, "that any citizen, coming home triumphant from victory, was received by so vast a concourse of people, or such unqualified demonstrations of regard, as he was upon his return from banishment; for by universal consent he was hailed as the benefactor of the people, and the *father of his country*." Cosimo showed his prudence and foresight by using his perhaps temporary popularity to purchase durable security. He executed a simple but effective reform in the electoral system; in place of the lottery previously used he caused a committee to be appointed to choose the members of each new bimonthly Signoria. This committee he took care to fill with reliable men and had it awarded a term, not of two months, but of five years, renewable. He further demonstrated his political sagacity by sugaring the electoral pill with two measures of class reconciliation: he ended the bitterness between *Grandi* and *Popolani* by declaring all the *Grandi* who had not been banished to be *Popolani*, and he gave a number of lesser governmental posts to citizens of the lower classes.

Though continuing occasionally to hold office, Cosimo ruled Florence for the next generation entirely by the weight of his influence. "For thirty years," wrote Voltaire, "his counsels were the law of his republic." He was listened to because of his wealth and power, and because his counsels were sound.

Cosimo was far from being the first businessman to appear on the political stage. But he exercised power equal to that of sceptered heads of European states, without even removing himself from the world of business; on the contrary, he divided his wisdom and energies between business and politics with outstanding success. His policy was politically conservative and financially expansionist; the generation of his political power represented a period of stability and order in Florentine politics and the heyday of the Medici bank.

In 1435 Cosimo carried out a business reorganization. Giovanni d'Amerigo Benci and Antonio di Messer Francesco Salutati became his chief executives (Cosimo's oldest son, Piero, being just twenty). These men replaced the Bardi who had for more than thirty years been associated with the Medici firm; the fact that the leading member of the Bardi family was among those exiled on Cosimo's return to Florence makes it possible that politics had separated the two financial dynasties, Cosimo's own marriage to Contessina de' Bardi notwithstanding. Benci had served as manager in Geneva, Salutati in Rome; they were now made full partners in the new contract, which raised the firm's capitalization from 24,000 florins to 32,000. The capital of the Venice and Geneva branches was likewise increased, and an office opened in Basel, where a Church council was meeting.

The year 1436 saw another major decision. For years the Medici had used other Florentine firms to handle their business affairs in Flanders and England; these had now grown to the point where Cosimo resolved to open a Medici branch in Bruges. It was placed in charge of Bernardo di Portinari, son of the former head of the Venice branch. At the same time, he expanded the firm's cloth manufacture in Florence by opening a new wool shop, and purchasing a silk shop. A new branch office in the small Adriatic port town of Ancona was opened primarily to supply funds to Francesco Sforza, whose band was camped nearby. Cosimo thus held the condottiere in permanent reserve, in his own pay.

When the firm's books were balanced in 1441 following the death of Cosimo's brother Lorenzo, total investment amounted to 73,956 florins. Of this sum, only 32,000 represented the original investment of 1435; profits for the six years, including withdrawals, had amounted to over 100,000 florins, about 17,000 a year on invested capital of 32,000.

Cosimo determined to expand further. In 1442 a branch was opened in Pisa, where previously the firm had used the facilities of a Medici cousin Averardo. Four years later a branch was opened in London; Italians had retained a healthy apprehension about the English capital since the Frescobaldi, Bardi, and Peruzzi debacles of a hundred years earlier, and the Medici London office, managed by an Italian experienced in English affairs, remained modest in scale. The same year a branch was established in Avignon, which despite the departure of the papal court remained the most important commercial center in southern France.

All the new branches exhibited the sharp-eyed prudence that had characterized Medici operations from the beginning. In 1451, when the next major accounting took place, profits since 1435 were shown to be 290,791 florins. The rate of profit had remained remarkably steady throughout the whole period since Cosimo's return to Florence. Profits in Rome were 30 percent, as in Giovanni di Bicci's day, though for the decade of the 1420s they rose to over 50 percent. The branches in Venice and Geneva had done well, and the other branches had returned reasonable profits; even the office in Ancona, presumably in business mainly to sustain Sforza's mercenaries, had made 5,000 florins. The two wool shops in Florence had contributed small steady sums, while the silk shop had proven a rather brilliant success, earning nearly 20,000 florins in the fifteen-year period, or almost double the two wool shops' profits— another reflection of the affluence of the age.

During these years Cosimo guided the affairs of Florence no less successfully than those of his firm. In 1439 the council of Florence made the city temporarily the capital of Christendom as the patriarch of Constantinople and the emperor of Byzantium met the pope and the Roman prelates there in an effort to end the Great

Schism; their success was recorded—alas, overoptimistically—
on one of the giant piers of the Duomo. The same year war broke
out with Milan, whose bellicose duke, the last of the Visconti,
backed Rinaldo degli Albizzi in a bid to recover power in Florence.
A Milanese army invaded Tuscany. The Florentines now perceived
the wisdom of Cosimo's keeping Francesco Sforza in rations; concluding an alliance with Venice to help defray expenses, Cosimo
picked up the Visconti gauntlet. Sforza's mercenaries performed
doughtily, the Florentines won a notable victory on their own account, and a satisfactory peace was signed in 1441. Sforza got the
plum of the campaign in the form of Duke Filippo Maria Visconti's
legitimatized daughter Bianca. Cosimo backed his soldier of fortune,
establishing a new Medici branch in Milan to assure him financial
support, and brought about a diplomatic revolution; thenceforward,
Sforza as son-in-law of the duke and heir apparent made Milan a
firm ally of Florence.

It was a timely stroke. Venice, never a completely reliable Florentine ally, was splitting off. It was the moment when the Ottoman
Turks were threatening Constantinople, and Venice, with her special position in the Greek capital, wanted to organize resistance.
Florence, unencumbered with bases and privileges in the Levant,
had no difficulty in establishing commercial relations with the
Turks. The diplomatic chill between Venice and Florence turned to
the heat of war when Venice supported an ambitious southern
prince, Alfonso of Naples, in an invasion of Tuscany. Cosimo made
a rare appearance in the Signoria to reproach the Venetian ambassadors, then sent posthaste to Sforza in Milan. The ex-condottiere
gave invaluable support. Venetian diplomacy, active and skillful, enlisted the German emperor Frederick III and two small Italian states,
Montferrat and Savoy. For a moment the situation looked desperate.
To Paris Cosimo sent an ambassador to remind Charles VII of the
old Anjou claim to Alfonso's Naples. In the classic diplomatic pattern, Cosimo attracted allies by offering them the enemy's territory.
Charles's interest sufficed to check Savoy and Montferrat, and after
the battle of Castillon in 1453, a veteran French army crossed the
Alps and made short work of the Venetian mercenaries. The fall of

Constantinople the same year nudged Venice toward peace at home. Statesmanlike Cosimo granted reasonable terms. The Florentine populace accepted the sacrifices of the war no more enthusiastically than it had those of Rinaldo's wars twenty years earlier. "The citizens have raised a great clamor about the new taxes," wrote the Venetian ambassador, "and have uttered abusive words again Cosimo and others." The same writer added a few days later that two hundred respected families had had to sell their property to pay their taxes, and that "Cosimo had to proclaim that no one was to raise his voice in complaint, because he himself was going to advance the money, and that he would reclaim it only according to the convenience of everyone. . . . Cosimo has had to distribute daily many bushels of grain among the poor, who were crying out and grumbling because of the rise in prices."

Cosimo was ready to make peace, but Charles VII's relative René of Anjou, commander of the victorious French army, was eager to invade Naples and claim the throne. That part of the allied enterprise Cosimo now regarded as much too speculative; treating the French prince with all the courtesy and consideration in the world, he delayed action until René, bit by bit disillusioned, went back home, his irritation at his Italian ally just sufficiently appeased by the appointment of his son to a Florentine military command. On April 9, 1454, the peace of Lodi guaranteed the status quo with a 25-year nonaggression pact among Florence, Venice, and Milan. More negotiations were required to settle Alfonso, who was finally bought off with the promise of a free hand against Genoa.

Peace came barely soon enough to stop trouble at home. Cosimo permitted his autocratic election committee to lapse that year and in 1457 an increasingly independent Signoria restored the *catasto*, a tax on wealth that enraged all the rich. Angry opposition formed at once, centering among the hardest-hit parvenus. The masses favored the new tax, and Cosimo again put his reliance on their backing. He arranged for a loyal and energetic patrician, Luca Pitti, to be made gonfaloniere, and requested Sforza to dispatch a band of reliable troops to stand by outside Florence. Pitti arrested the heads of the opposition, extracted confessions of treason, and banished them; assembling a balia, he caused the electoral committee to be restored for ten more years. Cosimo, who had quietly taken the precaution of having his Milan branch rent him a house in Pavia, rewarded Pitti with 20,000 gold florins, enough for the gonfaloniere to begin work on a mammoth new palace on the left bank of the Arno.

The Medici firm was by now the largest in Europe. Few events of significance are recorded in its steady sway during the last ten years of Cosimo's life. The Geneva branch was transferred to Lyon, where a new cycle of fairs had been set up. The London branch moved to Southampton and eventually quit the country when a new wave of the chronic English trouble—defaulted royal loans, riots against the Italians, and seizure of their goods—broke out.

Elsewhere the Medici financial empire continued to enjoy stability. In addition to the branches (Florence, Rome, Pisa, Venice, Ancona, Bruges, Basel, Geneva, and Avignon), and the factories (the two wool shops and the silk shop), profits were made from distant correspondents in such places as Barcelona, Valencia, and Lübeck; indeed, the firm's ultimate dealings reached to Bergen and Moscow, one of whose recurrent fires sent up the price of sables sold by the Medici in Florence. The death of Cosimo's friend Pope Eugene IV made no difference to the firm's standing in Rome; Eugene's successors Nicholas V and Pius II remained steadfast friends and faithful depositors.

Still upright and handsome in old age, Cosimo de' Medici in the 1460s personified the apogee of the medieval moneyman. He had the kingly rather than patrician quality of democratizing without stooping. His palace in Florence (completed in 1453) and his villa on the Fiesole heights were built not by fashionable Brunelleschi but by more utilitarian but also gifted Michelozzo. Like his own dress (and his family's) Cosimo's houses made no outward display, because, unlike Luca Pitti, Cosimo felt no need for display. What he wanted was classic simplicity, copied after the ancient buildings of Rome which he admired, and which some years before he had sent Donatello to measure and sketch. The resulting Medici residence in Florence has been called the "first great palace of the Renaissance."

The Medici Palace in Florence. Classically simple and restrained in style, reflecting the tastes of Cosimo, who felt no need for outward display, this residence, completed in 1435, has been called the "first great palace of the Renaissance." (Ente Provinciale per il Turismo, Florence)

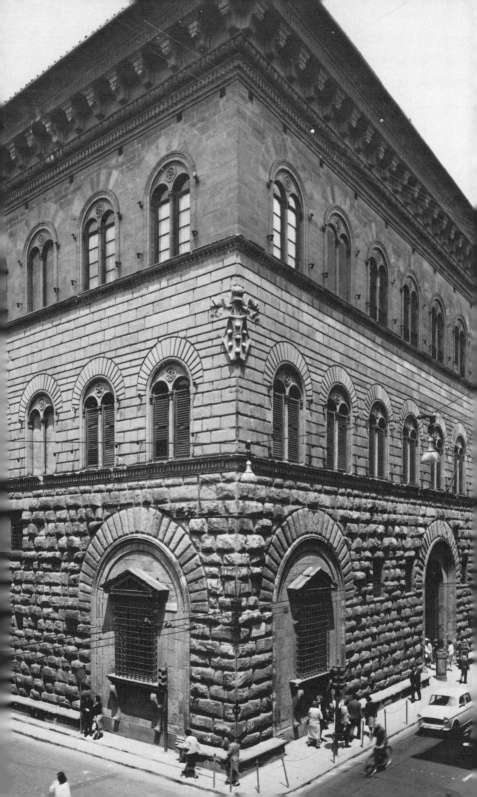

A guest at Careggi, the older villa west of Florence, was overwhelmed not by the lavishness but by the charm of the place: "It delighted me not only for the way the gardens have been laid out, but also for the wonderful planning of the house. . . . After dinner we retired to another room to hear Maestro Antonio sing to the lute. . . . I do not know whether Lucan or Dante ever produced anything more beautiful. . . . There were stories of ancient times, myths, poets and the Muses. When that was over a delightful little show was given by the ladies, the wives of Piero and Giovanni, a grown-up daughter of Piero's . . . and a few country women. They all did dances in the Florentine manner." Many illustrious guests stayed in the villa, including Emperor Frederick III.

A book collector since youth, Cosimo took advantage of the Church council meeting in Florence in 1439 to expand his library, and sent scholars to Constantinople, Chios, Syria, Rhodes, Egypt, and Athens in search of Greek manuscripts. His friend Pope Nicholas V assisted him by formulating a canon for collecting: theological works, first priority; Aristotle and his Greek and Arabic commentators, second; philosophers such as Maimonides, and mathematicians, third; humanist works, fourth. In spite of this severe program, Cosimo's library, which came down to posterity as the Laurenziana, included works of Boccaccio, Dante, Petrarch, and other recent and contemporary authors, as well as Ovid, Cassian, Livy, and other Latin classics. He also gave numerous books to monasteries and other ecclesiastical collections.

He appreciated artists as much as writers. The chapel of the Medici palace was decorated by Benozzo Gozzoli with frescoes depicting the members of the Medici family as models for holy figures. Fra Angelico was commissioned to decorate the monastery of San Marco, while Fra Filippo Lippi was paid to create madonnas which a critic described as seeming to ask for kisses rather than prayers. Andrea del Castagno painted one of the first great equestrian frescoes, of Cosimo's friend the soldier of fortune Niccolo da Tolentino. The works of Paolo Uccello, master of perspective, decorated Cosimo's own palace. Flemish master Roger van der Weyden, who visited Italy in 1450, was commissioned to paint a madonna with Cosimo's name saints, St. Cosmas and St. Damian, for the private chapel. Luca della Robbia fashioned terra-cotta reliefs depicting the labors of the field for each month, a work now in the South Kensington Museum in London. Cosimo recognized the talent of Donatello, an old democratic rebel, and sponsored his study in Rome. Donatello cast a statue of David for the Medici palace, the first bronze fountain piece of the modern world, and many other works, including a terra-cotta bust of Cosimo. So close was the friendship between patron and artist that Piero de' Medici had the sculptor buried by Cosimo's side in San Lorenzo.

Scholars too received patronage; in his old age Cosimo was comforted by Marsilio Ficino, a brilliant young man whom he had sent to Bologna to study Plato; Marsilio brought back his own translation which they read aloud together.

To the end he remained the bourgeois aristocrat, the latter-day Roman senator. A good father and husband (despite the Circassian slave girl whose son Carlo was now archpriest of Prato), he was especially devoted to his son Giovanni, whose early death he bore stoically: "Nicodemo [Tranchedini], don't try to comfort me," he told an old friend, Sforza's agent in Florence, "for I should shame myself could I not bear this, as I have often exhorted others to do in similar circumstances. There are two kinds of men who need sympathy in such cases—those who have not made their peace with God and those who have lost their heads." He allowed himself only the pathetic remark that his palace was now "a house too large for so small a family." He loved his grandchildren, too; an embassy from Lucca was interrupted when a grandson entered the room and asked his grandfather to make him a whistle. Cosimo took knife and stick and adjourned the discussion, saying, "My lords, know you not the love of children and grandchildren? You are surprised that I should make the whistle; it is as well that he didn't ask me to play it, because I would have done that too!" He acted the prince if occasion called for it, entertaining Sforza's son in Florence and at the Villa Careggi with tourneys, balls, hunts, mock combats, and torchlight processions. He married his sons to daughters not of the landed nobility, but of his own burgher class, not out of class modesty but out of class self-respect.

On August 1, 1464, Cosimo died. Despite his request that the funeral be kept simple, "the whole city," Machiavelli records, "followed his corpse to San Lorenzo," where the Signoria caused to be inscribed on his tombstone:

> Cosimo de'Medici by public decree is hereby declared
> Father of His Country
> He lived to the age of 75 years, 3 months, 20 days

Neither Florence nor the Medici firm was the same after the death of the Father of His Country. The glitter of Cosimo's grandson Lorenzo the Magnificent is misleading, as is his title, which is merely the normal appellation given the head of the firm in correspondence, as contrasted with "respected and distinguished," for the lesser partners. Lorenzo, who succeeded his grandfather Cosimo in 1469 on the death of his father, Cosimo's sickly younger son Piero, acted the role of a leading European statesman, bequeathed by his grandfather, with ability and courage. But he was less adept at business. The manager whom he allowed to usurp all the functions of the head of the firm proved incompetent, and Lorenzo was unable to restore stability. In 1494 Lorenzo's son Pietro ended through his political ineptness sixty years of Medici rule in Florence just as the firm reached the verge of bankruptcy.

The family had by then acquired such prestige, through the financial ability of Giovanni di Bicci, the financial and political ability of Cosimo, and the political ability of Lorenzo the Magnificent, that their less competent successors recovered and legitimatized the Medici rule of Florence as dukes of Tuscany, marrying into the families of the kings and emperors of Europe, and placing sons and daughters on many thrones, including that of the Holy See.

19

Cely and Sons,
Merchants of the Staple

In the 1470s and 1480s, the men of the Cely family divided their
time between their London house on Mark (Mart) Lane near London Bridge and the Tower, where lived many wool exporters, and
Calais, the staple town that had been the solitary English prize of
the Hundred Years' War. Richard Cely, Sr., the head of the family,
presided in London, while his three sons, Richard, Robert, and
George, shuttled back and forth to the Continent and made frequent trips into the English countryside to buy wool and skins.
Their ship, the *Margaret Cely*, named after the boys' mother, plied
the Channel to Calais, Holland, and Flanders, and down the Bay of
Biscay to Bordeaux, transporting the usual cargoes of salt, wine, and
fish. Its complement consisted of a captain, boatswain, cook, and
crew of sixteen sailors, armed against pirates with bows and arrows
and a small cannon.

One member of the family or another was nearly always in residence in Calais, sometimes the eldest son, Richard, Jr., sometimes
George, sometimes Robert, the black sheep of the family; and after
Richard, Sr.'s death in 1481, a cousin, William Cely. The young
men lived in licensed lodgings controlled by the Company of the

Staple, but with a degree of freedom of which they took full advantage. Robert was always in debt. He borrowed thirty shillings to pay his landlord and lost it at dice. His wife refused to join him in Calais, pleading the dangers of a Channel crossing, but evidently with other reasons; the next year Richard, Jr. wrote to George, "There is a division fallen between our brother Robert and she that should be his wife and he has given her over." A month later Richard, Sr. reported that Robert was in Bruges and was afraid to return to Calais for fear of action being taken in the Bishop's Court "for the lewd matter of Joan Hart." Joan, an English girl living in Calais, was pregnant and her relatives were trying to extort money from Richard, Sr., but the girl finally agreed to a settlement and even returned some of Robert's presents, including a gold belt with a silver and gilt buckle and pendants, a gold ring set with a small diamond, and a damask carpet. Four months later Robert wrote George that he had been sick and still had to walk with a cane, and asked George to pay £14   15 s. which he had borrowed from a London mercer.

George also had a mistress in Calais; in January 1482, when George had returned to London, his servant wrote him that "Margery" was with child; in August he reported that she wanted a new dress for her churching, the ceremony performed after childbirth, "as she had the other time." At the end of August the servant wrote that the child was dead. Richard, Sr. was apparently ignorant of this affair. But he was dissatisfied with George as a correspondent. "I greet thee well and I marvel much what is the cause that you send me no letter from Calais," he wrote, "neither thy brother nor thyself for the which I think right strange in so much that I am so worried about my goods recently shipped, it were great comfort for me to hear how you do and in what case my goods are in Calais." After Richard, Sr.'s death, the younger Richard wrote to George, "Our mother longs sore for you."

Calais was a half-English town. After its capture, many of the native inhabitants had been driven out, and their houses assigned to English merchants and craftsmen, like the family of Robert Cely's mistress. Calais had a good harbor, accessible from Dover and Hythe

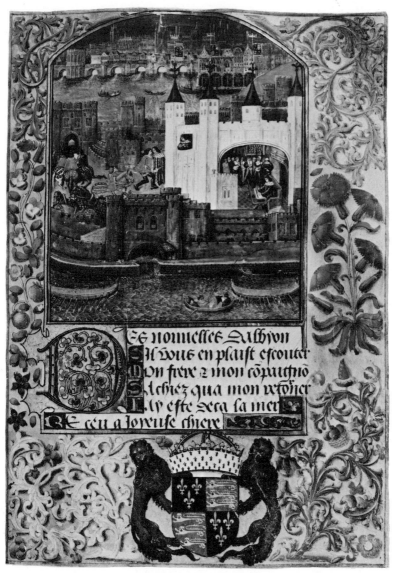

at times when the prevailing southwest winds made it difficult for ships to make other French ports. It was ideally situated as a marketplace for trade with Flanders. The town government was military, headed by a captain and a lieutenant.

The capture of Calais had been made possible by the loans of the Italian bankers, whose resulting bankruptcy had shaken the European financial world in the middle of the fourteenth century. The Italians were succeeded by a group of English financiers, among whom William de la Pole and Walter de Cheriton were prominent. Following in the footsteps of the Frescobaldi, Bardi, and Peruzzi, de la Pole and Cheriton were enriched and ruined in their turn. It was in their catastrophic wake that the true English moneymen of the new age emerged. Not great capitalists, although men of substantial wealth, their life style contrasted with that of the Riccardi branch manager who slept in Edward I's wardrobe, or the "beloved merchants" of Edward II and III.

The Cely family, representatives of this new class of English merchants, probably originated in Cornwall, but by the fifteenth century were settled in London, with a country place, Bretts, in Aveley parish, Essex, northeast of London. Social climbers, they had coats made of the livery of a distinguished neighbor, Sir John Weston, Prior of the Hospitallers, a decadent Crusading order (which arose from the hospital founded by Amalfitan merchants in the days of Pantaleone), even though they lacked any feudal connections with him.

The Celys were members of the Company of the Staple of Calais, a royally licensed monopoly set up at the beginning of the fifteenth century as a compromise among many elements with interests in the wool trade. The king wanted a closed company of merchants to have the monopoly on the export of wool in order to facilitate collection of export duties, his best source of income, and in order to borrow from them against customs receipts. For this purpose it was convenient to have a "staple," a fixed market where all the raw wool for export would be sold. A class of English middlemen, the "woolmen," had grown up, who bought from the monasteries and sheep farms in Lincolnshire and the Cotswolds and sold to exporting merchants. These woolmen wanted to keep foreigners from buying wool directly from the growers. They proposed that staple towns in England should be the only places where alien merchants could buy wool, thus barring the Flemings and Italians from their centuries-old practice of contracting in advance for the clip of the great abbeys and estates. Like the woolmen, the manufacturers of English cloth, growing ever more numerous and powerful, were interested only in the domestic market, and wanted staple towns in England. The Italians and Flemings were of course opposed; they wanted free trade. The English wool growers were also opposed to the staple, either in England or abroad: a domestic staple restricted competitive buying and lowered prices to the growers; a foreign staple passed on the king's export tax to them in the form of lower wool prices. English exporters like the Celys, who bought from the woolmen, wanted the Flemish and German merchants to be restricted to buying from them, and at prices fixed at the maximum. Formation of a staple company would enable them to travel in convoys and to wrest privileges and protections in Flanders.

Fiercely contested by the opposing forces, the staple went through a series of phases. In the 1290s, it was established at Dordrecht, in Holland, and later moved to Antwerp, where English merchants handled wool, paid the king a huge export tax known as the *maltote*, and loaned him money on their sales. This staple was not compulsory; wool was still shipped to Bruges and elsewhere, and the merchants were not yet a monopolistic company. Twenty years later the first compulsory staple was set up at St. Omer, moving about between that city and Antwerp and Bruges until 1326. For the next ten years free trade alternated with home staples in England. During the period between 1337 and 1399, a compulsory staple was gradually established again to finance the Hundred Years' War; at the end of that time emerged the Company of the Staple of Calais.

The Company of the Staple presented a compromise among king, exporters, middlemen, wool growers, and cloth manufacturers. It provided the king with a safe and secure source of loans. It satisfied the exporters by establishing the staple abroad in Calais, an

English town, and unlike the cities of Flanders, not closely con-
nected with any manufacturing area, so that no single group of
English merchants with connections in Bruges, Antwerp, Ypres, or
Ghent was favored, and no group of foreign buyers could conspire
to monopolize the market and hold down prices. Even the free-trade
parties were not dissatisfied. Foreign merchants were allowed to buy
wool in England, provided they took it directly to Italy by sea
without touching the staple market of western Europe. Almost a
fifth of the English wool produced in the fifteenth century was carried from Southampton, Sandwich, and London down the Atlantic
coast and through the Straits of Gibraltar (Francesco Datini bought
English wool this way). The wool dealers, growers, and cloth manufacturers, meanwhile, were appeased because the rapidly growing
English cloth industry provided an increasing demand for raw material. The high export tax paid by the Staplers to the king provided
English cloth producers with an unplanned benefit: low wool prices
in England and high wool prices abroad, an effective protection for
the nascent industry. Wool was taxed at thirty-three percent, cloth
at less than two percent. The years of the Staple Company's preeminence were accompanied by a steady decline in the export of English raw wool, while English cloth manufacture expanded and prospered.

In Calais, the Staple Company paid customs and subsidies
directly to the king, afterward collecting the money from the individual merchants. The Staplers had their own law court, which
handled all civil suits involving members of the company. They supervised the packing of wool, inspected it, and regulated its sale. A
certain amount of "old" wool, defined as wool brought to Calais before February of any year and unsold by April, was to be sold with
each lot of new.

Wool growing had itself undergone a small revolution during
the fourteenth century. In the thirteenth century, large-scale sheep
farming, both by monasteries and lay lords, was the rule. The
bishop of Winchester's estates supported no fewer than 29,000
sheep; the earl of Lincoln had over 13,000. Depression, the Black
Death, and the heavy wool taxes exacted by Edward III to pay for

his wars wreaked drastic changes; the great landowners, pressed for cash, leased their lands to tenant farmers who took over sheep-raising. The multiplication of wool growers complicated marketing; it was no longer possible for the agent of a Boinebroke or a Datini to operate by simply buying up the clip of a monastery or estate. The new class of English woolmen, which had evolved to meet the situation, circulated in their local districts, buying on credit, and in turn selling to three groups: the foreign importers, chiefly Italian and Flemish, who had formerly monopolized the English market; the English cloth manufacturers, once an insignificant part of the market, but now becoming important; and the English exporters, of whom the Celys were an example.

The Celys bought most of their wool from middlemen in the Cotswolds. In the course of the fifteenth century several families of woolmen grew wealthy, and built the handsome churches of the Cotswold market towns, Northleach, Cirencester, Chipping Campden, Stow-on-the-Wold, and Chipping Norton. Many of the woolmen were depicted on the church walls and floors in a unique English art form, memorial brass engravings, popularly "brasses," often with one foot on a sheep, the other on a wool pack, sometimes with their merchant's mark, sometimes with their wives and children, sometimes with memorial verses. William Midwinter, a woolman who did business with the Celys, is shown with his wife and four children in a brass in the Church of St. Peter and Paul in Northleach. Thomas Busshe, another Northleach dealer with whom the Celys had dealings, had a brass bearing the arms of the city of Calais and, a fifteenth-century visual pun, sheep hiding in a bush. Another brass in the Northleach church was erected to woolman Thomas Fortey, his wife Agnes and their four children, and Agnes' first husband and their children. William Grevel's brass in the Chipping Campden church, one of the largest of such monuments in England, bore the inscription, "Formerly a citizen of London and flower of the wool merchants of England, who died on the first day of October Anno Domini 1401," followed by his merchant's mark and his arms, a combination symbolic of the businessman who had become a country gentleman.

Rubbing of a brass commemorating Thomas Busshe, a Cotswold dealer who sold wool to the Celys, and his wife, each with feet resting on a wool pack and a sheep. Busshe's merchant's mark is below. (British Publishing Co.)

The Celys' relations with the woolmen were not always cordial. The Staple merchants were in the position of being pressed for payment by the woolmen while waiting to collect from their Continental purchasers. If the importers were dilatory, which was by no means unusual, the Celys had to stall the woolmen. At one moment William Midwinter complained that he had sold the Celys wool cheaper than he could buy it, was completely without funds, and wanted to be paid. On another occasion, Richard Cely wrote his son George that William Midwinter was in London, "God rid us of him."

The old debtor-creditor situation had been reversed. In the thirteenth and early fourteenth century, credit was from buyers to sellers; the Italian and Flemish merchants advanced cash to the abbeys and estates. Merchants were rich in liquid capital and growers poor in it. Now, in the Celys' time, the seller gave credit to the buyer. The purchaser paid no more than one third of the price, the remainder being incorporated in a promissory note, usually due six months later, discountable, and carrying interest. The Midwinters bought on credit from the grower; the Celys bought on credit from the Midwinters; Dutch and Flemish customers in Calais bought on credit from the Celys, with payment due at the Antwerp Fair. The sequence of payment began when the Celys presented their bills and collected their money at Antwerp, or one of the other Low Country fairs. The money was sent back to England, usually through the medium of an importer who needed cash to make purchases in the Low Countries, and who gave the Celys bills on his London office. The Celys received this money in time to pay Midwinter, who paid the growers. When there were delays in the payments of foreign buyers at the fairs, the Celys' payments were delayed, and the Cotswold middlemen became threatening.

The Cotswold wool was shipped by pack animal in canvas bales through Surrey and Kent to the southeast ports of Milhall, New Hythe, Halling, and Maidstone, where customs collectors weighed, labeled, and assessed it; or it traveled to London, where it was weighed at Leadenhall, not far from the Celys' London house. Ships from Boston and Ipswich brought the northern wool from Lincolnshire and the Midlands, where the Celys did not normally deal.

The Celys' business was carried on at one of the worst times and places in the Middle Ages as far as security of commerce was concerned. The intermittent war between France and Burgundy-Flanders spawned pirates up and down the length of the Channel. On May 14, 1482, William Cely wrote George at Bruges that an English ship had been pursued by two French corsairs off Calais, but had escaped; a patrol from Calais gave chase and captured both ships, one of which was brought into Calais, the other taken to England. A month later he reported that another English ship had been chased by Scottish pirates between Calais and Dover. That fall he wrote George in London to reassure him that the report that his ship had been plundered by the Flemings was false; it was another ship in her company. In March 1484, English goods were seized at Nieuport in reprisal for English piracy against Ostend ships. At Calais it was proposed that they arrest a Fleming in retaliation, but the military command vetoed the move. Instead a deputation was sent to Ghent to remind the Flemings of an old agreement that Englishmen and Flemings were answerable in Flanders and Calais only for their own misdoings and not for those of their countrymen; goods were to be free from retaliatory seizure. Later a Flemish delegation came to Calais to complain that their goods had been confiscated and taken to Sandwich, and to ask for the Staple's cooperation in recovering them.

The incidents multiplied: "certain banished Englishmen" seized Spanish ships laden with wine bound for Flanders; a French ship chased an English vessel into Dunkirk, a Flemish port. In March William Cely wrote to Richard, Jr. and George in London, "On Friday last past . . . Richard Awray that was master of my Lord Denman's ship . . . took on merchants and set them on land at Dover and at Dover took men in passage to Calais again, and as he came to Calais two men of war of France met with him and fought him and there he was slain and divers more of his company, they say eight or nine persons on whose souls Jesu have mercy." Shortly afterward, two Frenchmen drove other passenger-carrying ships into the Calais harbor.

Three years later, William Cely wrote that because of the Flemish insurrection against Maximilian of Habsburg, he had escaped from Bruges with difficulty and had been forced to spend two days at Nieuport; he was finally able to proceed only because he had passage on a ship carrying goods belonging to the English ambassador. He advised his cousins to abandon this trade and instead invest their money more safely in madder, wax, and fustian cloth, shipping in Spanish bottoms.

On occasion, the Staple merchants did not hesitate to practice piracy themselves. One of the Celys' associates, Thomas Dalton, wrote George begging him to pay a bill of £80 for him in London, "for I look every day for tidings out of Holland for my ship and my prisoners, and brother, this payment lyeth my poor honesty upon." Apparently Dalton was waiting for ransom money with which he planned to pay his debts.

Merchants in the Anglo-Flemish wool trade had other problems besides piracy. The Flemings charged that the English contrived matters so that foreigners lost on the exchange rates, and that English merchants shopping at the Low Country fairs bought nothing until the last day when the Flemish merchandise went at bargain prices. Among the offenders undoubtedly were the Celys, who although they were not importers nevertheless made many purchases at the Flemish fairs. They executed dozens of commissions for family, friends, and business acquaintances—Louvain gloves, ginger, saffron, sugar loaves, saddles, armor, tapestries, furs, Bordeaux wine, goshawks, pickled salmon—and bought supplies used in their own business, canvas and pack thread to make their wool packs.

In Calais the Flemish wool purchasers, by contrast, were forbidden to offer less than the price fixed by the Staple; the only flexibility was that the Staplers raised their prices even higher if they were not paid cash. Washed and unwashed wools, said the Flemings, were mixed together; wool was packed fraudulently; false descriptions of its origin were given on the bale; and they were forced to buy old wool when they wanted new.

The Merchants of the Staple, on the other hand, claimed that the clever Flemings swindled them. English merchants, trying to recover debts in Flanders, ran into such tricks as this: the Flemish debtor sent a penniless ne'er-do-well who owed him money to Calais to buy wool from his own English creditor's agent, with a cash down payment. The man brought the wool back to the Flemish town where the English creditor was dunning his Flemish debtor. The sly Fleming now seized the wool in recovery of his loan to the ne'er-do-well, and paid the Englishman with his own wool. When the bewildered Englishman tried to collect the money owing him on the wool bought by the ne'er-do-well, he found that the man owned no property worth seizing.

The English merchants were evidently no more above question in ethics than the Flemings. In April 1484, William Cely wrote from Calais to his cousins in London that a Fleming named Willikin, with whom he had had dealings and from whom in fact two months before he had received a token—"a God's penny"—for the Celys' wool, was in England, and that Willikin and a fellow countryman, Peter Bale, were trying to buy wool there, contrary to the Staple Ordinance, to avoid paying the usual subsidy. The Celys should be careful to make sure they were paid in Calais—which was evidently not always the case—for the authorities had been alerted as to the Flemings' intentions; "but as for your dealings, knoweth no man without they search Peter Bale's books."

William showed his cunning on another occasion when the lieutenant, second in command to the military governor of Calais, chose a particular sample of Cely wool to test its quality. Knowing that it was poor, William had his packer, William Smith, secretly substitute a sample of good wool and change the labels, writing to George, "Item, sir, your wool is awarded [judged] by the sarpler [sample] that I cast out last." Not long after, George Cely was appointed to a commission to protect the standards of the company.

Eldest son Richard was still unmarried when his father died in 1481. He at once set about looking for a wife. He was a good, if not a brilliant, match; in 1484, for instance, cousin William Cely reported that Richard and George had grossed £2,000 in the past year, with a profit of ten percent, an income of £200 between them from business, in addition to their landed property. Although Richard's first overture came to nothing, his account presents an interesting glimpse of fifteenth-century courtship.

Richard was in the Cotswolds buying wool, in the village of Northleach, a rendezvous of woolmen and exporters. William Midwinter, whose presence in London had provoked Richard on another occasion, urged him to go courting. There was a "young gentlewoman whose father's name is Lemryke and her mother is dead and she shall inherit by her mother £40 a year. . . ." Her father "is the greatest ruler and richest man in that country," and great gentlemen had courted the heiress. Richard made representations to the magnate, who sent a message that if Richard would stay in Northleach until May Day he could meet the young lady. The father was scheduled to sit as Justice of the Peace that day in Northleach, but discreetly sent a clerk in his place and took himself off to Winchcombe, to be out of the way. The girl and her stepmother presented themselves at Northleach church, where Richard by prearrangement attended Matins with a friend. When the service was over the ladies went to "a kinswoman of the young gentlewoman and I sent them a pottle of white romney and they took it thankfully for they had come a mile on foot that morning." Richard stayed for Mass, after which the ladies invited him to dinner. "I excused myself," but he promised to come and have a drink with them after dinner. He sent them a gallon of wine, they riposted with a roast heronshaw. After dinner Richard and his friend called on the ladies. He found the girl in every way attractive: "she is young, little and very well favored and witty." Her father agreed to come up to London to settle the affair, but somehow it fell through. Ten days later Richard was inquiring about another young woman. He was married in the course of time, but to neither of these girls.

At home in Essex, the Celys led the life of country squires, hunting and hawking. Riding down to Gloucestershire to buy wool, Richard carried his hawk on his fist, ready to let fly at heron or partridge. When George was abroad, the brothers kept him posted on the health of his horses—his great horse, his young horse, his horse Bayard, his horse Py. Richard, Sr. wrote, "The horse is fair, God save him, God send you a buyer for him," after remarking that

Richard, Jr. had sold his sorrel for four marks. George's gray bitch had fourteen whelps and died forthwith. George wrote that he had at last sold Py for five marks, and the buyer was "full beguiled"; he reported that hawks at Calais were four or five nobles each, so expensive that only "my Lord Chamberlain" could afford to buy them.

Once their sporting blood got the two Richards into trouble. Richard, Jr. wrote George that he, his father, and "Brandon's men" were indicted for "the slaying of a hart," which was driven over the Thames from Essex and killed at Dartford, along with two hind calves, by the Celys' hounds. Brandon had informed on them, but was himself involved, and had been accused of killing two harts and several calves. The Celys did not want the case to come into court, and Richard went to Sir Thomas Montgomery, Steward of the Forest of Essex, "to have us out of the book before it be showed to the King." He gave Sir Thomas a hundred shillings, and paid a small bribe to one of his gentlemen. Sir Thomas promised to become their "special good master in this matter," and to protect them; George was to call on him and thank him when he arrived in Calais presently, and doubtless add to the bribe. The elder Richard decided to get rid of the greyhounds who had killed the hart; when George next returned to Calais after a visit to England, he took the dogs with him for himself and the lieutenant, "for he [Richard, Sr.] will keep no more greyhounds, he will be agreeable to keep a hawk and spaniels." Furthermore, Sir Thomas Montgomery's favors had taxed Richard, Sr.'s resources, and he would welcome money from Calais. The experience, however, had made him some useful connections: "I am come into acquaintance of divers worshipful men that will [do] much for us for his sake."

What became of Robert and George Cely we do not know; Richard, Jr. died in 1494, leaving three young daughters. One of them died childless, one remained unmarried, and a third was twice married and inherited Bretts Place, which remained in the hands of her family until 1531, when it was sold. A subsequent lawsuit over a will caused the Celys' business correspondence to be brought to Chancery, where it remained to provide posterity with a picture of a family of Merchants of the Staple.

Comfortable, or at best affluent, seeking security rather than power, this typical Staple family, like the Cotswold woolmen, had the social outlook of the country squire rather than the business magnate. The Celys had a healthy respect for the king, in whose antechamber they would never have dreamed of sleeping; they were flattered to rub elbows with Sir John Weston and Sir Thomas Montgomery. The Staple Company, acting as a leveling agent, had an important effect on the English middle class, lowering the heights, while broadening the base. Its members represented an important aspect of rising capitalism, its democratic side.

20

Jacob Fugger,
the First Modern Capitalist

Among the several momentous events of the decade of the 1450s were two with a close, if not readily apparent, connection: the perfection of a smelting technique for separating silver from copper, and the birth of Jacob Fugger.

The first of these events took place in the Austrian Tyrol, and the second a few miles north, in Augsburg, an ancient Roman campsite on the River Lech which had grown into a city of some 20,000 inhabitants, with a prosperity based on fustian. This was a new cheap, durable cloth made by weaving locally grown flax fibers through cotton imported from Venice. Jacob's grandfather Hans Fugger moved his family from the village of Graben to Augsburg to take advantage of the more promising business climate; Hans's son Jacob married a local girl, Barbara Baesinger, daughter of a master of the mint, and fathered eleven children, the youngest of whom was the Jacob Fugger known to history.

When the elder Jacob died suddenly in 1469, widow Barbara followed a tradition of medieval women of manfully shouldering the family burden until her sons were old enough to take over. Her husband and her father-in-law had expanded their cloth shop to deal in other merchandise; Barbara mastered the business while holding the family together and, in token of the family's improved status, sending young Jacob, born in 1459, off to Rome to become a novice priest. First Ulrich, the eldest son, and then George succeeded their mother in managing the business. In 1478 the deaths of other children caused Ulrich and George to entreat their mother to recall the novice (whose character and intelligence may well have been already observed). Although assured of a benefice, Jacob still had the option, as a clerk in minor orders, of returning to the secular world, and he did so with apparent alacrity. Quitting Rome, the ecclesiastical capital, he transferred his studies to Venice, the business capital, reporting to the Fondaco dei Tedeschi, the "German shop," where he quickly mastered Francesco Datini's art of double-entry bookkeeping.

Though Jacob's operations soon eclipsed them, Ulrich and George Fugger were themselves competent businessmen. Under their leadership the Fugger firm had already undergone a considerable expansion. They had known how to take advantage of a visit to Augsburg by the old Emperor Frederick and the crown prince Maximilian to supply silk and wool cloth to the Imperial party en route to a diet at Trier, and had received in return confirmation of the family coat of arms—gold and azure lilies in an azure and gold field. The emblem briefly caused this branch to be known as the Fuggers of the Lily, in distinction to the family of Hans Fugger's other son Andreas, whose coat of arms featured a roebuck. But Andreas' sons proved incompetent and the Fuggers of the Roe disappeared from the business scene, while those of the Lily opened offices in Italy, the Netherlands, Silesia, and Poland.

The firm had acquired the privilege of collecting the revenues of the Holy See in Germany and Scandinavia, thanks largely to the application of another clerical brother, Mark, who had become secretary of the Service of Requests of the Apostolic Chancellery; Mark himself died prematurely, but not before inaugurating a long, profitable and dramatic relationship between the Augsburg firm and the Holy See. Young Jacob's first coup was to win for the firm the right to collect the Church revenues of Poland and Hungary as well; the profits on the transactions arrived through assigning a fa-vorable exchange rate between the local currency, in which the tithes were collected, and the ducats paid out in Rome by the Fug-gers, who now established a branch bank there. By 1494, when a new contract was drawn up under the name of "Ulrich Fugger and Brothers," the voice of thirty-five-year-old Jacob had become the decisive one in the family council.

It was a voice that rarely had to be raised in anger. If ever a being came into the world as a natural leader of men, it was Jacob Fugger. Handsome, personable, good-humored, and unassuming, Jacob commanded by force of his superior intellect, his swift grasp of complexities, and penetrating analysis of their possibilities. The readiness with which his mother and older brothers accepted his direction is extraordinarily revealing, and prefigures the docility with which his nephews later submitted to the autocracy he spelled out by contract.

Jacob's managerial ability came decisively into play in directing part of the firm's capital into mining. The opportunity arose through a combination of technological advance and the financial difficulties of Duke Sigismund of the Tyrol. Son of *Friedrich mit den Leeren Taschen* (Frederick with the Empty Pockets), Sigis-mund had begun his reign with equally empty pockets. The exploi-tation of his mines, suddenly made possible by the new smelting process, offered a welcome opportunity to replenish the exchequer. Medieval law granted the sovereign the right to a tithe of all min-eral ores extracted, as well as the seigniorage on silver. But Sigis-mund wanted to lay hands on the money at once, without waiting for the tedious mining operations. To do so he had recourse to Hans Baumgartner, wealthy moneyman of Kufstein, in Bavaria, who ad-vanced the duke a large sum to be repaid (with substantial interest) out of the silver royalties. The duke, fond of luxury and addicted to fighting with his Swiss neighbors, was immediately trapped in the familiar princely vicious circle of successive borrowings against future royalties.

Hans Baumgartner owed his role as the duke's banker partly to his Bavarian nationality. Sigismund's heir was his Habsburg cousin

Jacob Fugger, the first modern capitalist, portrayed by Dürer. Modest and personable, but tough, shrewd, and perceptive, he built his family's business into an international mining, commercial, and banking empire. (Bayerische Staatsgemäldesammlungen, Munich)

Maximilian, heir-presumptive also to the Empire; but Sigismund had apprehensions that Maximilian might come to collect his inheritance before it was due. Therefore he made an alliance with anti-Habsburg Bavaria. In an injudicious moment he interrupted his skirmishes with the Swiss to start a war with the more formidable Venetians. The result was the overthrow of his pro-Bavarian counselors and a new, more conservative orientation toward the Habsburgs. The duke's director of finances was a certain Anton vom Ross, known in his native Genoa as Antonio de Cavallis. Ross may have approached Jacob Fugger, or been approached by him; in any case the two rapidly concluded an agreement by which Bavarian Hans Baumgartner was unceremoniously dumped as the duke's moneyman, and the firm of Fugger, of the Imperial City of Augsburg, given his place. The Fuggers advanced a large loan (150,000 florins), to be paid in monthly sums, against all metal-ore royalties from the rich silver mines of the Schwaz region until principal and interest were paid. Thus virtually without risk, Jacob Fugger succeeded in obtaining a steady supply of silver-copper ore at a price substantially below the cost of mining and separation.

These transactions took place in the late 1480s; in 1490 Duke Sigismund abdicated in favor of his cousin Maximilian. From the point of view of the Fuggers, this was another brilliant turn of events. Maximilian was an ambitious and soldierly prince who knew nothing about money. In the wars he waged continually over the next thirty years, he seldom enjoyed any support from the Imperial Diet, whose princes and free cities were equally opposed to strengthening their sovereign and voting him revenues. Inevitably Maximilian fell into the hands of Jacob Fugger. At his accession to the Tyrol, Jacob presented Maximilian with a bill for 46,000 florins in Sigismund's unpaid debts. On such occasions princes often declined responsibility, but Maximilian accepted it in full because he needed instant cash to pay his army, which was suppressing a rebellion in Flanders. Jacob Fugger advanced the money, under highly favorable conditions. It was the first of a long series of loans, once more against futures in Tyrolean metal; Maximilian's councillors did their best to obtain better terms, but they were no match for Jacob Fugger, who held all the cards in his hands. In 1496, Jacob, with a show of reluctance, agreed to lend Maximilian 121,600 florins, a deceptive sum, for Jacob began by deducting almost half to satisfy the firm's previous claims, which only two years earlier had been reckoned at no more than 40,000 florins. For another 27,000 florins, Jacob accepted additional ore futures. He went further; when the Habsburg envoy appeared in Augsburg in 1499 with a new request, Jacob boldly explained that he could only meet such demands if he had a monopoly of copper throughout Imperial Germany.

Maximilian could not escape. Jacques Coeur and nearly all his bases of financial operation had lain within the potent grasp of Charles VII, and the Italian bankers had enjoyed only a fragile asylum in Edward III's England. In contrast, Jacob Fugger possessed a base that was virtually unassailable by political authority. Augsburg's status as a free city within the confederation of the Holy Roman Empire put such proceedings as those against Coeur and the Italians out of the question. Maximilian could exert pressure on Jacob to lend him money, but the pressure was limited, and more than balanced by the potential of Jacob's counterpressure.

So successful were the monopolistic Fugger Tyrolean operations that Jacob Fugger resolved to enter another metal-mining region, Hungary, although conditions were quite different. The risks were greater, owing to the frequent incursions of the Turks into Hungary and the even more frequent combats among the turbulent Hungarian magnates. Transport from the slopes of the Carpathians was also difficult. Worst of all, the Hungarian mines, which had been worked for centuries, the copper and silver going to Hanseatic merchants via the Polish king's staple town of Cracow, had now reached depths where they were chronically flooded by water inrushes. Until the water could be controlled the rich mines could not be worked.

The seven Hungarian mining cities of the Carpathians, with the backing of their warlike (and revenue-hungry) king, Matthias Corvinus, submitted their problem to the leading mining engineer of the day, Johann Thurzo of Cracow, offering him a substantial share in the mining profits. Thurzo studied the problem and designed machinery consisting of an endless bucket-chain circulating around two large drums, the lower in the mine and the upper, on the surface, powered by animals. The solution was practical, but a large amount of capital was needed to convert it from paper into working machinery in the mines. King Matthias' war with the Habsburgs temporarily prevented a search for backing in the most likely place, South Germany; when the war ended (with Matthias still in possession of Vienna, but promising to give Hungary to the Habsburgs if he died childless, which he in fact did), the opportunity was presented to Jacob Fugger, who investigated it thoroughly and accepted.

Possibly inspired by the example of the Habsburgs, who adroitly exploited the marriage contract to expand their holdings, Jacob cemented an alliance with Thurzo, the mining genius, by arranging a marriage between Anna, daughter of Ulrich Fugger, and Thurzo's son George. A new firm was founded, the Fugger-Thurzo Company, whose mission was to mine and sell mineral products to two firms, the Fugger Company of Augsburg and the Thurzo Company of Cracow. It was also empowered to buy from the Fugger firm such merchandise as silk and wool cloth and precious stones, which it might sell in Hungary or use as good-will gifts to great Hungarian landlords.

The ore mined by the Fugger-Thurzo Company in Upper Hungary was mostly "black copper," containing silver and lead. At Neusohl, Johann Thurzo designed and constructed a smelting furnace and rolling mill capable of processing most of the company's ore. Jacob Fugger spent several weeks deep in the Thuringian forest, where charcoal was plentiful, personally supervising construction of another plant. A third processing establishment was set up at Fuggerau in Carinthia.

The Neusohl plant, completed by Thurzo in 1495, employed hundreds of workers, producing mainly copper sheets and plates, but some silver, most of which was sold to the Hungarian mint. The copper was marketed principally in western and central Europe, especially via Breslau and Cracow to Stettin and Danzig, whence it progressed in Hanseatic or Dutch ships through the Danish Sound or via Lübeck and Hamburg to Novgorod (a little) and Antwerp (the bulk). From Antwerp the metal progressed to France, Portugal, Spain, and Italy. The Fugger-Thurzo copper also traveled via Zengg or Trieste to Venice. By 1496 the Fugger firm had branches in Breslau and Lübeck; to circumvent the Hanseatic resistance to foreign penetration, Jacob skillfully planted a bank in Lübeck in partnership with natives, which transferred funds from the papacy and did commercial business. Within a few years Fugger offices were opened in Stettin and Danzig, then in Hamburg, and finally in distant Livonia. In Danzig, Jacob formed an alliance with Jacob Vetter, leading copper importer, who defended the Fugger interests before the town council. With the aid of the Teutonic Order, the firm got a foothold in the East, establishing commercial contacts with the Russians. Throughout the Baltic they bought wax, furs, and other merchandise, selling not only copper but spices and cloth.

The Hansa was slow to take alarm at the inroads on its own monopolistic traffic in Swedish copper by the highly competitive rival monopoly from the south. In 1511, an aroused diet at Lübeck forbade transit of non-Hanseatic goods through Hansa cities. A Dutch fleet carrying Fugger copper was attacked off Danzig. Jacob Fugger protested to the king of Hungary, the pope, and Maximilian, and enlisted Vetter's aid with the king of Denmark; the Hanseatic lawyers argued vehemently against the Fugger monopoly, theoretically illegal in the Holy Roman Empire, but in the end, though Jacob did not recover damages, Fugger copper was allowed to supply the Baltic. Through Vetter's assistance the Fugger firm obtained from the king of Denmark the right to trade in the Danish Sound and in Scandinavia (1515).

The success of the Fugger-Thurzo enterprise had long since sealed Jacob Fugger's ascendancy within his own firm. The contract of 1494 had specified that on the death of one or two of the three brothers, the heirs could not withdraw capital for a period of three years, and even then only gradually. The arrangement was aimed at forestalling Jacob Fugger's nephews from pulling the props out from under his expanding mining business. Jacob himself, thirty-five years old, had no children. He had taken a wife, Sybille Artz, daughter of a fellow businessman, but the couple remained childless. Underlining the anti-nepotic nature of the contract of 1494 was the stipulation that heirs could take no part in management for three years.

Jacob Fugger's strong-willed personality, discernible in the contract of 1494, was unmistakably spelled out in the contract drawn eight years later, in 1502, by which time the immense value of the Hungarian enterprise had become evident. Despite the competence with which his mother had served the business, he summarily excluded his own wife from it, along with the wives and daughters of his brothers. It was his business; he alone was responsible for its sensational success, and although he gave his older brothers their due, he made sure that their families were totally subordinated to the interests of the firm. By the terms of the 1502 instrument a "Preferred Share" of the business was established, based principally on the Hungarian enterprise, to be awarded to the male heirs only, and to be unalienable. In the event of the death of one of the three brothers, it was specified that the two survivors should have unrestricted freedom as directors, and would be free to choose from among all the nephews (not merely from the sons of the deceased partner) the young man most fitted for leadership and to educate him appropriately so that in case of the death of a second brother the remaining partner would have a capable assistant.

Ulrich and George were already middle-aged, and perhaps suffered impaired health; Ulrich died four years after the new contract was signed, George eight years later. In 1506 Jacob and George had become all-powerful codirectors, with Jacob unquestionably the superior voice; in 1510 Jacob survived as sole director. Summoning his nephews, he had them confirm his unchallenged power by solemn oaths on the newly printed Bible. Two years later , in 1512, he dictated a new contract, in which the firm was rechristened *Jacob Fugger und seine Gebrüder Söhne* (Jacob Fugger and his brothers' sons) and in which Jacob's absolute sovereignty was triply underlined, with t's crossed and i's dotted: "[The nephews] shall accept in their entirety the amounts which I shall allot to them or their heirs, and shall waive all further advances, and shall give me a complete quittance in the matter. Furthermore, shall my above-mentioned four nephews collectively and each in particular recognize and look upon me as the head of this my business, together with such trade as I give them to do and accomplish; they are also faithfully bound to be true and obedient in all things, in whatsoever form and for whatever things this may be required, and . . . to hold the business in complete secrecy and tell no one. . . . They . . .

shall do nothing but what I command and give them permission to do. And if I direct one or all of them to do something, and afterward recall it to myself, they shall not dispute it. And what I alone arrange, or bind the association to, to that shall they also nonetheless be committed, and shall be bound to its accomplishment. . . ."

The death of this absolute monarch was foreseen and provided for: Ulrich and Raimund Fugger, sons of Ulrich and George, would become codirectors; Jacob however took care to provide himself with the option of changing this decision at any time he saw fit.

At the time of this definitive contract, Jacob Fugger had a dozen years to live; these proved the most profitable of all. Yet already in 1512 the Fugger firm stood foremost among all business enterprises in Germany and had few if any rivals elsewhere in Europe. The capital listed in the 1494 contract, 54,385 Rhenish gold gulden, had grown to nearly 300,000 gulden; an accounting of February 4, 1511, gives a net total of 269,091, probably a low figure. Not all of the money was invested in business; a sizeable proportion (70,884 gulden in the 1511 accounting, probably a conservative evaluation) was in houses and estates. For several years, Jacob had pursued a policy of acquisition of large estates throughout Swabia. In 1507 Maximilian, planning an expedition into Italy, borrowed 50,000 florins by mortgaging his revenues as count of Kirchberg and lord of Weissenborn, two vast properties which as a predictable result passed into the hands of the Augsburg moneyman. In 1509 Jacob bought the Hofmark Schmiechen with its castle from Maximilian, and in 1514 acquired the domain of Biberbach, near Augsburg. Altogether Jacob put 92,000 gulden into landed property, thus following the traditional policy of nearly all moneymen. The universally imputed motive was social climbing, and all over Europe successful merchants' sons and grandsons were indeed slipping into the nobility. But there were other motives; land was safe from taxes and market fluctuations and at worst one could always live on it. Furthermore, land values could not help rising. By the same token that land brought status it enhanced power; a moneyman who owned large estates was in a stronger psychological position when a prince's envoys came to borrow money. Probably foremost among Jacob's considerations in acquiring huge estates was the prestige of immense visible wealth—wealth which also had the advantage of not being available for Maximilian to borrow.

That Jacob Fugger might have aspired to rise, like the contemporary Medici, to a dukedom, was no more than reasonable, but Jacob's character was against so gaudy an ambition. He contented himself with the title of count, bestowed by his faithful Imperial debtor Maximilian.

He passed little time on his estates, but built a house in Augsburg that became known as the first Italian Renaissance palace in Germany. Fronting for more than three hundred feet on the Maximilianstrasse, the principal street of the city, with open galleries on the upper two floors, its façade was decorated with frescoes by a notable local artist, Hans Burgkmair. The inner Ladies' Court, set off by graceful red marble columns, was the scene of ball playing, dancing, and feast-day celebrations; on the walls under its arcades were life-size representations of spectators and droll figures of musicians.

Jacob continued to press expansion of the business, yet always within prudent bounds, rarely incurring an avoidable risk. He established the most widespread and reliable courier service in the European business world; all important commercial and political news arrived promptly in Augsburg, supplied partly by his Habsburg and papal connections. Much of it he passed on immediately to his branches and correspondents, but he was a master at keeping vital information to himself. His favorite motto, reminiscent of Jacques Coeur's, was "Silence is best" (*Stillschweigen stehet wohl an*).

His strength of personality and character as well as his financial power made him the acknowledged leader of the South German business community. When Maximilian, at war with Venice and desperate for money, succeeded in extracting a forced loan of some 150,000 florins from the businessmen of Augsburg, Nuremberg, Memmingen, and Ratisbon, Jacob Fugger led the opposition which forced the emperor to pledge the crown lands and furthermore never again to resort to such a procedure.

Jacob's extraordinary position with the Habsburgs was illus-

The Emperor Maximilian, Jacob Fugger's great princely client. Portrait by Dürer. (Kunsthistorisches Museum, Vienna)

trated at the Congress of Vienna of 1515. On this occasion Maximilian arranged a double marriage between two of his grandchildren and the children of King Vladislav of Hungary, guaranteeing the annexation of Hungary to the Empire, an outcome very much in Jacob Fugger's interest. In return, Jacob underwrote Maximilian's expenses for the showy Congress, personally distributing gold rings, necklaces, silks, and other baubles (his expense account on his return to Augsburg showed 10,000 Rhenish gulden), and himself transporting to Vienna Maximilian's gold and silver dinner service, which had been in pawn to an Augsburg merchant. A letter from Maximilian to his counselors at Innsbruck, pointing out the benefits of the marriage arrangement and the need for spending money on the Congress, entreated the counsellors to sign the contract for the covering loan from Jacob Fugger: ". . . so soon as our friend the Cardinal von Gurgk writes that the main agreement . . . and our meeting, have been concluded, we are to move on immediately. But we cannot do this unless the loan from the Fuggers is carried through. For without this we cannot go on, but will have to drop all the above dealings . . . and abandon the plan for our children and theirs, and cancel all the arrangements; and it will probably bring about the disadvantages and injuries suggested above if we finally abandon our meeting with them. If we knew any other method of finance, we would have been only too glad to spare you this; but we know of no other way. . . ."

Maximilian promised to pay in December what he borrowed in May, but in October he sent two diplomats to ask Jacob for an extension, and also for another loan. Jacob received them cordially, but gave them no satisfaction. Reminding the emissaries that Maximilian owed him a king's ransom of 300,000 gulden, he averred that he was short of cash to meet his own obligations. The 12,000 gulden borrowed in May he needed to cover his tax payment of 10,000 gulden to the treasury at Innsbruck. As for another loan to the emperor, he expressed pained surprise. In accordance with carefully rehearsed instructions, the negotiators brought out Maximilian's final hope: a new loan based on more future royalties from the Tyrolese copper and silver. Unmoved, Jacob reminded them that Maximilian's copper royalties were already pledged for the next four years and his silver royalties for the next eight, and furthermore that silver production in the Tyrol had declined from 14,000 marks a year to 7,000. To soften the rebuff, he told the crestfallen envoys that if their master could make shift until Easter, by which time various sums owing the Fugger firm would have come in, perhaps a fresh arrangement could be made about the mining royalties.

Such was the relationship between the moneyman of Augsburg and his sovereign when Maximilian begån to turn his attention to the matter of a successor. The Habsburgs had no constitutional basis for their succession to the Holy Roman Empire; tradition alone, and their position as leading German princes, led to their election by the seven princely electors. Maximilian's heir to the Habsburg crown lands was his grandson Charles, who by dynastic accident had succeeded Ferdinand, Columbus' patron, as king of Spain. The prospect of Charles uniting Germany, Hungary, Spain, Burgundy, the Netherlands, part of Italy, most of America, and much of the Indies, under one crowned head was enough to stimulate a rival, and no mean one at that. Francis I of France, head of a strong, united kingdom, accompanied the announcement of his candidacy with the promise of lavish bribes to the electors. Whatever their German patriotism, the seven German princes welcomed Francis's candidacy with undisguised pleasure. The three bishops and four secular princes all offered their votes for sale. In this situation it was practically inevitable that Jacob Fugger of Augsburg should play a decisive role.

This fact was not at once apparent. At the moment that Maximilian put forward Charles's candidacy, Jacob had no connections with the young Habsburg. A rival Augsburg financial dynasty, the Welsers, had the inside track. The Welsers had originally moved into the Iberian peninsula with a consortium that financed the Portuguese fleet organized in 1505 with the object of exploiting the Indies route pioneered by Vasco da Gama. The expedition was altogether too successful; the Portuguese king henceforth ruled out foreign participation in his ventures. The Iberian Welsers moved from Lisbon to Madrid, at which court they had been active for several years by the time Charles became king, and shortly after, candidate for the Imperial crown.

In the opening clash of the battle of gold pieces, Maximilian promised the Elector of Brandenburg 100,000 gulden, with the

Charles V, Habsburg king of Spain, whose election as Holy Roman emperor was financed largely by Jacob Fugger, in the form of funds to bribe the seven German Electors. (Staatliche Museen, Berlin)

backing of Jacob Fugger. But Maximilian died shortly after, January 1519, and the contract was voided while the tension heightened. In Spain the nineteen-year-old Charles entrusted to the Welsers and the Genoese the transfer of funds from Spain to Germany for the bribes. Jacob Fugger was chagrined not merely at losing the profits of the exchange transactions but at losing his financial preeminence with the Habsburgs. He at once moved to recover it. Writing Charles, he recounted, without going into unnecessary detail about interest and profits, the many services he had performed for Maximilian. With boldness bordering on effrontery he threatened the consequences of the House of Fugger going over to the support of Francis I.

Jacob then turned his attention to the electors. Promises were cheap, he pointed out, but who actually had the cash? Their bribes would be far more secure if they carried the pledge of Jacob Fugger of Augsburg. The Elector archbishop of Mainz saw the point at once, and proposed to cancel the pledges of the Imperial cities of Antwerp and Mechlin which Charles had offered and substitute for them that of Jacob Fugger. The Elector of Brandenburg, possibly the greediest of the lot, seconded the motion, refusing to accept guarantees even from the Welsers. In the end Jacob underwrote Charles's bribes to the Electors to the tune of more than half a million gold gulden, almost three times the amount the Welsers had been able to extend. When on June 28, 1519, young Charles was elected Emperor Charles V, he had old Jacob chiefly to thank.

At that Jacob was not entirely satisfied. The tenacity of the Welsers and the Genoese prevented him from totally monopolizing the loans to Charles. Not that he considered Charles a better debtor than Maximilian, a point on which Charles did not surprise him. Early in 1523 Jacob addressed a letter more in sorrow than in anger to the original sovereign "on whose empire the sun never set":

"Your Royal Majesty is undoubtedly well aware of the extent to which I and my nephews have always been inclined to serve the House of Austria, and in all submissiveness to promote its welfare and its rise. . . . We cooperated with the former Emperor Maximilian, Your Imperial Majesty's forefather, and, in loyal subjection to His Majesty, to secure the Imperial Crown for Your Imperial Majesty. . . .

"It is . . . well known that Your Majesty without me might not have acquired the Imperial Crown, as I can attest with the written statement of all the delegates of Your Imperial Majesty. . . . If I had withdrawn my support from the House of Austria, and transferred it to France, I should have won large profit and much money, which were at that time offered me. What disadvantage would have risen thereby for the House of Austria, Your Imperial Majesty, with your deep comprehension, may well conceive.

"Taking all this into consideration, my respectful request to Your Imperial Majesty is that you will graciously recognize my faithful, humble service, dedicated to the well-being of Your Imperial Majesty, and that you will order that the money which I have paid out, together with the interest, shall be reckoned up and paid, without further delay. . . ." The letter omitted to mention that although the money had been loaned in Flemish gulden, repayment was contracted in Rhenish gulden, worth two kreutzer more apiece.

However dilatory the account-settling, the Habsburg connection promised to be even more profitable under Charles than it had been under Maximilian. Magellan's voyage (1519–1522) had opened the Moluccas, the fabled Spice Islands, to Spanish-German exploitation. Jacob Fugger headed a group financing expeditions by Garcia de Loaisa and Sebastian Cabot. Both enterprises failed, and the Fugger firm lost 4,600 Spanish ducats. But the loss was more than made good by other ventures, especially the mortgage of the Spanish mercury mines of Almada, made over by Charles to Jacob. The Fugger firm, drawing on its Tyrolean-Hungarian experience, introduced improved mining techniques, and soon reaped rich profits.

Still another part of Europe was drawn into the Fugger net when Jacob loaned money to Charles's brother Ferdinand in 1521 to fight the Turks and in 1524 to suppress the peasants' rebellion in Germany. To repay principal and interest, Charles assigned his brother the government revenues of the kingdom of Naples; Ferdinand turned them over to Jacob Fugger.

By this time both Jacob and Charles V were deeply embroiled

with the new, unexpectedly intractable, and rapidly spreading movement in German religious circles, which the Medici pope Leo X had considered a mere monks' quarrel, but which developed into the Protestant Reformation.

Jacob's role grew out of the decades-old connection of the House of Fugger with the papacy. In 1507 Pope Julius had deposited 100,000 ducats in the Fugger bank in Rome. Many other members of the Curia became Fugger depositors. The Fuggers were given the Roman mint privilege; on many papal coins of the period appears the Fugger mark, an "F" rising out of a ring. The firm became involved in all aspects of Vatican finance, from the collection of papal revenues in northern Europe to the payment of the pope's mercenaries.

In 1511-12 two proposals of unequal merit were made to Jacob in connection with the Rome branch. The first was an application from Maximilian for a large new loan with which to bribe cardinals; the emperor had conceived the idea of getting himself elected pope. The death of his second wife, Bianca Sforza (the condottiere's granddaughter had become an empress), had led him to the bizarre notion. "We have resolved never again to lie beside a naked woman," he informed his daughter, "and are sending tomorrow to Rome to the Pope to find a way . . . to take us as coadjutor, so that after his death we can be assured of having the Papacy and becoming . . . after that a saint." He confidently signed himself "your good father, Maximilian, future Pope," but Jacob Fugger declined to lend substance to the imperial whim, even though promised the key to the papal treasury.

The second scheme offered to Jacob in 1512 came from a more hardheaded source. His factor in Rome was a certain Johannes Zink, whose activities on behalf of the firm reveal a combination of qualities similar to Jacob's own. Zink was adept at the sale of benefices, driving the best possible bargain for the pope, the firm's client, with eager aspirants to vacant bishoprics. Zink's new inspiration was based on the popularity of the convenient remission of sin known as the indulgence. Indulgences had a long history in the Church, but in earlier times had been granted for fighting the infidel, as in the

First Crusade. In the jubilee year of 1500 the pope had offered in-dulgences to the citizens of Rome on a different basis; although true repentance was insisted upon as a condition of the deal, the payment of a sum of money appeared to be the more significant element. The Jubilee indulgence proved so popular both with sinners and with the bishops who shared in the revenues that it was extended all over Europe. In 1501 the House of Fugger handled the transmission to Rome of the receipts from indulgences in Germany and Lorraine, skimming off the profits on exchange in addition to a five percent commission.

But although indulgences were peddled everywhere, they did not everywhere bring the same returns. In the strong monarchic states—France, Spain, and England—the government kept a tight rein on sales, not only to prevent the pope from robbing them of revenues, but to stop abuses that might stir discontent. Hungary successfully claimed retention of indulgence money to finance de-fense against the Turks. Poland, threatened by the schismatic Rus-sians as well as the Turks, did the same. That left Germany, with a diffuse secular authority and no threat from Turks or Russians, as the ideal hunting ground for the Church's salesman. The Emperor Maximilian, unable either to forbid or permit the practice in the ter-ritories of the German princes, sought merely to share in the profits.

It was against this background that Johannes Zink had his happy inspiration in 1512, just before Medici Leo X's accession as pope (1513). The bishopric of Constance was rebuilding its cathe-dral, destroyed by fire, with the aid of a promotion of indulgences, one third of whose revenues, in accordance with custom, went to Rome. When Constance applied for a renewal of the indulgence li-cense, Zink proposed increasing the pope's share (and thus the Fug-ger revenues from commissions) from one third to one half. Jacob Fugger's influence helped win acceptance in Constance, and the pope rewarded the Fugger firm by giving it the exclusive right to negotiate with cathedral chapters in Germany for similar grants. Jacob at once set his agents to work.

The new commerce in indulgences dovetailed neatly with the other Church business in which the firm specialized, the sale of benefices. Agostino Vespucci of Florence wrote Machiavelli from Rome: "Benefices are for sale here more readily than melons, wafers or drinkable water." Albrecht of Brandenburg, younger brother of the most rapacious of Charles V's Electors, had acquired three simony-rich bishoprics with the aid of Fugger loans; to help Albrecht pay back principal and interest (disguised in the contract by the standard form of "trouble, danger, and expense"), Jacob Fugger arranged for him to be made commissioner for indulgences in Saxony. A monk known as the Pardoner Tetzel journeyed through the land accompanied by a Fugger agent, who kept the key to the indulgence chest into which the coins of the sinners were dropped; as soon as the chest was full it was opened and the contents forwarded to Andreas Mattstedt, the Fugger agent in Leipzig. Thence half the proceeds went to Rome and half to Augsburg. Cardinal d'Aragone wrote in his diary in 1517 after a visit to Augsburg that the chief source of wealth of the Fugger firm was loans to those "who have to make payments to Rome for appointments to bishoprics, abbotships and great benefices." That was an exaggeration, but Jacob himself admitted, or rather boasted, to the cardinal that "he had been concerned in the appointment of all the Germam bishops; often indeed two or three times."

The ostensible purpose of the indulgence revenue was to build the new St. Peter's in Rome, a project in itself not entirely agreeable to carping critics. When in addition indulgence money went to pay for the extravagances of local bishops, the critics raised their voices, and when finally the spectacle was presented of half the money going into the coffers of "Jacob the Rich," notorious throughout Germany and indeed Europe, Martin Luther loosed his wrath. Luther's followers took up the angry theme, and were joined by more orthodox Catholic clergy and ordinary laymen. The old medieval resentment of fortunate businessmen was redoubled; the name "Fugger" was turned into a verb signifying to deal sharply or fraudulently. The great German nobles already hated Jacob Fugger because of his power at the Imperial court, which diminished theirs, just as Edward II's barons had hated the Frescobaldi. The petty nobles hated him because through him they lost status and preferential treatment in both state and Church to sons and daughters of moneyed burghers. Above all, everybody hated him because of rising prices, which one and all blamed on the Fugger penchant for monopoly and cartel.

His unashamed practice of holding goods off the market for a rise in price came in for violent Lutheran invective. "It is not right to say, 'I will sell my wares as dear as I can,'" declared Luther, "but 'I will sell my wares dear as I should or as is right and proper.'" Stung, Jacob sponsored a champion of his own brand of theology, Dr. Konrad Peutinger, also a native of Augsburg, and a distinguished scholar. Dr. Peutinger flatly contradicted Luther: "Every merchant," he declared, "is free to sell his wares as dear as he can and chooses. In so doing, he does not sin against canonical law; neither is he guilty of antisocial conduct. For it happens often enough that merchants, to their injury, are forced to sell their wares cheaper than they bought them." Jacob induced the Augsburg council to pass a resolution in favor of complete freedom of businessmen from all restraint, and persuaded Dr. Johann Eck, Luther's foremost adversary, to come out in favor of an interest rate of five percent. When Luther made his break in 1521 the populace of Swabia and central Europe remained true to the old Church, but they did not love Jacob Fugger.

"Many are hostile to me," he admitted in a letter to Duke Albert of Saxony. "They say I am rich. I am rich by God's grace, without injury to any man." Jacob had some reason to feel aggrieved. By all accounts he had many of the qualities of Cosimo de' Medici. His bearing was modest; he was frank and plainspoken to superiors and inferiors alike. His integrity was beyond question, and at least in his own eyes his business methods were above reproach. He never "had any hindrance to sleep," he wrote, but laid from him "all care and stress of business with [his] shirt." Like Cosimo, he was hospitable to his guests, but simple in his own tastes; he especially enjoyed giving skating parties and dances. He donated generously to the Church, especially St. Ann of Augsburg, which, ironically, went over to the new faith. He was a generous bestower of alms, and one of his philanthropic ventures was truly unique: at the edge of the city he built a garden village of some fifty cottages, each designed to house two families, at nominal rent, for workers of the poorest class. Surrounded by a wall and provided with its own church, the picturesque "Fuggerei" survives in Augsburg today. On his death Jacob left to each family of the settlement with children a Rhenish gold gulden, and to each childless couple a half gulden.

Charity and philanthropy notwithstanding, in the summer of 1525 Jacob's unpopularity made it possible for the king of Hungary to strike a severe blow against the firm. Alexius Thurzo, incompetent son of the able engineer Johann Thurzo, acquired and misused the Hungarian mint privilege, debasing the coinage and aggravating an inflationary situation. Mobs broke into the Fugger-Thurzo offices, and King Louis forced Alexius to cancel all the royal debts and hand over 125,000 gulden.

In Augsburg, Jacob received with mounting rage the succession of bad reports from his courier service. But unlike earlier moneymen cheated by royalty, he was not helpless. Even when his firm was in the wrong he had political power of his own to bring to bear. His debtors, the German princes, and above all the Emperor Charles, intervened, partly in gratitude for past favors, partly in hope of future ones. In addition, Jacob threatened to boycott Hungarian copper throughout Germany. King Louis was forced to conclude a new agreement for the exploitation of his mines by the Fugger firm.

In October 1525, Jacob was still hard at work on the Hungarian problem, bargaining, threatening, bribing. Disdaining any delegation of authority, the aging potentate continued to run his empire in person. Suddenly in November a rumor spread through the European business world: the head of the Fugger firm was seriously ill.

He was in fact dying. Early in December, Charles V's brother Ferdinand, who ruled the Habsburgs' German possessions, entered Augsburg for the session of the provincial legislature. As the head of the royal procession neared the Fugger house in the Wine Market, Ferdinand ordered the trumpeters and kettle drummers to leave off, and the parade passed in respectful silence the house where Jacob lay.

The man who in his youth had consecrated his life to another

world found it difficult to quit this one. Not till his failing body
warned him that a day's delay might be catastrophic did he dictate
his last testament. Three days before Christmas, he turned over the
headship of the House of Fugger to his nephew Anton. He fought
on a few days longer, but on December 30 the greatest of medieval
moneymen breathed his last. He was buried in the chapel of St. Ann,
where his older brothers already rested, in a suitably sculptured
tomb, with a glowing epitaph:

> *To God, All-Powerful and Good*
>
> Jacob Fugger of Augsburg, ornament
> to his class and to his country, Imperial
> Councillor under Maximilian I and Charles
> V, second to none in the acquisition of
> extraordinary wealth, in liberality, in
> purity of life, and in greatness of soul,
> as he was comparable to none in life,
> so after death is not to be numbered
> among the mortal.

The firm continued to expand and prosper, until it reached an
apogee in 1546, twenty-one years after Jacob's death, a year in
which its property was inventoried at 5,000,000 gold gulden. Under
the reign of Jacob's nephew Anton, the House of Fugger gained its
richest luster. Anton was the Lorenzo to Jacob's Cosimo; his book
collections turned into libraries, and his patronage decorated
churches and cathedrals. But as with the Medici, the House of Fugger shone the most brilliantly when it was past its prime. Anton was
a capable businessman, but he lacked Jacob's iron character; the
loans to popes and Habsburgs grew ever larger without growing
more profitable. In the end, after Anton's death (1560), national
bankruptcies ultimately brought down the House of Fugger, though
the family retained its immense landed property, acquired long before by farsighted Jacob.

Jacob Fugger was to businessmen what Napoleon was to generals; his acumen on the battlefield of finance was surpassed only by
his energy and determination. Like his predecessors, he dealt with

powerful sovereigns, but he revolutionized the relationship. The Emperor Charles V, beside whom Edward III of England was a pigmy, was reduced almost to the status of a pawn by Jacob Fugger, and his bold exploitation of the finances of the Church contributed no little to bringing on the Reformation. In type of activity, in scale of enterprise, in attitude and personality, Jacob Fugger carried the businessman out of the Middle Ages and into the great age of capitalism, in which European businessmen (and their American heirs) came to dominate history.

After the Commercial Revolution

About A.D. 1000, just as the Italian maritime cities began the counteroffensive against the Muslims which launched a half-millennium of commercial revival, Europeans first set foot on the continent of North America. But the Viking bridgeheads in Labrador and Newfoundland were feeble and unproductive. Despite their skilled shipbuilding and seamanship, the Norsemen were the transmitters of a primitive, rural, backward economy. What they brought to the New World was small improvement over what was already there.

Five centuries passed before Europe returned to America, but the second time it came to stay; in the interval the Commercial Revolution had taken place. In 1001, as Leif Ericson's broad-beamed, square-sailed *knörr* crossed the Davis Strait, the Italian cities were stirring. Amalfi, trading with Muslim North Africa, established commercial colonies all over the Mediterranean world. Milan prospered, doing business across the Alps with Germany and down the Po with Venice and the Levant. Even in backward northwest Europe, commerce began to revive, and traveling merchants like Godric of Finchale sailed to Norway and Flanders, carrying English wool and bringing back cloth, spices, and wine.

The Crusades, in which Venice, Pisa, and Genoa seized control of the luxury trade with the East, quickened economic growth. At first a satellite of Byzantium, Venice rose to the status of rival, and finally in the Fourth Crusade conquered Constantinople itself.

At the beginning of the Crusades, the balance of Mediterranean trade favored the rich East over the underdeveloped West. The growth of Western industry, especially in the manufacture of cloth and arms, altered this ancient economic geography. Raw wool from England, woven and fulled in the cities of Flanders, was sold at the Champagne Fairs to Italian merchants. At first businessmen from Asti and Genoa journeyed to the Fairs to meet their counterparts from Arras and the Flemish cloth towns; later the Italians stayed home and did business through agents, using credit instruments and paper transactions developed at the Fairs.

In Flanders, cloth manufacturing, foreshadowing modern industrial capitalism, developed many of the ills of capitalistic society —class conflict, market crisis, and an unbridgeable gulf between rich and poor. Bankers of Arras capitalized on the financial difficulties of the northern cities, brought to the verge of bankruptcy by loans to the count of Flanders and by the corruption of their own patrician governments.

In the late thirteenth century, Genoa defeated Pisa and became the reigning power in the Tyrrhenian Sea. Merchants from Genoa and Venice penetrated the Black Sea, establishing themselves in the Crimea, whence the Polos made their fabulous trip to Cathay. Inland Florence came to the fore, as the merchants of its Calimala Guild progressed from cloth finishing to international banking, developing new forms of partnership, financial instruments, insurance, business information services, and techniques of administration. At the same time, accounting underwent an evolution from the old-fashioned journal to double-entry bookkeeping.

By the fifteenth century, Europe was economically and technologically ready for an Age of Discovery. Perhaps it was even overdue. The voyage of the Vivaldi brothers of Genoa in 1291 down the Atlantic coast of Africa, anticipating da Gama, might well have been followed by successors with happier results. Before another explorer could round the Cape (or be blown to Brazil, like Cabral in 1500), the catastrophes of the fourteenth century put an end for the moment to the European expansion.

Italian bankers, financing the English kings in their wars in Scotland and Wales, and in the first battles of the Hundred Years' War, went bankrupt, shaking the financial world to its foundations. Flanders, caught between the count's feudal loyalty to France and its dependence on English wool, was torn by revolution. But the cataclysm that dwarfed all the other disasters of the century was the Black Death, wiping out a third of the population of Europe and leaving an aftermath of social disorder and depression. A ray of light in the economic gloom was the institutional emergence of the North German Hansa.

Some medieval scholars have had the temerity to suggest that the Renaissance, despite its dazzling cultural explosion, was, compared with the peak decades of the Middle Ages, a period of economic stagnation, and that no merchant of the fifteenth century, the Medici included, achieved the stature of the earlier Bardi and Peruzzi.

As far as the impact of the Middle Ages is concerned, the question is academic. What the Middle Ages bequeathed to the modern world was not so much prosperity as techniques—the tools for future growth and ultimate abundance. In the words of Robert S. Lopez, "The startling surge of economic life in Europe in the High Middle Ages is probably the greatest turning point in the history of our civilization."

In the fifteenth century, the economic currents certainly shifted. Although Italy still had its great magnates, like Cosimo de' Medici, Italian merchants no longer monopolized European banking and exchange. France produced its first international financier, Jacques Coeur. The metal industry of Milan declined, that of South Germany advanced, bringing with it a towering financial giant, Jacob Fugger. Italian wool cloth manufacturing contracted, and silk took its place; the English wool cloth industry flourished. In England, the fifteenth century saw the emergence of the Staple Company, to be followed in the sixteenth by the Merchant Adventurers, selling cloth where the Staplers had sold raw wool, and traveling all over Europe where the Staplers had confined themselves to Calais and the Flemish fairs. Holland profited by social and political disorders in Flanders and by the weakening of the Hansa, taking over northern markets. Spain and Portugal sprang into prominence with their discoveries of overseas treasures.

The successors of the Embriaci, the Zaccarias, the Alberti, the Boinebrokes, the Veckinchusens, and the Celys were Magellan, the conquistadors, the Merchant Adventurers, the Dutch, French, and British India Companies, the Massachusetts Bay Company, and the other profit-making seafarers, colonizers, and sedentary financial strategists who carried the banner of imperialism from western Europe to the shores and hinterlands of worlds new and old. The markets they opened and the raw materials, especially precious metals, they recovered, gave new momentum to the rallying economy of Europe, and rapidly thrust the world into the modern age.

APPENDIX 1

Medieval Money

The basic coin of the Middle Ages was the silver denarius. From the time of Charlemagne until the thirteenth century, this small, thin penny and the even smaller half-penny or obole were virtually the only pieces in circulation. The solidus, equal to twelve denarii, and the libra, equal to twenty solidi or 240 denarii, were "moneys of account," ghost currency used in figuring, rather than real coins. The dozen and the score were chosen as easy groups for reckoning.

Modern equivalents of medieval money cannot be assessed except with gross qualifications. The value of the denarius, and therefore of the solidus and the libra, varied from mint to mint and from year to year. One medieval scholar, Urban Tigner Holmes, estimated that a denier minted in Paris in 1177 contained four cents' worth of silver at the 1952 U.S. price; therefore, on the basis of silver value, not taking into account alloys or purchasing power, a livre (a twelve-ounce medieval pound) would be worth about ten dollars, and a sou fifty cents. A gold bezant, minted in Constantinople, or in southern Italy or Spain, had a value in gold, at Professor Holmes's calculation, of about five 1952 U.S. dollars; in 1199 in England the bezant could be exchanged for twenty-four pennies, or two shillings.

Perhaps the most useful approach to the value of medieval money is through wages and purchasing power. It has been calculated that a skilled workman earned 4½ denarii a day up to 1350 (the time of the Black Death), 6d. from 1350–1500. The day's pay of a workman could usually buy a chicken or a peck of wheat or pay a week's house rent. A sheep in the thirteenth century sold for three or four solidi, a pig for about the same, a goose for six denarii, a rabbit seven, a liter of wine for from two to six denarii, honey a solidus per pound, slippers two solidi and up, a sheepskin two solidi. (Further information on prices may be found in Vicomte G. d'Avenel, *Histoire économique de la propriété, des salaires, des denrées et de tous les prix en general depuis l'an 1200 jusqu'en l'an 1800*, Paris, 1898.)

In Italy and France the denarius slowly but steadily declined in value. In the beginning of the thirteenth century, it was replaced by a new, finer, and larger silver coin, the "grossus denarius" (great penny), or groat. In Verona, Florence, and Milan the groat was the equivalent of the solidus, in effect turning that ghost money for the first time into a real coin. Introduced into England in 1279, the groat did not take hold at first, probably because the English penny was less debased. It was reintroduced in 1351 by Edward III. Holland, Flanders, and the princes and cities of the Holy Roman Empire soon followed.

The resumption of gold coinage in the 1250s, after long centuries, did little to simplify the complexities of medieval currency; on the contrary it made it even more bewildering. The Florentine florin, the Genoese genovino, and the Venetian ducat were designed to give flesh to the ghostly medieval pound, but they quickly wandered from their designed relationship to the old denarius. So did the French écu, meant to realize the ghost livre tournois, and the English noble, a third of the ghost pound sterling. To correspond to the groat and to the gold coins, new ghost moneys of account developed. Venice kept its old system while introducing a money of account based on the groat, maintaining a wavering relationship between the two systems. Yet the new gold coins had great importance in commercial and financial transactions, above all because the standard gold coins of Florence, Venice, Genoa, France, Spain, England, Portugal, Hungary, and Bohemia, whatever their varying and uncertain relationships with their own silver coins and ghost currencies, were equal in fineness and weight, and so interchangeable.

Principal medieval coins

SILVER

Denarius (*penny, denier, denaro, pfennig*). Minted from Merovingian times in France, from Carolingian in the Holy Roman Empire, Italy, England. Money of account pegged to the denarius: solidus (shilling, sou, soldo, schilling), worth twelve denarii; libra (pound, livre, lira, pfund), worth twenty solidi; in twelfth-century Germany, the mark (a unit of weight for gold and silver equal to eight ounces), worth 160 Imperial pfennigs.

Grossus denarius (*groat, grosso, gros, groschen, groot*).

First minted in Venice, 1202, worth twenty-four Venetian denarii or two solidi.

1203, Verona, worth one Veronese solidus.

1237, Florence, worth one Florentine solidus.

About 1250, Milan, worth one Milanese solidus.

1266, France, gros tournois, worth one sou tournois (12 deniers).

1279, England, worth four English pennies. Dropped, reintroduced in 1351.

GOLD

1252, Genoa, genovino. ⎤
1252, Florence, florin. ⎬ All approximately equivalent, at first worth a
1284, Venice, ducat. ⎦ libra, later more.

1385, France, écu, worth one livre tournois.

1344, England, noble, worth one-third pound sterling (the mark, money of account, equal to two nobles).

1354, Germany, gulden, Rhinegulden, Rhenish florin, approximately the same as Florentine florin (Cologne mark, money of account, equal to 66 Rhinegulden).

APPENDIX 2

Original Texts of Translated Poems

Adam de la Halle on Arras

Arras, Arras, ville de chicane
Et de haine et de denigrement,
Qui naguere etiez si noble,
On dit partout qu'on vous ruine,
Et si Dieu n'y restaure la vertu
Je ne sais qui retablirait la concorde;
On y aime trop l'argent.
Chacun fut stupide en cette ville
Au point qu'on y est dans le petrin.
Adieu, plus de cent mille fois,
Ailleurs je vais entendre l'Evangile
Car ici on ne sait que mentir!

Baude Crespin's Epitaph

Chy gist uns homs de boin renom;
Sires Baudes Crespins fu son nom;
D'Arras, [et] fu valles le Roy.

....
.... hostel.
Jamais ne trouvera on tel.
De luy vivoient plus de gens
A grand honneur que d'austres cent.
Pour luy doivent a Dieu prier
Gens gaignans et manouvrier.
En l'an de l'Incarnation
Mil trois cens et XVI, dit-on
Trespassa li preudhom sans guille,
XVIII jours el mois de guille.
Or, prions Dieu l'esperitable
Qui'il li doint joie permenable.

Giovanni de' Frescobaldi's Advice to Italians Visiting England

Ricordo per chi passa in Inghilterra:
Vestir basso colore, essere umile;
Grosso in aspetto ed in fatto sottile;
Male sia all'inglese se t'atterra;
Fuggi le cure e pur chi ti fa guerra;
Spendi con cuore e non ti mostrar vile;
Pagare al giorno, a riscuoter gentile
Mostrando che bisogno ti sotterra;
Non far più inchiesta ch'abbi fondamento;
Compera a tempo se ti mette bene,
Nè t'impacciar con uomini di corte;
Osserva di chi può'l commandamento,
Con tua nazione unirti t'appartiene,
E far per tempo ben serrar le porte.

BIBLIOGRAPHY

General

ADELSON, HOWARD L., ed., *Medieval Commerce*. Princeton (N.J.), 1962.

Cambridge Economic History of Europe. Vol. II, *Trade and Industry in the Middle Ages*, ed. M. M. Postan and E. E. Rich. Cambridge, 1952. Vol III, *Economic Organization and Policies in the Middle Ages*, ed. M. M. Postan, E. E. Rich and Edward Miller. Cambridge, 1963.

GRAS, N. S. B., "Capitalism—Concepts and History." *Enterprise and Secular Change*, ed. Frederick C. Lane and Jelle C. Riemersma. London, 1953.

HEYD, W., *Histoire du commerce du moyen âge*. Leipzig, 1936.

LEWIS, ARCHIBALD R., *Naval Power and Trade in the Mediterranean, A.D. 500–1100*. Princeton (N.J.), 1951.

———, *The Northern Seas: Shipping and Commerce in Northern Europe, A.D. 300–1100*. Princeton (N.J.), 1958.

LOPEZ, ROBERT S., *The Birth of Europe*. New York, 1967.

LOPEZ, ROBERT S. and I. W. RAYMOND, *Medieval Trade in the Mediterranean World*. New York, 1955.

LUZZATTO, GINO, *An Economic History of Italy from the Fall of the Roman Empire to the Beginning of the Sixteenth Century*. New York, 1961.

————, "Small and Great Merchants in the Italian Cities of the Renaissance." *Enterprise and Secular Change.**

MISKIMIN, HARRY A., *The Economy of Early Renaissance Europe, 1300–1460.* Englewood Cliffs (N.J.), 1969.

PIRENNE, HENRI, *Economic and Social History of Medieval Europe.* New York, 1937.

RENOUARD, YVES, *Les hommes d'affaires italiens au moyen âge.* Paris, 1949.

REYNOLDS, ROBERT L., *Europe Emerges, Transition Toward an Industrial World-Wide Society.* Madison (Wis.), 1961.

————, "Origins of Modern Business Enterprise." *Journal of Economic History,* 1956.

SAPORI, ARMANDO, *Le marchand italien au moyen âge.* Paris, 1952.

WHITE, LYNN, *Medieval Technology and Social Change.* Oxford, 1963.

YVER, G., *Le commerce et les marchands dans l'Italie meridionale au XIIIe et au XIVe siècle.* Paris, 1903.

I. Stirrings

FAHMY, A. M., *Muslim Sea Power in the Eastern Mediterranean from the Seventh to the Tenth Century A.D.* London, 1950.

GANSHOF, F. L., "Notes sur les ports de Provence du VIIIe au Xe siècle." *Revue historique,* 1938.

LATOUCHE, ROBERT, *The Birth of Western Economy: Economic Aspect of the Dark Ages.* Trans. E. M. Wilkinson. London, 1967.

————, *Les grandes invasions et la crise de l'Occident au Ve siècle.* Paris, 1946.

LOPEZ, ROBERT S., *The Birth of Europe.**

————, "Mohammed and Charlemagne: a Revision." *Speculum,* 1943.

————, "Still Another Renaissance?" *American Historical Review,* 1951–52.

————, *The Tenth Century: How Dark the Dark Ages? Source Problems in World Civilization.* New York, 1959.

LUZZATTO, GINO, *An Economic History of Italy.**

MONTANELLI, INDRO and ROBERTO GERVASO, *L'Italia dei secoli bui.* Milan, 1970.

* indicates earlier citation.

PIRENNE, HENRI, *Mohammed and Charlemagne*. New York, 1957.

RABINOWITZ, L., *Jewish Merchant Adventurers, a Study of the Radanites*. London, 1948.

REYNOLDS, ROBERT L., *Europe Emerges.** ,

SABBE, E., "Quelques types de marchands du IXe et Xe siècles." *Revue belge de philologie et d'histoire*, 1934.

THOMSON, JAMES WESTFALL, "The Commerce of France in the Ninth Century," *Journal of Political Economy*, 1915.

WHITE, LYNN, *Medieval Technology and Social Change.**

The passage from Cassiodorus's letters is taken from Thomas Hodgkins, *The Letters of Cassiodorus*, London, 1886; the story of Suleiman the Merchant from E. Renaudot, "The Travels of Two Mohammedans Through India and China," in *A General Collection of the Best and Most Interesting Voyages and Travels in All Parts of the World*, ed. John Pinkerton, London, 1811; Ibn-Khurdadbih's description from L. Rabinowitz's *Jewish Merchant Adventurers.**

1. Pantaleone di Mauro, a Merchant from the Amalfitan Eagle's Nest

CAMERA, MATTEO, *Memorie storiche e diplomatiche sull'antica città ducato di Amalfi*. Salerno, 1876–81.

CASSESE, LEOPOLDO, *Amalfi e la sua costiera*. Rome, n.d.

CITARELLA, ARMAND O., "Patterns in Medieval Trade: the Commerce of Amalfi Before the Crusades." *Journal of Economic History*, 1968.

———, "The Relations of Amalfi with the Arab World Before the Crusades." *Speculum*, 1967.

CONIGLIO, G., "Amalfi e il commercio amalfitano." *Nuova rivista storica*, 1944–45.

HOFMEISTER, A., "Maurus von Amalfi und die Elfenbeinkassette von Farfa." *Quellen und Forschungen aus Italienischen Archiven von Rom*, 1932–33.

———, "Der Übersetzer Johannes und das Geschlecht Comitis Mauronis in Amalfi." *Historisches Vierteljahrschrift*, 1932.

NORWICH, JOHN JULIUS, *The Other Conquest*. New York, 1967.

PONTIERI, E., "La crisi di Amalfi medioevale." *Archivio storico per le provincie napoletane*, 1933.

Liutprand of Cremona's report to Otto I appears in *The Early Middle Ages, 500–1000*, ed. Robert Brentano, *Sources in Western Civilization*, New York, 1964. Paperback.

2. The Rozos of Milan, Masters of the Mint

PRINCIPAL SOURCE

LOPEZ, ROBERT S., "An Aristocracy of Money in the Early Middle Ages." *Speculum*, 1953.

OTHER SOURCES

BLOCH, MARC, "Le problème de l'or au moyen âge." *Annales d'histoire économique et sociale*, 1933.

LOPEZ, ROBERT S., "Continuità e adattamento nel medioevo: un millennio di storia delle associazioni di monetieri nell' Europa meridionale." *Studi in onore di Gino Luzzatto*. Milan, 1950.

———, "The Dollar of the Middle Ages." *Journal of Economic History*, 1951.

SPUFFORD, P., "Coinage and Currency." *Cambridge Economic History*, Vol. III.

STRADA, M., *La zecca di Milano e le sue monete*. Milan, 1930.

VIOLANTE, CINZIO, *La società milanese nell' età precomunale*. Bari, 1953.

3. An English Peddler-Saint: Godric of Finchale

PRINCIPAL SOURCE

Reginald of Durham, *Godric of Finchale (Libellus de Vita et Miraculis S. Godrici, Heremite de Finchale)*. London, 1845. (A selection from this book, translated by G. G. Coulton, may be found in paperback in *Sources in Western Civilization, the High Middle Ages, 1000–1300*, ed. Bryce D. Lyon, New York, 1964.)

OTHER SOURCES

BLAIR, PETER HUNTER, *An Introduction to Anglo-Saxon England*. Cambridge (England), 1966.

DOUGLAS, DAVID C., *The Norman Achievement, 1050–1100*. Berkeley (Cal.), 1969.

———, *William the Conqueror*. Berkeley (Cal.), 1964.

LEFEBVRE, LUCIEN, "Fils de riches ou nouveaux riches?" *Annales d'histoire économique et sociale*, 1946.

PIRENNE, HENRI, *Economic and Social History*.*

TOMKEIEFF, O. G., *Life in Norman England*. New York, 1967.

VOGEL, WALTHER, "Ein seefahrender Kaufmann um 1100." *Hansische Geschichtsblätter*, 1912.

II. Adventurers and Profiteers

Businessmen of the Time of the Crusades

BYRNE, EUGENE H., *Genoese Shipping in the Twelfth and Thirteenth Centuries*. Cambridge (Mass.), 1930.

LOPEZ, ROBERT S., *Storia delle colonie genovesi nel Mediterraneo*. Bologna, 1938.

MC LAUGHLIN, T. P., "The teachings of the Canonists on Usury." *Medieval Studies*, 1939.

REYNOLDS, ROBERT L., "The Market for Northern Textiles in Genoa, 1179–1200." *Revue belge de philologie et d'histoire*, 1929.

———, "Merchants of Arras and the Overland Trade with Genoa in the Twelfth Century." *Revue belge de philologie et d'histoire*, 1930.

Guibert of Nogent's views on usury are taken from John F. Benton's *Self and Society in Medieval France, the Memoirs of Abbot Guibert of Nogent*, New York, 1970. Harper Torchbook.

4. A Genoese Crusader: Guglielmo Embriaco

PRINCIPAL SOURCE

LOPEZ, ROBERT S., *Storia delle colonie genovesi*.*

OTHER SOURCES

BACH, E., *La cité de Gênes au XIIe siécle*. Paris, 1955.

BYRNE, EUGENE H., "Commercial Contracts of the Genoese in the Syrian Trade of the Twelfth Century." *Quarterly Journal of Economics*, 1916.

———, "Easterners in Genoa." *Journal of the American Oriental Society*, XXXVIII.

———, "Genoese Trade with Syria in the Twelfth Century." *American Historical Review*, 1920.

CESSI, ROBERTO, *Le colonie medioevali italiane in Oriente*. Padua, 1942.

LOPEZ, ROBERT S., "Aux origines du capitalisme génois." *Annales d'histoire économique et sociale*, 1937.

ROTH, CECIL, "Genoese Jews in the Thirteenth Century." *Speculum*, 1950.

SAYOUS, ANDRÉ, "Aristocratie et noblesse à Gênes." *Annales d'histoire économique et sociale*, 1937.

Ibn-Jubayr's description of the customs house at Acre appears in R. J. C. Broadhurst, ed., *Travels of Ibn-Jubayr*, Jonathan Cape, Ltd., London, 1952; Raymond d'Aguilers's story of the siege of Jerusalem in *Historia Francorum Qui Ceperunt Iherusalem*, translated by John Hugh Hill and Laurita L. Hill, American Philosophical Society Philadelphia, 1968; Caffaro's account of the taking of Caesarea is translated from Lopez's *Storia delle colonie genovesi.**

5. A Merchant of Venice: Romano Mairano

BROWN, HORATIO, "The Venetians and the Venetian Quarter in Constantinople," *Journal of Hellenic Studies*, 1920.

CESSI, ROBERT, *Le colonie medioevali italiane.**

———, *Politica ed economica di Venezia*. Rome, 1952.

CRACCO, GIORGIO, *Società e stato nel medioevo veneziano (secolo XII–XIV)*. Florence, 1967.

DE ROOVER, RAYMOND, "The Organization of Trade." *Cambridge Economic History*, Vol. III.

LUZZATTO, GINO, "Les activites économiques du patriciat vénitien (Xe–XIVe siècles)." *Annales d'histoire économique et sociale*, 1937.

———, *Economic History of Italy.**

———, *Studi di storia economica veneziana*. Padua, 1954.

MACLAGAN, MICHAEL, *The City of Constantinople*. London, 1968.

MOLMENTI, POMPEO, *Venice, Its Individual Growth from the Earliest Beginnings to the Fall of the Republic*. Trans. Horatio F. Brown. *Part I, the Middle Ages*. Chicago, 1906.

MORO, ISA, *I Dogi di Venezia: congiure, eroismi, torture*. Milan, 1968.

PACELLI, VINCENZO, "Il contenuto economico della commenda nei documenti pisani e genovesi del secolo XII." *Bolletino storico pisano*, 1937.

Geoffrey de Villehardouin's description of the attack on Constantinople appears in *Chronicles of the Crusades*, translated by M. R. B. Shaw, Baltimore (Maryland), 1963. Paperback.

6. The Royal Milch Cow: Isaac of Norwich

PRINCIPAL SOURCE

LIPMAN, V. D., *The Jews of Medieval Norwich*. London, 1967.

OTHER SOURCES

DAVIS, BRENDA, "The Story of a House." *Wensum Lodge*, Norwich, n.d.

EVANS, M. CAREY, *The Legend of St. William, Boy-Martyr of Norwich.* Norwich, n.d.

ROTH, CECIL, *History of the Jews in England.* Oxford, 1964.

7. Symon di Gualterio, a Patron of the Champagne Fairs

PRINCIPAL SOURCE

FACE, RICHARD D., "Symon de Gualterio: a Brief Portrait of a Thirteenth-Century Man of Affairs." *Economy, Society and Government in Medieval Italy, Essays in Memory of Robert L. Reynolds,* ed. David Herlihy, Robert S. Lopez and Vsevolod Slessarev. Kent (Ohio), 1969.

OTHER SOURCES

ALENGRY, CHARLES, *Les foires de Champagne.* Paris, 1915.

BAUTIER, R. H., "Les foires de Champagne." *Recueils Jean Bodin*, Vol. V, *La foire*. Brussels, 1953.

BOURQUELOT, FÉLIX, *Études sur les foires de Champagne au XIIe, XIIIe et XIVe siècles.* Paris, 1865.

CHAPIN, ELIZABETH, *Les villes de foire de Champagne.* Paris, 1937.

FACE, R. D., "Techniques of Business in the Trade Between the Fairs of Champagne and the South of Europe in the Twelfth and Thirteenth Centuries." *Economic History Review*, 1958.

GIES, JOSEPH and FRANCES, *Life in a Medieval City.* New York and London, 1969.

LAURENT, H., *Un grand commerce d'exportation au moyen-âge. La draperie des Pays Bas en France et dans les pays mediterranéans.* Paris, 1935.

REYNOLDS, ROBERT L., "Genoese Trade in the Late Twelfth Century, Particularly in Cloth from the Fairs of Champagne." *Journal of Business History*, 1931.

———, "Merchants of Arras and the Overland Trade with Genoa, Twelfth Century." *Revue belge de philologie et d'histoire*, 1930.

SAYOUS, ANDRE, "Les operations des banquiers italiens en Italie et aux foires de Champagne pendant le XIIIe siècle." *Revue historique*, CLXX.

VERLINDEN, O., "Markets and Fairs." *Cambridge Economic History*, Vol. III.

III. Affluence

DE ROOVER, RAYMOND, "The Commercial Revolution of the Thirteenth Century." *Enterprise and Secular Change.**

———, "Aux origines d'une technique intellectuelle: la formation et l'expansion de la comptabilité à partie double." *Annales d'histoire économique et sociale,* 1937.

LOPEZ, ROBERT S., *Storia delle colonie genovesi.**

PIRENNE, HENRI, *Belgian Democracy, Its Early History.* Manchester, 1915.

———, *Histoire de Belgique,* Vols. I, II. Brussels, 1922, 1929.

SAPROI, ARMANDO, "The Culture of the Medieval Italian Merchant." *Enterprise and Secular Change.**

8. *A Flemish Merchant Prince: Sire Jehan Boinebroke*

PRINCIPAL SOURCE

ESPINAS, GEORGES, *Les origines du capitalisme, I; Sire Jehan Boinebroke, patricien et drapier douaisien.* Lille, 1933.

OTHER SOURCES

ESPINAS, GEORGES, *Les guerres familiales dans la commune de Douai aux XIIIe et XIV siècles: les trêves et les paix.* Paris, 1899.

———, *La vie urbaine de Douai au moyen âge.* Paris, 1914.

PIRENNE, HENRI, *Belgian Democracy.**

———, *Histoire de Belgique.**

VAN WERVEKE, HANS, "The Rise of the Towns." *Cambridge Economic History,* Vol. III.

9. *Benedetto Zaccaria, Genoa's Merchant-Admiral*

PRINCIPAL SOURCE

LOPEZ, ROBERT S., *Genova marinara nel duecento: Benedetto Zaccaria, ammiraglio e mercante.* Messina-Milan, 1932.

OTHER SOURCES

BRATIANU, G. I., *Recherches sur le commerce génois dans la Mer Noire au XIIIe siècle.* Paris, 1929.

CESSI, ROBERTO, *Le colonie medioevali italiane.**

DE ROOVER, RAYMOND, "The Organization of Trade." *Cambridge Economic History*, Vol. III.

LOPEZ, ROBERT S., *Storia delle colonie genovesi.**

10. The Polos of Venice

PRINCIPAL SOURCE

The Travels of Marco Polo, trans. Henry Yule, ed. George B. Parks. New York, 1929.

OTHER SOURCES

GALLO, RODOLFO, "Marco Polo, la sua famiglia e il suo libro." *VII Centenario della nascità di Marco Polo.* Venice, 1955.

HART, HENRY, *Marco Polo, Venetian Adventurer.* Norman (Okla.), 1967.

LOPEZ, ROBERT S., "Venezia e le grandi linee dell'espansione commerciale nel secolo XIII." *Civiltà veneziana del secolo di Marco Polo.* Florence, 1955.

LUZZATTO, GINO, "Il mercante veneziano del tempo di Marco Polo." *VII Centenario della nascità di Marco Polo.* Venice, 1955.

OLSCHKI, LEONARDO, *Marco Polo's Precursors.* Baltimore (Md.), 1943.

POWER, EILEEN, *Medieval People.* New York, 1954.

RENOUARD, YVES, "Mercati e mercanti veneziani alla fine del duecento." *Civiltà veneziana del secolo di Marco Polo.* Florence, 1955.

Pegolotti's advice on travelling to Cathay is taken from Francesco Balducci Pegolotti, *La pratica della mercatura*, ed. Allan Evans. Cambridge (Mass.), 1936.

11. Cities and Bankers: the Crespins of Arras

BIGWOOD, GEORGES, "Les financières d'Arras." *Revue belge de philologie et d'histoire*, 1924, 1925.

FRYDE, E. M., "Public Credit with Special Reference to North-Western Europe." *Cambridge Economic History*, Vol. III.

HIBBERT, A. B., "The Economic Policies of Towns." *Cambridge Economic History*, Vol. III.

LESTOCQUOY, J., "Les étapes du developpement urbain d'Arras." *Revue belge de philologie et d'histoire*, 1944.

———, *Patriciens du moyen-âge: les dynasties bourgeoises d'Arras du XIe au XVe siècle.* Arras, 1945.

———, "Les usuriers du debut du moyen âge." *Studi in onore di Gino Luzzatto.**

———, *Les villes de Flandre et d'Italie sous le gouvernement des patriciens (XIe–XVe siècles)*. Paris, 1952.
Adam de la Halle's verses and Baude Crespin's epitaph were translated by Frances Gies.

12. The Calimala Guild: the Alberti Company of Florence

PRINCIPAL SOURCE

DE ROOVER, RAYMOND, "The Story of the Alberti Company, 1302–1348, as Revealed in Its Account Books." *Business History Review*, 1958.

OTHER SOURCES

CARUS-WILSON, ELEANOR M., "The Woolen Industry." *Cambridge Economic History*, Vol. II.
DE ROOVER, RAYMOND, "The Organization of Trade." *
———, "Aux origines d'une technique intellectuelle." *
PEGOLOTTI, FRANCESCO BALDUCCI, *La pratica della mercatura.**
PERAGALLO, E., *Origin and Evolution of Double-Entry Bookkeeping.*
RENOUARD, YVES, *Les hommes d'affaires italiens.**
SAPORI, ARMANDO, "Gli Alberti del Giudice di Firenze." *Studi in onore di Gino Luzzatto.**
———, *I libri di commercio dei Peruzzi*. Milan, 1934.
———, "Il personale delle compagnie mercantili del medioevo." *Archivio storico italiano*, 7th ser., 1939.
———, *Merchants and Companies in Ancient Florence*. Florence, 1955.
———, *Studi di storia economica medioevale*. Florence, 1955.
The description of the Villa Paradiso appears in Boccaccio's *Decameron* (the Third Day).

IV. The Fourteenth Century

Capitalists in Crisis

DOLLINGER, PHILIPPE, *La Hanse, XIIe–XVIIe siècles*. Paris, 1964.
HIBBERT, A. B., "Economic Policies of Towns." *
MISKIMIN, HARRY A., *The Economy of Early Renaissance Europe.**
PIRENNE, HENRI, *Belgian Democracy.**
———, *Histoire de Belgique.**
ZIEGLER, PHILIP, *The Black Death*. London, 1969.

Agnolo di Tura's description of the plague in Siena is taken from "Cronica Senese di Agnolo di Tura del Grasso," in Muratori's *Rerum Italicarum Scriptores*, Matteo Villani's account of the aftermath from his *Cronica*, both passages as quoted in Ziegler's *Black Death*, William Collins Sons & Co., Ltd., London, and John Day Company, New York; Boccaccio's description of the plague in Florence comes from the *Decameron* (First Day).

13. Italian Companies Go Bankrupt: the Frescobaldi in England

PRINCIPAL SOURCE

SAPORI, ARMANDO, *La compagnia dei Frescobaldi in Inghilterra*. Florence, 1947.

OTHER SOURCES

FRYDE, E. B., "Public Credit, with Special Reference to North-Western Europe." *Cambridge Economic History*, Vol. III.
RHODES, W. E., "Italian Bankers in England and Their Loans to Edward I and Edward II." *Historical Essays by Members of Owens College.* Manchester, 1902.
RUSSELL, E., "The Societies of the Bardi and the Peruzzi and Their Dealings with Edward III, 1327–45." *Finance and Trade under Edward III*, ed. G. Unwin. Manchester, 1918.
SAPORI, ARMANDO, *La crisi delle compagnie mercantili dei Bardi e dei Peruzzi*. Florence, 1926.
Giovanni de' Frescobaldi's sonnet was translated by Frances Gies.

14. Moneyman in a Revolution: Jacob van Artevelde of Ghent

LUCAS, H. S., *The Low Countries and the Hundred Years War, 1326–1347*. Ann Arbor, 1929.
———, "The Sources and Literature on Jacob van Artevelde." *Speculum*, 1933.
PIRENNE, HENRI, *Belgian Democracy*.*
———, *Histoire de Belgique*.*
POWER, EILEEN, *The Wool Trade in English Medieval History*. Oxford, 1941.
VAN WERVEKE, HANS, *Jacques van Artevelde*. Brussels, 1943.

15. Francesco di Marco Datini of Prato, the Man Who Survived

PRINCIPAL SOURCE

ORIGO, IRIS, *The Merchant of Prato, Francesco di Marco Datini*. London, 1957.

OTHER SOURCES

BENSA, ENRICO, *Francesco di Marco da Prato: notizie e documenti sulla mercatura italiana del secolo XIV*. Milan, 1928.

BRUN, ROBERT, "Notes sur le commerce des objets d'art en France et principalement à Avignon à la fin du XIVe siècle." *Bibliothèque de l'école des Chartes*, 1934.

MELIS, FEDERIGO, "A proposito di un nuovo volume sul 'mercante di Prato' " (review of Iris Origo's *The Merchant of Prato*). *Economia e storia*, 1959.

———, *Aspetti della vita economica medioevale (Studi nell'archivio Datini di Prato)*, Vol. I. Siena, 1962.

ORIGO, IRIS, "The Domestic Enemy: the Eastern Slaves in Tuscany in the Fourteenth and Fifteenth Centuries." *Speculum*, 1955.

PERAGALLO, E. *Origin and Evolution of Double-Entry Bookkeeping.**

ZIEGLER, PHILIP, *The Black Death.**

Ser Lapo Mazzei's letters are translated from Cesare Guasti's *Ser Lapo Mazzei: Lettere di un notaro a un mercante del secolo XIV con altre lettere e documenti*. Florence, 1880.

16. Merchants of the German Hansa: Hildebrand and Sivert Veckinchusen

PRINCIPAL SOURCE

STIEDA, WILHELM, *Hildebrand Veckinchusen: Briefwechsel eines deutschen Kaufmanns im 15. Jahrhundert*. Leipzig, 1921.

OTHER SOURCES

DE ROOVER, RAYMOND, *Money, Banking and Credit in Mediaeval Bruges*. Cambridge (Mass.), 1948.

———, "The Organization of Trade." *

DOLLINGER, PHILIPPE, *La Hanse.**

POSTAN, M. M., "The Trade of Medieval Europe: the North." *Cambridge Economic History*, Vol. II.

V. The New Financiers

DE ROOVER, RAYMOND, "The Organization of Trade." *

LOPEZ, ROBERT S. and HARRY A. MISKIMIN, "The Economic Depression of the Renaissance." *Economic History Review*, 1962.

LUZZATTO, GINO, *An Economic History of Italy.**

MISKIMIN, HARRY A., *The Economy of Early Renaissance Europe.**

NEF, JOHN U., "Mining and Metallurgy in Medieval Europe." *Cambridge Economic History*, Vol. II.

POSTAN, M. M., "The Trade of Medieval Europe: the North." *

17. Jacques Coeur, the King's Moneyman

BOUVIER, R., *Jacques Coeur, un financier coloniale au XVe siècle*. Paris, 1928.

CHENU, CHARLES-MAURICE, *Jacques Coeur, le Royaume sauvé*. Paris, 1962.

MOLLAT, M., ed., *Les affaires de Jacques Coeur, Journal du procureur Dauvet*. Paris, 1952.

ROUSSEL, ROMAIN, *Jacques Coeur le Magnifique*. Paris, 1965.

18. Cosimo de' Medici, Father of His Country

ANDRIEUX, MARCEL, *Les Médicis*. Paris, 1958.

DE ROOVER, RAYMOND, *The Medici Bank*. New York, 1966.

———, "The Organization of Trade." *

GUTKIND, CURT S., *Cosimo de' Medici, Pater Patriae, 1389–1464*. Oxford, 1938.

JOURCIN, A., *Les Médicis*. Paris, 1968.

MACHIAVELLI, NICCOLO, *History of Florence and of the Affairs of Italy*. New York, 1966.

SCHEVILL, FERDINAND, *The Medici*. New York, 1949.

———, *Medieval and Renaissance Florence*. New York, 1963.

19. Cely and Sons, Merchants of the Staple

CARUS-WILSON, ELEANOR M., *England's Export Trade, 1275–1547*. Oxford, 1963.

LUCAS, C. P., *Beginnings of English Overseas Enterprise*. Oxford, 1917.

MALDEN, H. E., ed., *The Cely Papers, selected from the Correspondence of the Cely Family, Merchants of the Staple, 1475–88*. London, 1900.

322 BIBLIOGRAPHY

MILLER, EDWARD, "The Economic Policies of Government: France and England." *Cambridge Economic History*, Vol. III.

POWER, EILEEN, *Medieval People.**

————, *The Wool Trade.**

20. Jacob Fugger, the First Modern Capitalist

DOLLINGER, PHILIPPE, *La Hanse.**

EHRENBERG, RICHARD, *Capital and Finance in the Age of the Renaissance, a Study of the Fuggers and Their Correspondence.* Trans. H. M. Lucas. New York, 1928.

HERING, ERNST, *Die Fugger*, Leipzig, 1944.

MC GUIGAN, DOROTHY GIES, *The Habsburgs.* New York, 1966.

NEF, JOHN U., "Mining and Metallurgy." *

PÖLNITZ, GÖTZ, *Die Fugger.* Frankfurt-am-Main, 1960.

SCHICK, L., *Un grand homme d'affaires au debut du XVI siècle, Jacob Fugger.* Paris, 1957.

STRIEDER, JACOB, *Jacob Fugger the Rich.* Trans. Mildred L. Hartsough, ed. N. S. B. Gras.

INDEX

The World of the Commercial Revolution: 1000-1500